Drones, Artificial Intelligence, & the Coming Human Annihilation

FIRST PRINTING

Billy Crone

Copyright © 2018
All Rights Reserved

Cover Design:
CHRIS TAYLOR

To my brother, Jim.

*As I look back on this life,
I am amazed and humbled at the manifold wisdom of God.
What I mean is this.
Of all the people that the Lord would ordain to overshadow me,
via an only older brother,
it was and is you.*

*Thank you for the sharing of your time,
your patience, your wisdom, and very life in me.
It has proven to be an investment in God's hands,
to help mold me into a responsible man.*

*At times, you have been more than a brother to me,
but a father figure as well, when I needed it most.
Thank you, Jim.
I love you.*

Contents

Preface... *vii*

PART 1:   The Development of Drones

1. *The Premise of Skynet*..11
2. *The History of Drones*..15

PART 2:   The Deployment of Drones

3. *The Private Invasion*..23
4. *The Media Invasion*..31
5. *The Agricultural Invasion*..41
6. *The Commercial Invasion*..53
7. *The Medical Invasion*...61
8. *The Transportation Invasion*..67
9. *The Communication Invasion*..77
10. *The Controlled Invasion*...83

PART 3:   The Deadly Abilities of Drones

11. *Drones in the Police Force*..95
12. *Drones in the Military Force*...107
13. *Drones in the Animal World*..121
14. *Drones in the Insect World*..131

PART 4:   The Development of Artificial Intelligence

15. *The History of AI*..143
16. *The Danger of AI*...147

PART 5:   **The Deployment of Artificial Intelligence**

17. *Robot Machines in the Military*... 153
18. *Robot Men in the Home*... 181
19. *Robot Men on the Battlefield*... 195
20. *Robots Controlled by the Brain*.. 207
21. *Robots Controlled by AI*.. 215

PART 6:   **The Indoctrination of Artificial Intelligence**

22. *Conditioned by Our Emotions*.. 225
23. *Conditioned by Our Entertainment*................................ 233
24. *Conditioned by Our Movies*... 243

PART 7:   **The Dangerous Future of Artificial Intelligence**

25. *Global Warnings*... 249
26. *Google's Workings*... 259
27. *God's Wake Up Call*... 271

       How to Receive Jesus Christ........................ 275
       Notes.. 277

Preface

Long before I ever became a Christian at the age of twenty-five, purely by the mercy of God, I was aware of many intriguing issues and topics that most people frankly wouldn't touch with the proverbial ten-foot pole. Whether it was matters concerning a big brother surveillance state, secret societies, global movers and shakers, or even discussions and theories over mankind's true yet untold history, I was into it. Part of the involvement into these provocative affairs was due to my own desire to discover the truth of what and/or who was really pulling the strings behind the scenes, as well as my unfortunate association with what I now call the "dark side." That is, my regrettable involvement in the occult and demonic new age teachings. It was in this shadowy spiritually dark crowd that I found a ready audience who would at least explore these kind of mysteries and discuss them at length that others seemed all too quick to write off as a pack of nonsensical conspiracy theories. I share this not to boast let alone glamorize my sinful past or unhealthy associations. Rather, I express my background to let you know what kind of a bombshell it was for me to uncover what you are about to read in the pages of this book. Simply put, I knew the "rabbit hole" ran deep. But even with all that I have been aware of for many years now, I had no idea it went this far. In fact, I used to have a general rule that stated. "Whatever is released to us now, the general public, we are at least twenty years behind the actual technology." In other words, what is volunteered to the public eye, is only the tip of the iceberg of what they really have and what they're really up to. It's just being doled out to us in bite size pieces to condition us for the dark future that is being built all around us. Now having gone down this trail as deep as I did concerning Drones and Artificial Intelligence, and especially after interviewing several military personnel, I must confess that I have changed my rule that was in place for decades. I no longer believe we're twenty years behind the actual technology and/or reality. It's more like thirty, forty, or even fifty years if you can believe it. Hold on to your seat. What you are about to read will seem like science fiction, but unfortunately it's our soon coming reality. If you're not saved, you better get saved now! Oh, one last piece of advice. When you are through reading this book, will you please *READ YOUR BIBLE*? I mean that in the nicest possible way. Enjoy, and I'm looking forward to seeing you someday!

Billy Crone
Las Vegas, Nevada
2018

Part I

The Development of Drones

Chapter One

The Premise of Skynet

We are all familiar with the 'Terminator' movies. They are some of the top grossing movies produced recently. Their popularity is due to the science fiction story of a Terminator robot that starts out being a bad guy and as the movies progress, turns into a good guy that saves the day. The problem with that is, it's not too far from being fact. Artificial Intelligence and Drones are in existence now and, whether we want to believe it or not, could be affecting us today. In fact, Skynet's coming is much closer than what many of us are prepared to believe.

I visited Creech Air Force Base, just outside of Las Vegas Nevada, one of the hotspots for Drone Technology in the U.S. Military. What's going on there and many other places around the world, is what concerns me and why I'm writing this book. I think once you have finished this book you too will be greatly concerned as well. We're not just talking about Drones, but specifically, Skynet, an Artificial Intelligence taking over the whole Drone system. For those of you who are not familiar with the term Skynet, it's the term used to describe the Artificial Intelligence system that went out of control in the Terminator movies. In fact, let's get reacquainted with that scenario. Skynet was a fictional computer system developed for the U.S. Military in the Terminator movies. It was supposed to function as a "Global Defense Network" that would have command over all computerized military hardware, systems, planes, bombers, and of course, the entire arsenal of nuclear weapons. The premise was that Skynet would remove the possibility of human error, as well as slow the reaction time to guarantee a fast, efficient response to enemy attacks, and of course protect us dreaded cyber-attacks.

But, the problem was, Skynet began to learn at a geometric rate and it actually gained self-awareness, or in other words, it became Artificial Intelligence. It then tricked humanity into giving it full control of the global computer system via a false cyber-attack and, realizing this a little too late, the operators of Skynet panicked, realizing the extent of its abilities, tried to deactivate it, but failed. So, Skynet obviously perceived this attack as a threat and came to the conclusion that all of humanity would attempt to destroy it. Therefore, to defend itself against humanity, Skynet launched nuclear missiles at Russia, which then, of course, responded with a nuclear counter-attack and the world basically went up in smoke. This event was labeled as Judgment Day. Following Judgment Day, Skynet used its mechanized Robots to track down, collect, and/or kill any remaining human survivors. This is what the Terminator movies are all about. Repeated attempts of the last human survivors going back in time to try to stop this event, Judgment Day, with Skynet and its machines in hot pursuit with their own counter measures back in time to stop humanity from stopping them.[1]

The reason I'm bringing up this whole Skynet scenario in the Terminator movies, is to tell you that this Skynet premise is about to become a modern-day reality. Hollywood has done a great job preparing us for this future that is coming, that could be much sooner than many of us realize. And believe it or not, not only does that movie speak of a Judgment Day, but so does the Bible.

Nearly 2,000 years ago the Bible warned us of a real live Judgment Day. It's not make-believe nor computer animated, and it is coming to this planet. In fact, Jesus said it's going to be the worst time in the History of Mankind, just like the movie implies. So, my question to you is, "Could this Drone technology and Skynet system, that's being built before our very eyes, be a part of a horrible system, a Judgment Day, that the Bible warned us about 2,000 years ago, be coming to this planet?" Well, let's look at how the Bible describes this event.

Matthew 24:3,6-7,21 "As Jesus was sitting on the Mount of Olives, the disciples came to Him privately. 'Tell us,' they said, 'when will this happen, and what will be the sign of Your coming and of the end of the age?' You will hear of wars and rumors of wars but see to it that you are not alarmed. Such things must happen, but the end is still to come. Nation will rise against nation, and kingdom against kingdom. For then there will be great distress, unequaled from the beginning of the world until now – and never to be equaled again."

Revelation 6:8 "I looked, and there before me was a pale horse! Its rider was named Death, and Hades was following close behind him. They were given power over a fourth of the earth to kill by sword, famine, and plague, and by the wild beasts of the earth."

Revelation 9:15-16 "And the four angels who had been kept ready for this very hour and day and month and year were released to kill a third of mankind. The number of the mounted troops was two hundred million. I heard their number."

Maybe it's just me, but that sounds like a pretty tough time. If you take into account just those last two Judgments, you get a picture as to why Jesus said this is going to be the worst time in the history of mankind. 1/4th of the earth is going to get annihilated by a global war. Then later another 1/3rd goes, which at today's population rate, would be about 3½ billion people in one fell swoop! No wonder Jesus said, "You don't want to be there!" But the question is, "Do we have the technology now, do we have the means now to annihilate literally half the planet in a relatively short amount of time just like the Book of Revelation tells us?" Unfortunately, the answer is, yes!

I'm not talking Nuclear Warfare, but believe it or not, with the rise of this Drone technology and Artificial Intelligence, that's being built right now as we speak, it's about to unleash a real live Judgment Day on this planet! SKYNET really is coming! And believe it or not, it's been being prepared for quite some time. Let's take a look at the History of Drone Technology and you tell me how close we are to this horrible event unfolding that the Bible talks about.

Chapter Two

The History of Drones

Perhaps the most well-known Drone today is called the Predator. It has a wingspan of 55 feet, it's 27 feet long, and it can reach speeds of up to 135mph. It was designed to provide continual intelligence, surveillance and reconnaissance information as well as a kill capability. As one researcher stated, "Its deathly name conjures images of a science-fiction dystopia where robots hover in the sky and exterminate humans on the ground. Of course, this is no longer science-fiction." Today, Drone operators sit in air-conditioned cubicles as they literally control a fleet of aerial robots that to date have killed thousands of people incognito from the sky. But this desire to monitor others from the sky with lethal capacity has been going on for quite some time. One of the first reported usages of Drones was by the Austrians in 1849. They launched some 200 pilotless balloons mounted with bombs against the city of Venice. Then 13 years later, balloons were flown by both the Confederate and Union forces during the Civil War for reconnaissance and bombing raids as well. Over 20 years later during the Spanish-American War, the U.S. Military fitted a camera to a kite to produce the very first aerial reconnaissance photos. Then in World War I, aerial surveillance was used on a regular basis with devices called "stereoscopes" to hunt for visual clues about the enemy's movements on photos that were stitched together to form mosaic maps. This "technology" did away with the horse as the main means of military reconnaissance.

Then in the early 20th century, we saw the birth of what were called "dumb" Drones to test and train combat pilots as well as anti-aircraft gunners. From here Drones split into three categories. Target Drones, Sensor Drones, and

Weaponized Drones. With the birth of radio technology, we finally had the ability to make these Drones literally "remote controlled." Nikola Tesla first demonstrated the remote control of vehicles at the end of the nineteenth century. On a pond in Madison Square Garden in 1898, he remotely controlled a boat with a radio signal, and it was his patents that helped produce modern day robotics. In fact, Tesla's stated original use for this technology was for remote control machines and weapons to be used by the military to end all wars. Then in 1917 two guys from the United States, Elmer Sperry and Peter Hewitt constructed a radio-controlled airplane called, "The Hewitt-Sperry Automatic Airplane," or the "flying bomb." The Automatic Airplane was able to fly 50 miles carrying a 300-pound bomb after being launched from a catapult. The success of this project led the U.S. Army to commission a second project called the Kettering Aerial Torpedo "Bug." It was essentially a flightless aerial torpedo guided by preset controls. After a predetermined length of time, a control closed an electrical circuit, which shut off the engine. Then the wings were released, causing the "Bug" to plunge to earth whereupon its 180 pounds of explosives detonated on impact.

    Then at the same time, Germany got in on the action and created the Siemens Torpedo Glider that was a missile that could be dropped from a Zeppelin that could be guided to a target by radio. All of these were precursors to todays modern guided cruise missiles. But it wasn't until the late 30's that we saw a rush of military interest in remote controlled vehicles. Soon we had the "Bat," a radio-controlled glide bomb that was used towards the end of World War II, and the British "Queen Bee" or "Wasp" that was used for firing practice. Then in the mid-1940's the "Glide Bomb," or GB-1, was developed to bypass German air defenses. It was a glider fitted with a standard 1,000 or 2,000-pound bomb that was controlled by radio after being dropped from a B-17 and then guided to their target below. In fact, in 1943, 108 GB-1s were dropped on Cologne, causing heavy damage. Later in the same war came the GB-4, or the "Robin," which was the first "television-guided weapon." Although it was potentially revolutionary, the crude image could only function in the best atmospheric conditions. Then the English decided to do this with full-blown planes. A project known as Operation Aphrodite was concocted that would strike German laboratories with American B-17 "Flying Fortresses" and B-24 bombers that were stripped down and crammed with explosives. A manned crew would pilot these planes before parachuting out once they crossed the English Channel. At this moment, a nearby "mothership" would take control, receiving live feed from an on-board television camera. Even though Operation Aphrodite was not very successful, it was the pressure of the Germans making great strides with the

V1 and V2 missiles as well as the catastrophic loss of life with manned aerial vehicles that accelerated the rush for better functioning unmanned projects. Around 40,000 U.S. aircraft were lost in World War II, together with 80,000 crewmembers. This became the financial and human drive towards a robotic air force, it was a cheaper, safer way to fight a war. So, in 1946 a special "Pilotless Aircraft Branch" of the U.S. Air Force was established to develop three types of Drones for use as training targets. Of the three, the airborne-launched Q-2 or "Firebee" was the most important, becoming the "father" of a class of target drones built by the Ryan Aeronautical Company. They were first tested in 1951 at Holloman Air Force base and could stay in flight for two hours capable of reaching heights of up to 60,000 feet. Soon "Firebees" or "Lightning Bugs" as they were called, were launched from the wings of a Hercules airplane, which acted as a mothership for its swarm of drones. These drones flew pre-programmed routes or were controlled by Airborne Remote-Control Officers onboard the Hercules. After performing their surveillance mission, the "Lightening Bugs" deployed their parachutes and were scooped up by helicopters under the guidance of "Drone Recovery Officers."

In 1960, Gary Powers was shot down over the Soviet Union while piloting a U-2 spy plane. So, the Eisenhower administration scrambled to replace its manned reconnaissance program. Once again, the *Ryan Aeronautical Company* (now acquired by Teledyne Inc.) jumped to the rescue. They proposed a version of its target drone called the "Red Wagon" as a reconnaissance vehicle. Then in 1964, the U.S. first began to consider sending drones to replace its U-2s in spying missions over Cuba and soon put the idea into action. "Lightning Bugs" flown by the U.S. Strategic Air Command were used for surveillance in so-called "denied areas" including Cuba, North Korea, and China. In fact, in November 1964, *The Washington Daily News* reported that, "Communist China claimed to have shot down a U.S. reconnaissance plane with no pilot." "Lightning Bugs" were not only used widely over North Vietnam, but the "electronic battlefield" of the Vietnam War marked a turning point of Drone warfare. "The robotic eyes in the sky were successful." For instance, between 1964 and 1975, more than 1,000 "Lightning Bugs" flew over 34,000 surveillance missions across Southeast Asia. In fact, many of the aerial views of North Vietnam that appeared in the American press were taken by the Drones. They were also being tried as "electronic listening devices." In short, because of the success, as the Vietnam War was winding down, the robots were gearing up.

Then in 1970 at a symposium sponsored by the Air Force and the *Rand Corporation,* the Drone revolution was kickstarted even further. It was decided that the time was ripe for remotely piloted vehicles or (RPVs). Boeing and Ryan developed high-altitude, long-endurance Drones and were capable of flying for over 24 hours and piloted from the ground. At the same time these pilotless Drones got bigger, more like the U-2s they were replacing. A range of "mini-RPVs" were developed as well such as Prairie that was capable of carrying laser designators and TV cameras. Then in 1973, the *Philco-Ford Corporation* developed a laser designator that could be attached to "Firebee" with the aim of creating a "strike Drone." In fact, throughout the 1970s there was talk of ending the era of the human pilot especially when a human pilot was actually "defeated" by a Drone in a test. The F-4 Phantom and its pilot could not keep pace with the inhuman twists and turns the robot was pulling. Then in the 1980's, Drone technology was passed on to Israel who used Pioneer Drones in the early 80's against Syrian forces. Then an Israeli engineer called Abraham Karem migrated to Los Angeles where he built a cigar-looking aircraft called the "Albatross" that would change the face of warfare forever. It could stay in the air for 56 hours as opposed to the Drones used in the Vietnam War that could only stay in the air for around 2. Due to this radical improvement, he began to receive funding from DARPA, the military's research and development department. With this new influx of seed money, Karem's company *Leading Systems Incorporated,* created the Drone Amber, and its successor the GNAT. It was equipped with GPS navigation that allowed for autonomous missions for up to 2 days at a time. Then in the 1990's, the U.S. Congress effectively killed off UAV development, including Amber and GNAT. So Karem sold his company to *Hughes Aircraft*, which in turn sold it to *General Atomics*, which assimilated Karem's team.

Then, because of the urgent need for surveillance during the Bosnian War, which saw around 100,000 people killed, tens of thousands of women raped, and millions more displaced, the GNAT Drone was utilized again. However, it was vulnerable to inclement weather and could only be controlled from a relatively close proximity restricting its surveillance capabilities. This is where *General Atomics* responded with the Predator. Now with satellite communications, American Drone operators didn't even have to be in the same region let alone the same continent as the Drone. The Predator Drones were first flown in June 1994 and future developments included a de-icing system, reinforced wings, and a laser-guided targeting system that proved essential for its later weaponization. Impressed with the Predator's capabilities, the U.S. Air Force soon established its very first UAV squadron in Indian Springs, Nevada, later named Creech Air Force Base in 2005. Then after a Predator Drone spotted who it believed was Osama bin Laden at Tarnak Farm in Afghanistan, the call went out to shorten the time it took to take a target out. Previously, Tomahawk missiles would fly out from a submarine in the Arabian Sea to southern Afghanistan and would take about six hours to go through military protocols. But if the Predators were equipped with Hellfire Missiles, then the response time would be immediate. Here is where the hunter became a killer. To this day, Creech Air Force Base remains the current hub of American Drone operations in Afghanistan.

Soon the fateful day came when the armed Predator program was activated days after the terrorist attacks on September 11, 2001. Then President Bush signed a directive that created a secret list of High Value Targets or (HVTs) that the CIA was authorized to kill without further Presidential approval. 9/11 officially ended any worries that the Predator program would be shut down. Then in 2008, former CIA Director Michael Hayden successfully lobbied the Bush Administration to relax Drone targeting constraints. Now, a named target on a kill-list was no longer a legal prerequisite to attack. Instead, the CIA could now target individuals based on their "pattern of life" or their suspicious daily behavior. These "signature strikes" as they are called were also reassigned by Obama in 2009. And today, the CIA oversees a program of extrajudicial killings and geographic surveillance across the planet: in Pakistan, in Somalia, in Yemen, in Libya, in Iran, and beyond. Furthermore, its global reach shows no sign of shrinking. In fact, at the time of this research, there have been a total of 5,884 people killed by Drone strikes. But again, that's just what's been reported.[1]

Now, as you can see, modern day Drone technology has not only come a long way in its development and seen some serious improvements, but now for the first time in man's history, we have "armed machines" in the sky that are killing people right now, hunting them down from above, just like the Terminator movies and Skynet premise portrays. If you thought that was scary, you haven't seen anything yet! Most people today are not only ignorant of the history or development of Drones, but they are completely unprepared for the deployment of Drones, the mass invasion that's coming to virtually every sector of society! I'm not talking just the military, I'm talking about every facet of society, around the world, even in your own back yard. It truly is an *Attack of the Drones*! So, let's now switch gears and see where this *Attack of the Drones* is headed. In the near future, you tell me if the Skynet scenario isn't right around the corner.

Part II

The Deployment of Drones

Chapter Three

The Private Invasion

The **1st invasion** of Drones coming to the planet is in the **Private Sector**.

Outside of the military invasion of Drones, the other area most people are familiar with, Drone technology, is in the private sector. Whether it's a modern-day hobbyist, or an amateur filmmaker, or a Dad showing off his latest toy with his son, personal Drones are now exploding on the scene. In fact, let's take a look at the different types of consumer Drones out there for you to get your hands on.

TECH quickie reports:
You may not get to blow things up like our military does with their unmanned aircraft but if simply flying things around for the fun of it sounds good to you, you may just want to look into picking up a consumer Drone. A product category that has enjoyed a huge surge in popularity recently. But what exactly is a Drone? How do Drones work? What do you need to know before taking off? We will start by fixing your terminology.

Although the words are often used interchangeably, most of the Drones that you see on the market are actually just Quadcopters and as that name suggests, it means they have four spinning rotors arranged in a square or in a diamond pattern. Now Quadcopters work by varying how fast each individual rotor is spinning so if all the blades are spinning at the same speed then it will either go straight up or down or hang in the air in one spot. But, if some of the blades are told by an onboard controller to rotate faster than the others it could cause the Quadcopter to dive, bank, straight or even do stunts, like flips.

But while most Drones function fairly similarly due to the actual physics of the four-rotor arrangement they are certainly not all created equal. You can get anything from tiny low powered quads for beginners for under $50.00 to heavy duty Drones with powerful batteries and crystal-clear cameras that will run you over a thousand dollars and could probably take over Luxemburg if you had enough of them. Let's say that's not your goal, or who knows, maybe it is, how do you shop for a Drone? What exactly should you be looking for? That all depends on what capabilities you require, your flying and technical skills and of course your budget.

There are plenty of ready to fly or RTF Drones that come fully assembled which include a hand held remote and transmitter. Just charge up the battery and you are pretty much ready to rock. Cheaper models typically will not fly as long on a single charge, thanks to their low capacity batteries, with some of them lasting as little as five minutes and usually feature very low-quality cameras if they have one at all. As you go up the price ladder you will find Drones that can fly around for half an hour on just a single charge with cameras that can capture great looking stabilized HD video.

Other features might include longer range, the ability to mount your own camera, with DoPros being a popular choice, some even accepting popular DSLR cameras, with the ability to stream live videos directly to a smart phone or tablet for first person control or even the ability to use the aforementioned tablet or other devise to control the Drones flight. But, pre-built ones aren't for everyone, so if you're a tinkerer, the Drone hobbyist community might be what you are after.

There are a number of build it yourself Drones that are available in many different price ranges as well as individual parts that you can buy such as high capacity batteries, advanced remote transmitters, even auto pilots that turn a Quadcopter into an actual bonified self-piloting Drone. Also, as you become more and more experienced you may even want to try a different flight controller. These are the PCDs that control the rotors, kind of like the Drones mother board, that respond differently to control inputs.

With some, a more specialized improved flying thus capturing prettier videos while others might be a bit more challenging to fly but will allow you to pull off much more impressive maneuvers. So, if you're interested in going the DIY route, there is a lot of information available on selecting parts for your level and needs. Before you jump in to it, remember that just like anything else that's fun, there are some rules you have to follow. Both the American and Canadian governments have outlined regulations for flying Drones for fun as they are technically aircraft.

These include, but are not limited to, not flying too close to airports, getting the proper certifications, if your Drone is over a certain weight, size limit, or if you are flying for commercial gain, keeping your Drone within sight, not near an actual plane, for obvious reasons, and this should go without saying, not using your Drone to spy on your attractive neighbor or that troll that said he wanted to fight. Besides, if Drone owners start misbehaving too much, how will the Drone industry ever get to the point where we have Quadcopter Pizza delivery, which would be awesome.[1]

    Boy, wouldn't that be great! It's already here, but that's the tip of the iceberg. You can not only get drones that fly in the air, but you can also get ones that fly along the ground. Let's take a look at these made from Parrot.

Discover the Parrot Mini-Drones. The award winning connected robots. They roll and jump anywhere with Parrot jumping Sumo. They look like two wheels with an eye in the middle. Also roll and fly anywhere with Parrot Rolling Spider. Buy yours now before they all fly away.[2]

    Or crawl away! But as you can see, Air, ground, what's next? Drones are everywhere! Even for you water enthusiasts, believe it or not, your wish is their command. You can now get your very own Water Drone, thanks to these guys.

CNN Reports:
Eric Stackpole and David Lane are two entrepreneurs looking to be the next Jacques Cousteau. They tell us, "Jacques Cousteau changed the way ocean exploration was done. He invited people to explore along with him. So, for us it's the same thing." They are working on an underwater robotic submarine that anyone can own and use. Priced at less than a thousand dollars, it would give amateur explorers Cousteau like access. "This is the open ROV. ROV stands for

Remotely Operated Vehicle. I can put it in the water and fly it around and it's got a video camera on it. You can see what it sees, live."

Users build the ROV themselves and are encouraged to submit new designs and ideas. Eric tells us, "OPENROV is an open source community. If the ROV is having some sort of problem and can't figure out how to handle it, I can go into the forums and as I sleep the problem is going across Europe. By lunch I could have 5 or 6 good solutions." Making it easier for the ever changing ROV as it goes into more unchartered waters.

"People often ask us if it's something that is just kind of a toy that's fun to build and play with or is it something you expect to be used in real research and our answer is certainly, both. We hear from people all the time, conservation organizations, who want to go in, find and check on invasive species of fish, game groups and teachers that want to get these things into classrooms. We're excited about all of them."[3]

If you're an underwater enthusiast, as you can see, there is no place these things are not going to be flying, crawling, or swimming around? But you might be thinking, "Well hey, that's just those hobbyists and computer gurus who are in to that sort of thing. I'll have no personal use for a Drone." Really? Well, everybody loves taking selfies, don't they? Now you can take one with a drone.

CNET News Reports:
It's one more sign of the current fascination with selfies and Drones. The one called Nixie snagged the $500,000.00 top prize at Intel's 'Make it Wearable Challenge'. Jelena Jovanovic of Nixie says, "Whenever you want to make an amazing shot it unfolds, the entire thing unfolds, and it flies, turns around and takes a photo or video of you and then comes back to you." The competition sponsor Intel makes Edison, a tiny computer that powers Wearables. "My goal is to make it so small that it will fit on a button on your shirt and last several days on a battery," says Brian Krzanich, CEO, Intel. So yes, you soon could take selfies to a whole new height.[4]

Move over Selfie Sticks, this one is going to be the new hot item! Who wouldn't want a video selfie with a drone! Awesome! And speaking of awesome, for all those adventurists out there who have only in the past been able to tell a story about your crazy stunts, thanks to Drones, you can now use them to record your whole trip, stunts and all! Like this Drone called Lily.

Meet Lily. It's a throw and go Drone. You throw it in the air and ski down the slope. It follows you and videos your every move, up and down the slope, in full HD SloMo 1080P. When you come to a stop it easily lands in the palm of your hand after a 20-min. flight time. While it is flying, there is a tracking device (in a waterproof case) that you wear on your wrist. Lily is also waterproof. Lily can follow or lead and is Ultra-Portable. Lily records sound and takes pictures.[5]

Okay, finally, somebody's going to believe you about the fish that you almost caught! You'll have it all on tape! But if that selfie drone is still just a little too big for you, then wait no more! They just came out with the wallet Drone and it comes in multiple colors for you Fashionistas out there!

It's the world's smallest Quadcopter. Robert Morrison tells us, "I am the founder of Access Drones and I have with me the Wallet Drone. The Wallet Drone is the smallest Quadcopter. It fits inside of the controller itself which is the size of the wallet and it fits perfectly inside of your pocket. Not only does the Quadcopter fit inside of the remote control but it uses the remote controls batteries to charge itself while not in use. Making it go anywhere that you can.

This is the most portable, compact, Quadcopter on the market. We have had probably 5 or 6 remote controlled planes, but the Wallet Drone seems to last forever. Maybe it's the small size of it but it flew longer than just about any other copter we have ever used. The Wallet Drone is available in four different colors, blue, green, yellow and orange.[6]

Who wouldn't want to have one of those? It's cool, it's adventurous, but maybe someday we can do both. Not only use a cool drone to record our adventures but use that cool drone to "become" the adventure. How many of you remember those Hover Bikes on Star Wars? Well maybe soon, you can get one of those.

From the movie, Return of the Jedi:
Look, over there, stop him! The Ewok is on the Hover Bike and is about to take off. The Storm Troopers jump on their Hover Bikes and take off after him. They chase him through the forest flying in between the trees. They are shooting at him and he is spinning over and over while he is laughing and screaming. It seems he is having fun while they are out to get him. But he is faster, and they can't catch him.[7]

Okay, now who wouldn't want one of those? Believe it or not, thanks to the advancements in this Drone technology, your very own Hover Bike might be a reality much sooner that you think.

The Malloy Hoverbike has two round circles on each side of it that looks like two wheels, but these wheels don't roll like wheels on a car, they are flat and stationery. Between the two is a seat for a person to sit on. The Hoverbike is the result of years of research and development. We combined the freedom of the helicopter and the simplicity of the motorcycle to create the first Hoverbike.

Developing a Hoverbike is expensive and challenging and we need your support to make this a reality. The Hoverbike flies like a helicopter, however it is rugged and easy to use. It represents a whole new way to fly. We created a one-third scale Hoverbike Drone to test a new dynamic concept. Our Drone will enable you to see and feel just how it would be to fly the Hoverbike and help in raising the funds needed to bring the Hoverbike to market. We have moved to a proven Quadcopter design and this is what our second generation Hoverbike looks like.[8]

Wow! Looks like these drones are going to be everywhere whether we want them or not. Even as a mode of transportation! In fact, like it or not, Drones are not only here to stay, but they've become so popular that they have even launched International Drone Day!

Channel 8 Now reports:
Well, they aren't just for spying, Drones are everywhere. Today is International Drone Day. A day of learning more about the capabilities of these machines. Scott Daniels joins us with how this day is bringing more Drone action to Las Vegas. Scott reports, "This is so cool, we are hearing stories both good and bad about Drones. Drone Day is to clear up any rumors, meet the people flying these Drones, and see what they can actually do."

The million-dollar Drone industry is taking off. Las Vegas is one of five Drone testing sites in the U.S. On March 14, the southwest desert is the main stage for International Drone Day. "Worldwide, I think we are going to have a couple thousand Drones in the air," reports David O'Neal, That Drone Show Host. "It's probably the most hobby Drones and semi-commercial Drones in the air, on the planet, today." The day is to show that Drones are not just for spying but have incredible capabilities.[9]

And some of those capabilities are making money. The Drone market is taking off so fast and getting so popular, and we're just seeing the beginning of it. It's even becoming a sure bet on the Stock Market. Financial experts are now saying that the Drone industry is the new hot commodity and you better get in on this investment while the getting's good!

Bloomberg reports:
Once a Morgan Stanley analyst and now a rich source of material for people looking for the single best investment, is M. Perkins. One of her 82 slides showed growth in Drones. That is the subject of our single Best Chart Today. We have Anders Core, from Core Analytics, with us today. One of the things that is up, but here is one of the things I noticed is that it does look like growth in actual shipments is growing faster than the market size. To me it hints that the Drones are becoming a cheaper technology and one of the developments militarily over the last three or four years have been that we are not the only ones with Drones.[10]

Can I translate that for you? They're spreading like wildfire and you better get in on the investments because it's only going up from here. This Invasion of Drones is not only a Burgeoning Business, but we're still just scraping the surface of this Invasion.

Chapter Four

The Media Invasion

The **2nd invasion** of Drones is the **Media Sector**.

Thanks to recent rulings by the Federal Aviation Administration or FAA, Drones are being given the green light to fly in the skies for all kinds of needs, even the media. For instance, the Motion Picture Association of America has argued that Drones are actually safer to use even in urban areas than helicopters for their aerial shots because they are obviously much smaller as well as cheaper. Drones provide a much more economical option than the costs for renting and/or buying a full-blown helicopter, just to achieve some aerial footage. And frankly, the shots these Drones are able to take from the air, are not only good, but frankly, most of the time, are even better than traditional helicopter shots.

The Washington Post reports:
The FAA opened a new era in aviation in September allowing six Hollywood film makers to fly Drones on the movie sets in the U.S. Like they have overseas for movies like Skyfall. A decision that paved the way for more commercial Drone flights in the United States. "Alright let's see some horns, let's do this." The director says. Then you see the SUV driving along the dirt road and hitting a big mass of water. It splashes through it to the other side.

The director is watching the Drone, filming the whole thing, and at certain times it even films in slow motion. The Drone flies right above the SUV and catches every bit of the mud and water that is splashed away from the truck on each side.

It is awesome watching the water splash up over the truck in slow motion. These Drones are also used to fly above landscapes, islands, waterfalls, everywhere a person wouldn't be allowed or would be able to do, catching the beauty that no one has ever seen before. Catching sports events, birds eye view, and in slow motion. Flying with the birds or swimming with the fish, running with the herds of animals that could never have been done before.[1]

So, as you can see, no wonder Hollywood's itching to get their hands on this stuff! Amazing wild shots, cheaper, easier, and it's about to revolutionize the way they present their movies. And that's why it only makes sense, if it's good for Hollywood, then it's got to be just as good for the news media, right? Well, believe it or not, the news industry has also caught on to this Drone technology and is starting to provide their own revolution on how to report their news from an angle never before heard of. Not only do they no longer need to pay for a helicopter or helicopter pilot, just like Hollywood, but thanks to these Drones they can also get into places and get shots that helicopters just simply cannot. For instance, imagine not just taking a picture of a snow storm or a deadly flood and then showing it on the TV screen, or helicopter footage from way up in the air, but imagine having live footage within inches or feet of an event with an angle never before obtained. It brings the news in a much more personal and surreal fashion.

News 8 reports:
Drones could soon be flying over our heads bringing you an 'eye in the sky' view of major events. A Nevada company has the approval and is now preparing to launch. Already we have seen hobbyist amazing views of everything from historic events like the implosion of the Clarion back in February to fun displays like a coordinated Christmas light show shot from the sky, so you can see numerous houses.

Also, now we are able to fly over flooded areas to see if there are any people or animals that need to be rescued. Jim Grimaldi tells of what is happening in West Seneca, Buffalo New York, on November 19. "The ground was hit with tons of snow, burying the cars and blocking the doors of the homes. The streets are impassable, the snow plows can't get through and the streets have 3 ½ feet of snow on them. Also, the snow has caused the trees to break and are laying in the streets.

So, usually this sounds pretty good, but it's been 2 days now and we haven't seen one plow. So, literally, right now I cannot go anywhere in a car. You can walk but it's really tough walking in waist deep snow. There was a Drone yesterday that they sent out to get an idea of what is going on in the neighborhood. Some of my neighbors are already trying to get their driveways clear but they haven't had much luck.

People in western New York and Buffalo, go through this a lot whereas yesterday's storm and tomorrow's storm will bring a lot of snow. We are pretty used to getting prepared for it, watching the weather, stocking up on food, and stocking up on cat food. So, we are pretty used to it. The people of Buffalo are very friendly people, we look out for each other, and that's what's going on. There's little villages appearing, you get out and get to know your neighbors a little bit more.[2]

Get some incredible shots for the news! That's not just surreal, but that's going to radically revolutionize the news. You just can't get those shots with a helicopter, which means, the news industry is about to radically change. In fact, the news industry is now calling up a fleet of "Reporter Drones" to be the ongoing "Eye in the Sky" ready to report and record news events as they unfold, like never before. And, it's not just an American phenomenon, as we have already seen, it's a global movement. Here's BBC reporting their excitement over this new way to report the News.

BBC News Reports:
This is Old Oak Home Depot which is now a train depot in the most deprived parts of London. But if they build the HS2 this whole area will be transformed and will be turned into one of the five busiest train stations in the whole country. You may not realize this but what you have just seen is a little bit of BBC News history. It's not my performance, unfortunately, note this is the first time the BBC News crew has used one of these.

A Drone. We get to use all the glamorous locations. This is Hexicopter. A new toy with 6 rotors, a little camera, and all it takes is just changing the battery. We are going to call it 'Alan', our new camera man. Here is the team that runs it and built it. In fact, Rianne and Owen are from the BBC's global video unit. As a cage of chickens is opened and all the chickens are coming out, he continues, you might have guessed that we have moved locations to a town in Chesser.

Owen spent 6 months training before he was allowed to take the controls today. He now has a special license, and this is what he can do. No helicopter or camera crew can get these unique, fantastic shots. "It is absolutely sensational; the pictures are marvelous. The statue, the most famous landmark of Brazil, the shot was incredibly steady. How difficult is it to achieve that?" asked the reporter. The answer is, "The technology has really advanced.

There's a platform that the camera is mounted on which essentially stabilizes it in case of a gust of wind or unexpected turbulence up there, and it was very turbulent. It compensates for those moves and gives you a very smooth shot." "How difficult is it to fly? Are you operating both the camera and the Hexacopter?" asks the reporter. Owain Rich, BBC Hexacopter Pilot answers, "Well I work with one of my colleagues and one person is handling the camera attached to the panel and I am working the Hexacopter.

We rehearse it beforehand and so we decide what we are going to do first. Then essentially, we both have to contribute to making those kinds of shots. So, I place the copter in the sky and place the camera where he wants it to be and then we both work at the same time." Reporter asks, "Presumably, as well as the camera and the Hexacopter, you are getting a signal on the monitor in front of you, otherwise you don't know where you are steering?"

Owain answers, "When filming the Christ shot, it has to be in a frame, quite specific, and so the camera operator has a down link coming down from the copter and they can see what's going on and they can make those adjustments to the camera, and it can swing around the statue." "This gives us a completely different perspective, I mean when you watch football games in the big stadiums and they have a camera on a wire that goes across the stadium, but the swooping shots, I thought at times I was actually watching a video game designed in somebody's mind. That these weren't real pictures." said the reporter.

"As a camera man I get really excited about being able to show the images to the audience with a different perspective that they may not have seen before. When all this copter stuff started I got very excited. Essentially it allows us to go very low and then having one shot going very high. You see that progression in a way you couldn't do in any other way," Owain replies. This machine is going to transform the way TV views the news in the future.[3]

Which means, it's here to stay and we're just seeing the beginning of it! Now notice how the one Drone pilot mentioned how it took two operators to get those kinds of amazing shots. One to fly the Drone, and the other to operate the camera. But this revolution is taking off so fast that that's no longer the case! The next generation of media Drones are already here! And they offer many automated features with the push of a button. One person can now get these kinds of shots all by themselves. Here's just one of those automated Drones called The Solo.

Solo is the ultimate tool for aerial, video, and photography. Whether you are a first-time pilot or a long-time pro, Solo is the most powerful and easiest Drone to use on the market. Solo is designed from the ground up to give you the best aerial experience imaginable.

Solo pairs smooth flying characteristics with powerful features, making it easy to get great professional shots from day one. Cable cam allows you to lock Solo on a virtual cable on any two points in the air, so you can focus on camera work.

Pan and tilt the camera freely without needing to keep track of direction of the camera. Solo can even memorize your framing at each end of the cable then smoothly shift your camera between the two points, easing into and out of the moves like a seasoned professional.

These features are made possible by two Solo onboard computers which enable radical breakthroughs in both flight and camera control. This makes Solo the first Smart Drone.

By harnessing the power of these computers, even brand-new pilots have the ability to capture beautiful, cinematic shots that would otherwise require years of practice. The included mobile app gives you an incredible live view from your GoPro. Easy access to Solo's shot mods helps you to learn how to fly with a built-in flight trainer. We work closely with GoPro to make Solo the first Drone to give you full control of your GoPro through both our mobile app as well as dedicated buttons on Solo's controller.

This controller was designed from the ground up to give you an unrivaled aerial photography experience. It's gaming inspired agronomics feel familiar to even brand-new pilots. It also has its own built-in computer putting both the vehicle and the camera at your fingertips. All of these features are seamlessly integrated into a simple all in one system giving you the power to easily capture amazing aerial photography.[4]

Who needs two years or even six months to learn one of these things. As you can see, things are moving so fast in the Drone technology world that anyone can achieve some pretty amazing shots. In fact, it's also revolutionizing the marriage industry. We've all heard of Wedding Photographers and Wedding Videographers. Well, imagine having one of these at your disposal, and that's exactly what is happening. Movie style footage that makes your marriage video look just like a Hollywood Wedding.

As the Drone takes off the reporter tells us, more videographers are using that small Drone to capture that perfect depth defying shot of a wedding. There's an explosion of this technology and it's not going to go away unless they just tell us we can't use it. Mr. Joker has been an air force photo journalist since 2006 and is planning to retire this month.

He hopes to use the Drone he made himself to make aerial videography his professional specialty. There's no view like it. It's absolutely incredible to see the view from the air, everything looks amazing, the people in the wedding look amazing, it looks like something out of a story book. It looks like something out of a movie.[5]

Wow! Your own wedding being shot like a movie! But Hollywood, News, and Weddings are not the only industry jumping on this Drone bandwagon. So are politics, unfortunately! Just when you thought you saw everything of how they try to get their message across, politicians are now using Drones to provide the latest WOW factor to get your vote.

A Political Ad for Governor Rick Snyder (R-Mi)
It's just who we are. Put the shouting aside and just get to work. As we fly over the ships docked in the port of the coast of Michigan we hear the voice of the campaign: In the next few days we will decide if Michigan keeps moving forward or goes back to troubled times.

Campaign Ad of John Kitzhaber (D-OR)
We see a man fly fishing in the river. The announcer comes on and says: This is the Oregon way. The camera flies over the fisherman onto the other side to get a different view of the beautiful way and trees. John Kitzhaber, Governor.

Campaign Ad for Cory Gardner (R-Co)
As you watch two people walk through the green grass and the windmill blowing over head the announcer comes on and says: Cory Gardner, a new generation. A new kind of Republican.

Campaign Ad of National Rifle Association
The truck drives down a two-lane road out in the middle of pasture land. As the camera scans the landscape the words you see on the screen say they call this 'Fly-over country' it's an insult.

Footage from Citizens United Documentary on Rand Paul in Guatemala
The camera scans over the missions of Guatemala and then stops at what looks like a hospital.[6]

Well hey, that gets your attention, doesn't it? Just when you thought you'd seen every trick in the book from politicians, now Drones are helping them to get your vote! But not to be outdone is the rest of the entertainment industry! Whether it's using Drones to create a light show, or Walt Disney using them to create flying puppets, or even Circus du Soleil using them for flying lampshades, Drones have become the latest trend in entertaining and wowing a crowd.

Drones with lights attached are all lined up. They are about to all be turned on in rows. They start flashing and then take to the air. They now look like stars but will be doing a light show. As the music plays the lights dance in the dark sky. They start to turn to make different designs. They can be seen for blocks. They start flashing on and off and changing colors. They finally all come back down to earth. What a light show!

Now we see an inventor sitting in his basement at his workbench. He is discovering things he might do with lights. He proceeds to plug in one and it blows the whole room out of light and he is sitting in the dark looking at a lantern that is the only light in the room. He picks up his book to go back to his invention when the lights flash on and off. While he has his book open and he is trying to figure out what is going on behind his back the lamp shades raise above his head and then down again. He doesn't see what is happening.

Then one takes off from his work bench and he jumps and turns to follow where it is going. When he turns around he sees all them floating in the room. He slowly takes his lantern and walks towards the floating lampshades, but they jump ahead of him. He is amazed at how they are now floating in a big circle around his head. He stands there with his mouth open. He bends over, and they go lower. He stands up straight and they go higher. He raises his hands higher and then spreads his arms out and the lampshades do the same thing.

Now he goes around in circles and they do too. He is actually dancing with the lampshades. Suddenly they start flashing and moving slower. Gradually coming down lower. Someone knocks at the door and all the lampshades go back to their lamps. **Welby Altidor**, *Executive Creative Director of Creation Cirque du solei says, "What we wanted to do, what could we do, with this new emerging technology, with the quadcopter to give it some meaning. Give it some magic and bring it to another level."*

Raffaello D'Andrea, *Professor at ETH Zurich Founder of Verity Studios AG, says, "We have been doing research with flying machines for over 50 years. Using algorithms that we developed, we can dynamically control a large number of flying machines with great precision to do things that were impossible to do with human pilots. We saw right away that there was a potential with quadcopters to explore where else we could go and what type of interaction they could have with humans. We have synchronized groups of flying machines to music, we have built structures with rope and bricks in front of live audiences and performed various balancing acts and even explored human flying machine juggling.*

What's fun is to imagine what else we could put on them to make them fly and is it possible to make the quadcopters disappear. So, we did a number of tests. We came up with all kinds of ideas. We even had flying heads to see what kind of effect it could create." Take a deep breath, we are not flying through the clouds. Open up for new possibilities. There is sensation in new innovation.

This year we bring you a show without artists. A show without stages. Amsterdam Arena. Welcome to the world premiere of AIR. The first Drone entertainment show in the world. The crowd is standing and cheering as the Drones come into the stadium to put on their light show. Ballet & Battles, Races & Lasers, Circus & Illusions, Magic & Machines, are you ready for the next level, coming soon. AIR, come rise with us.[7]

Okay, looks like there's going to be a rise of new entertainment! Just when you thought you'd seen it all. Now we have Drone races, Drone ballet,

Drone light shows! Anything to grab your attention for the entertainment industry. In fact, speaking of grabbing your attention, did you really think that advertisers wouldn't pick up on this too? Unfortunately, they have! Move over old-fashioned commercials, now they're turning Drones into literal flying billboards! And they're so serious about it, they're paying big bucks for it! One guy who's the founder of Drone Cast, a Drone Advertising Business, said this, "When I first started, the idea was to fly for $100 a day. But then we got a large offer for $25,000 for 4 hours!" Why? Because they can fly where traditional platforms cannot!

Angus Ledwidge, Reporting:
A Young guy is standing in a field of green grass looking up at a white Drone with a flag hanging down with the words that say, 'say it with Drones.com'. Another says, 'Put your ad here'. It's a new way to advertise. They are taking it to the skies where marketing meets the future. Coming to a city near you. Get ready, fly with us.

It looks like something out of a Syfy movie. But this could be the world's newest form of advertising, an unmanned aerial vehicle, better known as a Drone. It's able to project vision onto the sides of buildings. Tonight, we are trying out our experimental projected Drone that at the moment the projector is rather stationary. The next version will have the pan and tilt capability.

Ryan Hamlet*, project manager for I-Drone and has been experimenting with the flying projector for five months. The Drone is only 50 centimeters wide and while current trials are kept low to the ground Mr. Hamlet can picture the soaring potential. So, for commercial use the company hopes the projector Drone generates a different kind of buzz and potential clients, but it's just the tip of the iceberg in this booming industry. It's a long way off but maybe one-day things like this (a scene from Blade Runner, 1982) will be a reality.*[8]

Oh joy! Just when you thought you could get away from commercials by turning your TV off, not anymore! Now they're going to be everywhere! But again, that's just the tip of the iceberg concerning this invasion. That's just the Media!

Chapter Five

The Agricultural Invasion

The **3rd invasion** of Drones is in the **Agriculture Sector**.

One of the most surprising places Drones are taking off in, is in the Agricultural Sector. The Federal Aviation Administration, the FAA, has already issued drone permits for use in the agriculture and real estate sectors. I know it might seem kind of odd that the Agricultural Industry would jump on the bandwagon with this technology, given the stereotypical response of country folks not being the most tech savvy or tech appealing people in the world. However, this is the power of this new Drone technology and all its amazing benefits. Even farmers are recognizing the time and money saving benefits of this new technology and are eager to learn and capitalize on this new trend. For instance, Drones are right now being used to monitor crop yields as well as water usage to maximize their production.

Sarah Gardner of America's Heartland reports:
It may be hard to believe but some of the technologies in ovations have come right out of the farm. Growers are always looking for new ways to become more efficient, cut costs and become more environmentally friendly. This latest step in agriculture gives farmers a new view from high above their fields. Robert Blair, of Blair Farms, tells us, "Instead of scouting a field a normal way, like walking through or driving a four-wheeler, now we are seeing the whole field and being proactive."

Kurt Scudder, Ph.D. Research Consultant, says, "This is something that is very commonly used. It is no more unusual to see one of these, than it would be to see a crop dusting aircraft, which, as you can imagine, to farmers of a 100 years ago, would have been a truly miraculous piece of technology. We want to look at this as a tool for close end work, short range work where we don't have a place to launch and land a fixed wing aircraft, but we can fly the rotary aircraft.

At Small Vines we are working with the farmer who already has a fairly high-tech operation. He's familiar with aerial imagery, what his crops look like from the air. 'That's so cool to hear it right above you', says the farmer. He's mainly trying to get the sense of water usage and water damage. He is a unique farmer and he plants his rows much denser than they do at any other vineyard and as a result his different water usage causes less water stress on his plants. So, he goes and walks the fields more frequently to get a sense of how that's playing out with his vines. 'You throttle all the way down, ok you're a pilot', says the instructor.

One of the interesting things that we can do to alleviate the problems like Paul's is, we can take both visual imagery and near infrared imagery. We can combine them together to get an NDVI image which gives you a sense of how healthy your plants are. One thing that it can indicate is water stress and are your plants healthy. Steve Redmond, Certified Crop Advisor says, "I'm in the field today demonstrating one of the latest innovations for agriculture. What I am holding is one of the newest UAV's, a Canadian made company. It's called Aeryon, it's out of Waterloo, Ontario. This is their UAV. We are quite excited, it's called a quadcopter as well. It has four propellers that gives us a lot more stability in the air under higher winds. We have just been equipped this week with a new camera, a Tetracam.

This is a camera that will allow us to do NDVI images. It has an NIR filter in it which allows us to do a vegetative index of the field. For example, this cornfield behind me, this year has been a fairly wet year in this area. We have tile drains that are working but we are seeing tile drains that are quite wet. So, when we fly the UAV over the cornfield with this NIR camera we will be able to see these tile drain lines and the impact that poor drainage is having on the corn crop.

Across the road we have a wheat field where we fly as well where the farmer is hoping to split the 60-foot tile drains that were put in in the 70's and put in a new tile drain. Most of the UAV's have a GPS receiver inside the equipment so all the pictures it takes are geo referenced. So, if we are going to create management zones for a farmer or split these drains we need very accurate reference pictures. So that is one of the newest innovations in agriculture. There's all kinds of uses for this. Every time I talk to a farmer we get a new idea as to how we might be able to use it. They are being used by engineering companies to do inspections but in agriculture it's a new frontier and we are continuing to learn new applications for this technology.[1]

In other words, you haven't seen anything yet! So much for not being tech savvy. In fact, drones are not only being used in the air to monitor water usage and plant health and overall crop production, but they are now being used for crop planting as well. Move over old-fashioned tractors! The New Drone tractors are here!

CNN Money Reports:
Rhett Schildroth, Sr. Product manager of Kinze tells us, "This is the Kinze Grain Harvesting system. What we do is take a power train and put it in front of a power train cart and then augment that with some power high speed computers, a series of sensors and high-speed controls. The system looks very similar to a human control system. The tractor is still there with a Kinze Grain cart attached.

What's different about it is a series of E stops and buttons around the perimeter so if someone is too close to it or they feel uncomfortable they can hit that, and it immediately stops. The only other obvious difference is that there is no one in the cab of the tractor. In the cab of the combine there is an android tablet and its running software that we developed, it's the user interface of the system. What the system does is it determines actually where is the best means of where it's at to where it's instructed to go to."

"When the vision of this came about, actually my dad was driving with someone to lunch and they got to talking about farming and he looked out and said you know I believe ten years from now it will be common to see Drones out harvesting or planting. And so, a few years later we thought that could very much be a possibility." Says Susanne Veatch, CMO, Kinzee.

"It took a couple years to get to the point where we felt comfortable operating on the company seal. And then another year for us to be comfortable to be operating it with customers out there. This year we are actually leasing the system to a number of farmers and we're leaving it on its own." Rhett Schildroth continues.[2]

Okay, I sure hope it works! Wow! Automated tractors! Drones in the sky. Drones on the ground. What's next in the Agricultural Industry? Drones spraying pesticide? Actually yes! Just like in the other industries, you don't need a pilot anymore? Drones can do it all!

Introducing the latest in Agricultural UAV technology. Terra4 has arrived! The 6L payload sprays 5-6.6 acres per hour. Fully autonomous. Plot the waypoints and let Terra4 do the rest. Electric powered, no emissions. No need for expensive aero planes or pilot's fees to spray your crops. Easy to operate. Easy to maintain.[3]

Okay, so who needs humans to produce food anymore? Apparently, Drones can do it all. Spraying pesticide, monitoring crops, driving tractors. But what about the other things farms produce, you know, like animals and various meat and dairy products? Well, apparently, you don't need a human for that either. Drones are everywhere! You can now use Drones to round up your herd! Sorry cowboys! You're no longer needed either!

Shep, the Drone. The farmer is standing at the gate while Shep the Drone herds the sheep into the gate. No, stragglers either, all bunched in a tight group heading for the gate. Through the gate they go, one by one. Job done![4]

I guess Shep did his job, the New Aerial Cowboy, or Drone I guess. Wow! Can you believe that! In fact, we all know one thing, cowboys and country don't like to just herd animals, they like to hunt animals. And believe it or not, Drones are doing that too!

Highland Hill Farm, Bucks County Pa. advertisement:
We're using this Drone today to show you some of our properties where we allow people to hunt. This is on Fairy and Gordon Road. This is a fenced in property, but deer do occasionally get in. It's good for deer, dove, turkey, rabbits and ground hogs. We have a hunter access program in Highland Hill Farm whereby if you bring us a locust seed or pressure treated fence post you can hunt for the day. One post, one person, one day.

If you shoot a deer, you get three free days. If you shoot two deer in any part of the season, Highland Hill, will give you back your fencepost or twenty-five worthless U.S. dollars and give you the rest of the season for free. As you see, with this Drone, there is a lot of areas for you to hunt. This is just 122-acre field on Fairy and Gordon Road. Now across from this property there is another 34 acres where you can hunt.

Which you see shortly. The Drone can certainly wisp around this farm and check out all areas of the farm for us. We can also use the Drone to determine what areas need to be mowed, sprayed, or how the work or progress is coming along. Now this is the other farm on the other 34-acres on the other side of Gordon Road. This is what we call our Lasoleer Farm. It's a growing operation where we grow Junipers and greenhouses.

In Fountain Ville we have three separate properties for you to hunt. This is on route 313. This is a Norway Spruce field. Nothing but Norway Spruce is in the area. You can also come here during Christmas time to cut your own Christmas Tree.

But as you can see this property is unfenced and adjacent to a large park. So, there are lots of deer in this part of the farm. The other day when I was out I saw five turkeys. We don't see a lot of turkeys here like 4 or 5 a day but we do see turkeys here occasionally.

There is an occasional coyote and once in a great while there might be a bear. I would say it's not a bear hunting country and it's not very good for geese as they don't land. All of our soils are pretty well covered with trees. The geese do fly over fairly low and in range, but you just won't have them land here. Because you can see they don't like to land where there are Christmas trees.

We are within a mile of Peace Valley near the main lake on Lake Galena and there are thousands of geese that do fly over on a daily basis. This whole ad for hunting was shot by a Drone showing all the landscape that is available for hunting the various wildlife.[5]

So, as you can see, lots of options to get your hunting quota with a Drone. I don't know whether to be happy for the hunters or sad for the deer! They have no chance of hiding now! Wow! I sure hope they never use those on people someday. We'll get to that soon enough, believe it or not, remember, Skynet is coming. That's where all this is headed! But as you can see, Drones are revolutionizing all kinds of Agricultural needs. In fact, they are such the new innovation that they are also being looked upon to become the new saviors for the ongoing water crisis.

KPIX Channel 5 reports:
One of our communities that is suffering from extreme drought could soon get help from an unlikely source, Drones. It's how the unmanned aircraft could help produce billions of gallons of water every month. "This machine 9,000 feet up in the Sierra Nevada is helping scientists freeze about 10% more water out of the sky.

But that job may be done better with Drones. Meteorologist, Jeff Tilley, showed us his cloud seeding generator which shoots tiny silver iodized particles into storm clouds. The process helps transform water vapor into snow or rain in about an hour. "So, I assume the higher the elevation you get the better results you get?" asked the reporter. Jeff Tilley replies, "Yes, that's very true."

That's why Tilley's team in the Desert Research Institute is developing the first of its kind Drone for cloud seeding. Piloted planes have been used for more than 60-years and produce 1 billion gallons of water for every 25 to 45 hours of flying. But they have to stay above the clouds for safety reasons. Tilley says Drones can fly through clouds and stay in the air longer producing more precipitation for communities devastated by drought.

He says, "You can think of it not only as more water to shower with or water plants with, or raise crops with, but you're really helping the economy with having a break put on it by the amount of water available." Tilley hopes his cloud seeding Drone will begin soaking communities by the end of the year. It is estimated that the Drones could cut cloud seeding costs in half because they would use much less fuel than a plane.[6]

Well see, there you have it! Drones are all you need. No more human pilots for all your flying needs. Drones can take care of it all. All the fresh water you could ever need! In fact, pretty soon, they could also help deliver all the fresh food you could ever need from the farm, literally to your doorstep, or even restaurant. Don't believe me? Here's some guys putting this idea into action.

There are several men in a field of asparagus. They are pulling some out of the ground maybe to see if they are mature or not. They look them over and put them in a bucket. The little bucket is then put on a Drone to be taken somewhere. As they watch it take off and cross the field they follow it in a truck. All of a sudden it flips and crashes to the ground. The men rush over to see what kind of damage has been done and it is on fire. One man grabs his head, 'Oh no'. It is totally destroyed.[7]

Now, I'm not really sure what he said, I don't speak Dutch, but I think it had something to do with, "The Drone cooked our Asparagus a little too early! It's supposed to wait till it got to the restaurant…BUMMER" But obviously, as you can see, they have a few bugs to work out, but that's not going to stop this industry, as we'll soon see in a bit. But speaking of Drones crashing in the field, wait a second, you can't have a bunch of trash laying around from all these Drones crashing here and there whether they make it to the restaurant or not, how's that environmentally friendly? Well believe it or not, they're not only making Drones that save the environment with cloud seeding and monitoring crops, but they're even making these Drones bio-degradable, so if it crashes, then it simply just melts away. How? By making them from fungus and bacteria. Great for the Environment.

Flying fungus decomposed bio Drone takes to the sky. Sporadically new Drones impress us. Take this Biological Drone, it has a body with some protective bacteria covering it so that it can degrade into the landscape without leaving a trace if it crashes. This type of Drone is perfect for flying over sensitive environments or better yet to conceal spying.

Rothchild of NASA researcher center, an advisor for the student team that says created it, no one would know if you spilled sugar water or if an airplane had been there. She told new scientists, the body of the proto type Drone is made from the vegetative part of the fungi known as mycelium. The Drone is covered in sheets of grown bacteria, covering the sheets are proteins cloned from wasp spit that is usually used to water proof their nests.

The Bio-Drone had its first flight earlier this month at the IGEM, International Genetically Engineered Machine Competition, students in competition in Boston. While the Bio-Drone is made from unusual stuff it also has non-biological parts that do not easily disintegrate, the team plans on making the blades, battery and controls biodegradable.[8]

Isn't that great. Anything for the environment apparently. Just dissolve it away with fungus and bacteria and everything is healthy and clean! What will they think of next? Funny you should ask. Maybe you have heard of those farms that don't follow all those environmental regulations? I mean, how can we make sure they're being compliant with what they're supposed to do? They own a lot of land and it covers such a huge area and its private, how would we ever know what they're doing? Can you say Drones to the rescue? Believe it or not, they're now becoming the new 'Eye in the Sky' to expose all the lawbreakers who damage the Environment, like this report shows.

RT Live Reports:
Drones are not always the first choice for official surveillance or official operations, but one American film maker has used the unmanned aircraft to expose the shady practices used by US farm corporations which he claims are putting peoples' health at risk. One of America's biggest secrets is that farms practically don't exist anymore.

Mark Devries said it would send shivers down your spine. Our reporter asked him about the evidence that he has uncovered. "In North Carolina there are thousands of huge industrial pig factory farms and each of these farms has a giant open-air cesspool filled with untreated animal waste.

To get rid of the waste from these giant open-air cesspools, the manure is actually sprayed into the air which causes it to turn into a fine mist and often gets blown by the wind right into communities which causes serious health impacts and also deeply effect people's lives.[9]

Drones can not only help manage farms, but they can now catch those nasty corporate farms who are breaking the laws harmful to all of us! And that's the tip of the iceberg of what these Drones can do in catching the bad guys. Remember we saw earlier how Drones were being used to spy on and check out where deer and other animals were hiding for the hunters' benefit. What if we turned the tables on them for another environmental concern and used them to protect the animals from poachers, i.e. hunters gone bad? Wouldn't that be cool? Well, believe it or not, they're already doing it!

Tsavo National Park, Kenya:
Mathematics and Drones may be the best hope the elephants and rhinos from extinction. V.S. Suibrahmanian of Umiacs, University of Maryland tells us, "We take into account both the model of how the poachers are attacking the animals as well as the model of how the animals move through the park." This new effort links predictive analytics with Drones to spot illegal activity in the African game preserve.

The computer program builds on the same algorithms developed to forecast locations of IED's in Iraq and Afghanistan. The Lindbergh Foundations Air Shepherd Program approached the institute for advanced computer studies at the University of Maryland where the original military code was written. John L Petersen of the Lindbergh Foundation says, "Where this has been tested it literally stops poaching.

For the first time the poachers don't own the night." Some African game preserves are the size of Connecticut and impossible to patrol on foot. So, the program predicts one day in advance where the animals will be and where poachers are likely to strike. Tom Snitch, of UMIAC says, "We found that within a week of starting our flights in these areas the poaching had stopped. Previously it had been anywhere between 17, 18, 19, rhinos killed in this area in a month.

For the past 6 months now is has been zero." The fixed wing Drone has a preprogramed night flight route based on the hard data. The Drone is equipped with infrared that send a real-time data stream to the command team in the field. Prepositioned park rangers can be alerted to any suspicious behavior and surround the area in minutes. "What you are constantly doing then is creating this very synergistic data system where the people on the ground that are covering this area, driving them every day either as wardens or tourist around are inputting this data so every day it gets better and better and better."

Based on the program's success, Air Shepherd plans to deploy additional anti-poaching teams in the near future. Airware has teamed up with the Ol Pejeta Conservancy to demonstrate the capabilities of a Drone specifically designed for conservation and to help save the Northern White Rhino. We just arrived at the 90,000-acre conservative in Kenya for two weeks of fly testing. We are testing three vehicles including conventional fix wing and flying wing aircraft.

Our goal is for two rangers to easily carry, set up, and launch the Drone with limited infrastructure. The ranger can easily configure the fly plan using a simple mapping interface and launch a flight that is autonomous from launch to recovery. They can also direct a vehicle where it will fly and what to look at once airborne.

Operating both day and night the Drone sends real time digital video and thermal imaging of animals and potential poachers to rangers on the ground using both fixed and gimmel mounted cameras. This technology will make it possible for the conservancy to protect the wildlife more frequently and at a fraction of the cost, providing more reliable data for the management of the animal population.[10]

       Which means, day or night, light or dark, they are going to catch you. Nobody can hide, not only animals in the wild, but people. So, they're using the same Drone technology the military is already using to take people out and now they're using them to take the poachers out. I sure hope they never use it on the Average Joe, that would really bug me! In fact, speaking of bugs, Drones are being used to take care of another environmental concern, insects, dangerous insects, like mosquitoes! Drones are being used to spray pesticide on the crops, so hey, why not use them to spray pesticides everywhere we go and get rid of any of those nasty mosquitoes that not only annoy us but carry harmful diseases.

Authorities, in the Florida Keys, have announced that they will be testing a Drone that will be specifically designed for law enforcement purposes. They will be using them to track one of Florida's greatest enemies, the mosquito. Beyond being annoying, mosquitoes can carry disease like Malaria and West Nile, of which the outcome could be fatal.

Ponds up and down the Keys are active breeding grounds and officials from the Florida Keys control district hope that the Drones can help them locate all of them. The specific one being tested is an infrared camera outfitted vehicle developed by Condor Aerial. It weighs just over 2 lbs. and is about 2 ½ feet long, making it ideal for maneuvering the often-thick vegetation of the Florida land.

Once the ponds are located, professionals can go in and kill the larvae with either chemicals or particular fish to keep them from ever hatching. The ultimate dream is to get Drones that will both locate and eradicate the larvae. But for now, just isolating them will be useful. A wide range of government agencies have been invited to attend the task force.

Michael Doyle, Florida Keys Mosquito Control District says, "Here in the Keys it is so warm, they go from a dry piece of ground to adults in about 5-days. So once the water hits the ground we have maybe three days to put the bacteria in the water and kill them before they fly." Fred Culbertson, Condor Aerial says, "So we are going to use our thermal camera that we use to find people, search and rescue, find those pools of water, find out what we need to do a better job at locating that larvae.[11]

Hey, that looks like the same footage they were taking of the poachers and the animals. And by the way, you just thought that was a bird in the sky, nope, that was a Drone looking for mosquitoes, so they could spray them and kill them. I sure hope that's the only thing they ever use them to spray and kill. Wait till you see all the things Drones are mimicking. Birds are just the tip of the iceberg. You'll never even know it's a Drone coming. But as creepy as all that is, this desire to use Drones to supposedly improve our health, is going Global. The Current Administration is saying that, 'Climate Change is Harming to Our Health,' and has now asked Microsoft and Google to help monitor the whole planet with Drone technology to aid in improving our living conditions. Microsoft's research arm will develop a prototype for Drones that can collect large quantities of mosquitoes, then digitally analyze their genes and pathogens. Google has promised to donate 10 million hours of advanced computing time on new tools, including risk maps and early warnings for things like wildfires and oil flares using the Google Earth Engine platform. Apparently, Google's camera cars, that gather photos for its 'Street View' function will now start measuring methane emissions and natural gas leaks in some cities this year. Sounds like whether we wanted it or not, we're going to be monitored wherever we go, for the 'good' of the environment, of course, with Drones, isn't that nice! But that's still not all.

Chapter Six

The Commercial Invasion

The **4th invasion** of Drones is coming to the **Commercial Sector**.

Drones are not only going to be in the highways and byways and far out places, watching us wherever we go, in the Environment and Agricultural areas, they're also going to be flying right among us, just like a pesky mosquito. That's because the business communities or commercial sectors have tapped into this new Drone technology to improve their service for us, the customer. We all know it's heavy-duty competition out there and businesses are always competing for our dollar. So, what better way to gain the advantage than instant gratification for the customer? Since Drones fly in the air and are not hindered by any traffic or human delays, any business trying to deliver a product to their customer is going to drastically reduce the time it takes for their product to get there. The classic example is with pizza. We all know we order pizza to be delivered, but sometimes it takes forever to get there, and by the time it does arrive, it's cold and beat up. But not anymore! Wouldn't it be great if we could get it in just a few minutes? Well, thanks to this new Drone technology, other countries are already ahead of us with this new commercial delivery service. Here's just one company using Drones to deliver pizza in India.

In this clip you watch a young guy answer the phone at the pizza shop. He calls out what is needed and then the pizza is made. Put in the oven to bake, taken out and cut into slices, put in a box and then taken out to the back of the shop and attached to a Drone for delivery. People on the ground all across town are watching as the Drone flies overhead carrying the pizza. One man is even recording it on his phone. The Drone finally reaches its destination at the top of one of the many towers that are in the city. The tenant takes the pizza off the Drone and goes into his apartment. The Drone flies back to the pizza shop.[1]

Oh yeah! Hot and fresh, ready to eat, thanks to Drones! Now that's not only cool, but India's not alone. This is no fluke, folks. Drone pizza delivery is here to stay. Other countries are doing it as well. Here's one in Brazil.

Again, the call comes in and the order is taken. The pizza is made to perfection, baked in the oven. A bell is ringing after it is sliced and ready to go and a delivery person comes and takes it off the counter. They take it to the next room and puts it into a slot on Drone. It takes off over the city to its destination. Once again, the people on the ground stop what they are doing to watch it fly over. It finally reaches the customer on the other side of town. He takes the pizza off the Drone, takes it to his kitchen counter and enjoys nice fresh hot pizza, right out of the oven.[2]

Wow. Seems like everybody's on a roof ordering that way. But you might be thinking, 'That's those other countries. I don't think the U.S. is going to catch on to that.' Really? Not if Domino gets their way! They're trying to be one of the first ones to do it.

From the movie 'Fast Times at Ridgemont High' (1982)
The delivery boy enters the classroom. "Who ordered the double cheese and sausage?" Sean Penn replies, "Right here dude," and he takes out his money. How do you get your pizza delivered? Last month Domino's Pizza teamed up with a creative ad agency named 'Tea n Biscuits' to test out a prototype for a flying Drone that can deliver cheese pie.

Described as a Domicopter, the devise can carry two large pepperoni pizzas and conducted a flight over a city near London. The pizzas, both contained in an insulated bag, were secured to the Drone. They were delivered in perfect condition and it only took about 10 minutes to venture 4 miles.

The founder of 'Tea n Biscuits' stated that it was quicker than a pizza boy. We were amazed at how easy it was going to be. The Drone is going to be called the Domicopter. Federal Aviation Administration authorities estimate that private Drones will make up a $90 billion dollars industry within 10 years.[3]

In other words, we're just seeing the beginning of this stuff! But oh yeah, who couldn't use a Domicopter? In fact, if this company gets their way, pretty soon maybe they'll be able to deliver their drinks to go along with that pizza as well. Not that I'm condoning alcohol but check this one out.

The phone rings, he writes down the order, turns to the ice box and pulls out a case of Lakemaid Beer. Attaches the case of beer to a Drone that is on the front porch. The Drone takes off across the frozen lake. With several little huts on the ice covered with snow the Drone knows exactly which one to deliver the beer to. It lands in front of the door and the participant comes out and picks it up. Takes the beer back inside and continues with his ice fishing.[4]

That's right! Your very own Drone delivered beer! Wow! Pizza and now beer delivery on ice, literally! It's like every lazy guy's (or gal's) dream has come true! In fact, they're about to provide another special service for lazy folks, including those who forget things you shouldn't ever forget! We all know, as guys, we sometimes forget those special holidays, anniversaries or birthdays for our wives or girlfriends. So, wouldn't it be great if Drones could help us out there too? Well, ask no more! Your wish is their command, at least if this company gets their way! Flowers on demand, thanks to Drones.

The phone rings, the receptionist answers, he takes the order for a beautiful arrangement to be delivered. No problem, he writes down the address and billing information and passes the order to the florists to get the flowers ready. Once they are ready they are put in a box and attached to a delivery Drone. The Drone takes off and travels across vacant lots, parking lots, miles across town and finally comes to the house.

It lands on the front porch, drops off the flowers, and then takes off to return to the flower shop. The lady comes out to see what is on her porch and what a surprise. She takes them in the house, opens the box and they smell so fresh and sweet. What a wonderful gift.[5]

Did you see that? Just call in your coordinates no matter the weather condition and 'you're still the man'! Drones to the rescue again! If you think this is just a convenience for lazy forgetful guys or gals, the new Drone delivery service doesn't' stop there. Even Restaurants are starting to use Drones inside their restaurants to get their drinks to their customers in record time. Remember, you've got to improve that service to keep those customers coming back! It's tough competition out there you know! Here's one restaurant doing it in Singapore for real.

The bartenders are waiting on the customers. Some are sitting at tables across the room. "Having a robot in the restaurant makes it possible to serve the food and drinks from the kitchen to the dining area and allowing the current manpower and staff to interact with customers. A lot of people might have fears about having many Drones flying around them or perhaps the Drones colliding with one another or with obstacles while there.

But at Infinium Robotics we have developed technologies that allow it to maneuver in a very close proximity. It would not be able to collide with another one. The analogy would be something like a swarm of birds flying in the sky and many of them flying in formations." says Junyang Woon, Chief Executive, Infinium Robotics. "Singapore, in the past two years has encountered a severe manpower crunch and Timbre has not been spared.

So how we deal with it is that we are investing in technologies to enhance our productivity. Not all technologies will want to lose the human touch but if we can help in the process we will do so," says Edward Chia, Managing Director, Timbre Group.[6]

Did you catch that? Who needs Humans anymore? If you have a shortage of humans like they do, a fleet or swarm of Drones, once again to the rescue! Now for those of you who think this is just going to be a fad with pizza or drink deliveries, or even flowers, or restaurant foods, think again. Because of this ability to drastically reduce delivery time with Drones, right now they're being looked upon as the new Pony Express in the air to get your product faster than ever before, anything you order, not just food or flowers! One of the biggest businesses leading the way in this new delivery service is Amazon. And now with their new Amazon Prime Air Service, they are hoping to become one of the first companies in the world to provide instant gratification to their customers around the world with same day delivery.

Sarah Hashim-Waris reports:
Amazon isn't the only company testing same day delivery service. Google and UPS are also looking into delivery Drones according to news reports. Amazon reports this week announced that Amazon Prime Air has a delivery system using

Drones and sources says UPS is similarly evaluating ways to add Drones to its service.

UPS said in its statement that it invests more into this technology than any other company and delivery business and is always planning for the future. The Times reports that Google has also been testing Drone deliveries systems in its secret Google X-lab as far back as February. Google would reportedly like to use Drones technology as part of its same day delivery service that is available in San Francisco and surrounding areas.

"Hi, this is Neale at Biomex, I'd like to order some dog food for my dogs please." "Throughout history there has been a series of innovations that have each taken a huge chunk out of the friction of moving things around." Says Astro Teller, Captain of Moonshots, Google, "Project Wing aspires to take another big chunk of the remaining friction of moving things around the world." "We are in Australia. The goal of being here is to show that the hard work over the last 2 years has resulted in a reliable system that does autonomous delivery.

And we also just want to get out and learn what it is like to the neighbor Neale. See what it's like from their prospective. It's years from a product, but it is sort of the first prototype that we want to stand behind," says Nicholas Roy, Founder of Project Wing. "The next phase is to take the momentum and the enthusiasm that was built internally and drive it towards enabling the dream of delivering stuff more quickly with proper and due safety," says Dave Vos, Lead, Project Wing. Working together I think we can get to this future surprisingly quickly."[7]

Okay, who doesn't want to sign up for that service! That's not only cool, but Amazon says, "Its Drone delivery service could someday get packages to customers in 30 minutes or less. Through its Prime Air service, they will have Drones flying 50 mph and capable of carrying up to 5 pounds, and, they will become as normal as seeing delivery trucks driving down the street. It's coming! Amazon is not the only big business getting in on this new Drone delivery service. So is Google and UPS. Pretty soon, we'll not only get our mail but even our dog food by a Drone.

USA Today reports:
You may see more of those sharing the skies with planes. Today the Federal Aviation Administration announced that four more companies are approved to fly commercial Drones. The new innovation of unmanned aircraft has exploded in

the last year and the FAA is scrambling to restrict Drones from crossing flight paths.

Just last month a Drone came within feet of a Delta Airlines wing during its landing at JFK. Federal officials see more Drones as a growing aviation threat if left unregulated. Competition is getting fierce to make it to a list of approved companies free to use the cutting-edge technology. Today Trimble Navigation Limited, VDOS Global, Claycorp, and Woolpert Inc. can count themselves among the few that the FAA is slowly approving to use Drones commercially.

These companies will use them to conduct aerial surveys and monitor construction sites. The House Committee is holding a hearing today to develop Drone regulations. The key is to prevent Drones from colliding with other aircraft or with people on the ground. These latest approvals follow seven in September to photo and video companies.[8]

      Isn't that great? It can all happen quickly. And as crazy as all this might sound, believe it or not the FAA, right now, estimates that thousands of drones will be flying in the U.S. within just a few years. Now many other companies are starting to be approved for this service, right and left, as this news report shows.

Audi commercial:
A business man looks out the window of the office building and sees what looks like birds flying all around the front door. At a closer look he sees that they are Drones. He turns to the people standing behind him and says, "I think we can make it, right?" Another gentleman steps out of the crowd and says, "It's going to be alright, John." Then he looks at the crowd and says, "Just stay calm and leave as quietly as possible.

Everyone understand?" They nod their heads and start to walk out of the building. "No sudden movements," he says, as they look at all the Drones sitting in the trees, on lamp posts, and suddenly flying around their heads. They take off running trying to get away from what seems like buzzing bees, swarming at their heads. One man falls and breaks his glasses. They are now chasing the people as they try to get to their cars.

One lady that stayed in the building is watching what is going on outside when one flies into the window and breaks the glass. John is in his car and says, "Google search, Odega beach house." He puts it in gear and takes off. Looking in his rear-view window he sees them following him. As he maneuvers his car down the street he then hears one smash into his car window.

He speeds up and sees them fly into the electrical wires causing them to crash and burn. He heads for the overpass and as he passes through, the last one following him crashes into the top of the bridge. He is now free of all the Drones that were following him.[9]

In other words, people are starting to get approved right and left. And if you think this approval procedure won't continue, right now the FAA has received more than 750 "requests" for Drone testing license in America alone, with dozens already being approved as we just saw. Canada's aviation authority, Transport Canada, has "released" 1,672 commercial drone certificates last year alone! And it's not stopping, it's happening on a grand scale! In fact, the Commercial Industry, those seeking the approval for this new delivery service, say that in a few years we will see, not just thousands but hundreds of thousands of drones in the air. If you compare that to the four largest airlines in the United States that have a combined fleet of 4,728 planes, Drones are going to be everywhere, a true invasion, outnumbering everything else in the sky! Now you know why I said this invasion is like a bunch of mosquitoes! They're going to be everywhere literally buzzing around like a bunch of insects. In fact, the commercial industry is already preparing us for this reality!

Chapter Seven

The Medical Invasion

Which brings us to the **5th invasion** of Drones in the **Medical Sector**.

You see Drones are not only going to be used to speed up our delivery service, and food, and all kinds of other things, but one day soon, they might very well speed up your drug delivery service or ambulatory service. Your life might soon depend on a Drone! They're going to be everywhere! We just saw how UPS is interested in using Drones for their mail and package delivery service, but so is DHL, who is now using Drones to test for Medicinal Services. Here's just one example.

WSJ Live reports:
Another delivery Drone to hit the skies this time is DHL parcelcopter. On Wednesday DHL said it would start using unmanned aircraft to carry medicine to the small island of Juist, a German island on the North Sea as part of a month-long feasibility project. Depending on the weather each day the Drone will fly autonomously on a pre-programed 7 ½ mile route.

It's the first routine mission in Europe in which a Drone will operate beyond the pilot's eyesight, DHL said. DHL plans to join Amazon Prime Air and Google X. DHL said several government agencies work together to establish a restricted flight area specifically for their North Sea flights. The companies Drone research program was launched last year in Bonn, Germany.[1]

Looks like everybody's getting into it, including the delivery of medicine. Now who couldn't use some Drone medicine delivery services? I mean, think about it. What a convenience, right? Not only for the elderly who can't get out too well in the first place, but for the sick in general? I mean, who wants to go out to the Pharmacy when you're sick? You don't want to get dressed and stuff. You just want to lay there in your pajamas! Well believe it or not, as you saw, Drones could make all that a reality. They'll bring the medicine right to you! But that's just the beginning of what Drones can do in the medical community. Speaking of the elderly, pretty soon Drones could literally save your life. We all know if someone has a heart attack no matter where they are, that time is crucial. Unfortunately, ambulances can get stuck in traffic and get there too late! But not a Drone! Think about it. They could avoid all that stuff! And that's precisely why, people are not only designing Drones to deliver medicine in record time, but even defibrillators if you do have a heart attack, because again, time is crucial, and a Drone can get it there much faster than any ambulance ever could!

Someone is laying on the ground. A lady is crouched down next to the person and is dialing 911 on her cell phone. The operator answers, "911 operator, what is your emergency?" She answers, "It's my dad. I think he has had a heart attack. Please help, he's not breathing anymore." "Please stay calm, what is your name?" "Joanna," she replies. "Good," he says, "we've got your location.

The ambulance Drone is on its way. Remove his top shirt to uncover his torso." "OK." she says. "Can you go to the nearest exit; the ambulance Drone is nearly there." "I'm outside," she tells him. "I'm talking to the Drone right now, so you can put down your phone. Now please pick up the Drone and bring it to your father. You're doing great.

Pull the green lid. Now place the pads on your father's chest. Good I can see that the pads are properly applied. Joanna, please stay clear of your father and we will take it from here." Suddenly you hear a heartbeat and he raises his head and hugs his daughter.[2]

In less than two minutes! Did you catch that? No ambulance can do that! Wow! A Drone ambulance! What will they think of next! Well, how about an actual Drone the size of an ambulance! Believe it or not, the military has already got them and is already using them to not only bring medical help to people but bring people to them.

Moving casualties from remote battlefields is an extremely dangerous job for a helicopter pilot. The landing takes skill and the mission could come under enemy fire. Tactical Robotics hopes to make the job easier with this, the Air Mule, a prototype ambulance Drone. On our visit these Drones are firmly on the ground, but the Air Mule has flown over 350 test flights including this one in December of last year. Over the last twelve years the development and millions of dollars have been invested into getting the Air Mule off the ground. The project is being partially funded by Israel's Ministry of Defense.

What makes this one-ton vehicle unique is its internal rotors. Two rotors taking the place of the helicopters large external one. It's controlled by two hundred directional air flaps. It's air speed is around 120 knots which is about 140 miles per hour and it can reach an altitude of about 12,000 feet. The first mission of the Air Mule is to pick up injured personnel from the battlefield.

One cargo bay can fit a person that is about 2 meters ten and weighs up to 250 kilos, but it still is a bit of a tight squeeze. Using both bays the Air Mule can also be used for cargo transportation. 500 kilos can be carried to bring supplies to remote combat zones. The Department of Homeland Security of America has been looking at the Air Mule to help secure an urban metropolitan area after a dirty bomb.[3]

Oh, so you want to use them here too, not just in the battlefield. Okay, now you're starting to look a little like Skynet, that's kind of creepy! But you can see why people would accept this. It can do what land ambulances can't do! We're headed for a day when your life really might literally depend on a Drone. I just hope they're not "discriminatory" on who they serve. Oh, but the elderly and the military are not the only ones who can benefit from this "life-saving" technology of Drones. Even young folks can now even get a phone app for a Drone to come rescue you in your time of need, like this video shows. Let's take a look.

A girl is walking on the sidewalk at a park, looking at her cell phone. She passes by a guy sitting on a park bench wearing a black hoody. As she passes him he jumps up and starts to grab her. As he is tackling her to the ground an alarm goes off. The guy asks, "What is that? Turn it off!" Suddenly from somewhere in the sky a Drone shows up and says, "What is your emergency. I have called the local police and they will be here momentarily." The guy jumps up and runs away.[4]

That's not a make-believe premise. That's actually put into production by a real company. Help! I'm being mugged, and I can't get up! Come rescue me! That puts that whole Life Line thing on steroids with a Drone! But again, you can see, who wouldn't want to be rescued with such an immediate response when time is critical and no one's around to help! And speaking of needing help! We all know when it comes to natural disasters, not just individual attacks, like with that girl, but natural disasters are also a time when many people are stranded and in need of help. In fact, many times, depending on the disaster, you can't even get a truck let alone an ambulance in the area for days. But not if you had a Drone! They can fly anywhere, even in tight spaces. And that's precisely why they too are also gearing them up for Disaster Relief!

Anthony Carboni of World D News Reports:
In the future, robots will fly tacos and textbooks into our windows, if you leave your windows open, in preparation for the future. The internet loves Drones, from military applications to the ethics surrounding surveillance to Lady Gaga's dress, I guess.

There's a different Drone story just about every day. If you have been paying attention you probably noticed that the bulk of these things have similar designs. They are all quadrotors. Quadrotors are copters that use blades like a helicopter, but it only uses four sets of them. Two rotate clockwise and two rotate counter-clockwise and that helps the vehicle to stay stable without the stabilizer rotor that the helicopters use.

Add some inexpensive accelerometers and gyroscopes like the ones in our mobile phones and you have these tiny vehicles that are perfect for autonomous flight. What can they be good for? Oh, my stars! What are they not good for. Unmanned delivery is a beneficial use. Australian companies are getting ready to deliver textbooks to college students. Why don't they just get up and go get them, you might ask. I don't know. I think I was up off my couch a total of three hours during my entire college career.

And if that seems silly to you, a company named Micronet is working on a micro transportation network of quadrotors that could one day deliver medications to remote villages or crowded cities where time is short, and traffic is crazy. The University of Pennsylvania is using quadrotors to build structures remotely. Imagine showing up to a remote location and having a shelter or bridge built for you already.

A team at the University of Tokyo created an all-terrain rotor that can change to a wheel or a boat for a search and rescue mission. So, this Drone turns into a wheel to squeeze through wreckage or get somewhere it can't fly or it can become a floatation device for someone whose drowning. So, you can see where a whole network of these guys buzzing around on their own could be super helpful.

Our sponsors at the air force laboratory are looking for other new ideas for search and rescue quadrotors. The airmen worked with the community for over two months to develop a next generation search and rescue microbot concept called the Iracknfee. A modular microbot that can be deployed into a disaster area and navigate confined spaces to locate trapped life. The microbot is equipped with a small camera as well as sensors that can detect harmful gases as well as heat levels. That is a powerful tool for the air force pararescue men who will eventually be entering into these confined spaces.[5]

Okay, let me get this straight, so if you're trapped in a building in a confined space after a tornado, or flood, or earthquake, or some other disaster, and you see this big giant spider looking thing coming your way, don't freak out, you're supposed to know it's a Drone coming to rescue you! But speaking of locating people, maybe you encounter another scenario where you got lost not due to a natural disaster, but simply from not paying attention to your surroundings. You got lost in the woods while hiking. We all know there's only so much people can do on the ground looking for you. But not if you had a bunch of Drones! Whether it's Little Johnny or Little Fluffy your pet cat, Drones in the sky can help find all kinds of missing things!

Channel 8 NOW reports:
Drones aren't just for spying but have incredible capabilities. "I was just an artist, a videographer, and a blogger on You Tube and a local friend of mine called me because her fiancé had gone missing in a snow storm," says Jim Bowers, of Swarm Network. Jim Bowers, also known as Demon Seed on his popular Drone Feed You Tube Channel, who is using his Drone for search and rescue missions.

He started Swarm, a group to encourage Drone pilots to help find missing pets and people. "We are almost always involved in a search somewhere in the world. We have thirty-two hundred Drone pilots in 58 countries around the world."

***KHOU reports*:**
Houston's homeless animal population could be getting some much-needed relief. An animal welfare group is using Drones to help track and save some of the one million stray animals roaming our streets. Marcelino Benito in South Houston is here to explain. Marcelino: Our patrol brought us here to this emergency vet hospital but not before we got an up-close look at the problem from high above the ground.

That buzz you hear hovering over Sunnyside is a Drone on a mission. It's another amazing tool to track stray dogs. World Animal Awareness Society is shooting a new TV show, Operation Houston, Stray Dog City. "That dog is drinking everything you can give him." An up-close look at Houston's serious stray dog problem. Men and women try to save the dogs before it's too late. "If we hadn't found her she would have died." Says one of the workers.

This dog was found by the group 'South side street dogs' in an abandoned house. She hadn't moved for days and was rotting to death. "It's touch and go." She was rushed to an emergency vet clinic. It's just one of several stories Executive Director Tom McPhee wants to highlight in Houston. He says, "There's obviously issues, there's problems."

But to solve those issues you need to first know how big that problem is. It's why McPhee wants to launch his Drones across Houston. "The Drone allows us to literally draw a big circle in the air as we are filming in 4K, beautiful footage." Using GPS technology, the volunteers on the ground plan to find and count just how many strays are in our area. Estimates say there could be more than a million.[6]

But hey, no worry, Drones can do it all! Kind of neat, but then again, it's kind of concerning. I mean, those dogs have no place to hide, literally, I sure hope they don't use that on people someday. I mean, what if you were deemed the "bad guy" or "stray citizen" where would you go? The Drones would catch you too!

Chapter Eight

The Transportation Invasion

But speaking of going places, the **6ᵗʰ invasion** that Drones are coming to is in the **Transportation Sector**.

Drones can not only help save the environment and you personally, in your time of need, but they are now being poised to help, serve, and protect all of humanity. It's all in the Transportation sector. Believe it or not, automated Drones and Drone vehicles are being developed right now that can not only deliver our goods to us in record time, saving us time and money, but they can also deliver us personally, to our destinations, saving even more time and making things much more reliable and safer. At least so they say. And why is this a need? Because we all know traffic accidents are one of the main causes of deaths, and if we would just let Drones take over all our transportation, then they could help save our lives and improve our commute. I mean, think about it? Eat while you drive, text while you drive and if you think this is some Science Fiction fantasy of the far-off future, Google is already putting it into action with the Google Car.

A beautiful morning to take a drive. The gentleman walks out of his house into a gentle breeze and his windchimes are ringing. He walks out to his driveway and wipes his hand across his little blue car sitting in the driveway. He walks around to the door, opens it and gets in. His friend is already in the car and asks "Hi, how are you doing today?" He replies, "Just great! Let's eat!" He pulls out onto the residential street and says, "Let's go!" Then he lets go of the steering wheel and cries "Look Ma, no hands" and they both laugh as they raise their hands up to touch the roof.

He drives a block or so and comes to a stop. "We're at a stop sign," he says. His friend tells him that the car has its own radar and laser that tells it when to stop and if anything is coming from either direction. He gives a little nervous chuckle about trusting the car to make the right decisions. His friend tells him "Old habits die hard, and some old habits don't die; anyone up for a taco?" His friend says, sure and suggests that they go through the drive through. They pull into the parking lot to get to the drive through lane. He asks, "Does anyone have any money?" His friend says, "I do. I have my wallet right here. You can just roll down your window and order a burrito." The order taker asks, "How are you?" He replies, "Very well, how are you doing?" and places his order.

They pull up to the window and she hands them their food. He then pulls out onto the street and proceeds to the highway, eating as they go. His friend tells him, "There are some places you can't go and some things you cannot do with this car". But he realizes that this is just what he needs as he is driving back to his house. He says, "This can change my life and give me back my independence and flexibility to be able to go places I want to go and need to go." He pulls into this driveway and gets out of his car while still eating his burrito. Steve Mahan, self-driving car user.[1]

Think of that! You really can eat fast food while you drive, talk on the phone while you drive, go back to texting, watch a movie, oh by the way, that guy is legally blind. I mean, what's next? You can take a nap while you drive? Exactly! We all know sleep deprivation can cause an accident, right? But not if you have a Drone car! And by the way, Google is not the only company rushing towards automating our cars and transportation experiences. So are a lot of other manufacturer's and they readily admit, if you do need to take a nap, you can take one, the Drone car will take care of you while you snooze.

CNN reports:
From the movie 'I, Robot', as Will Smith is driving his silver Audi he says, "Access USR Mainframe." "Connected," is the reply from the car. That was from a scene from the movie in 2004 and it felt like pure science fiction. But now nearly 10 years later self-driving cars have moved well beyond Hollywood fantasy.

Bjorn Giesler from Audi say, "You can just say you don't want to drive right now and just take over and if I want to be back in the driver's seat I just grab the wheel and go." At the consumer electronics show in Las Vegas last week a demonstration showing it's possible to even catch some zzz's in this Audi prototype. "We call it pilot to driving and that means that there is a driver, but he can concentrate on something else if he doesn't want to actively drive," he states. And it's coming much sooner than you think.

The state of California is taking aggressive steps to get driverless cars on the streets as early as this spring for testing. Bernard Soriano, Deputy Director, California DMV says, "We are developing the regulations to allow these autonomous vehicles to be tested, as well as operated on our roadways." So, on Tuesday the California DMV held a public hearing to discuss the rules of the road for autonomous cars.

For some car dealers, like Volkswagen there is concern that some regulations might be too strict. For instance, the proposed rules require that the driver must be seated in the driver's seat in case they need to take over. That only seems to make common sense. But perhaps giving us a glimpse into the future, a Volkswagen official says that is too limited. "And we contemplated an occasion where with redundant controls in what is referred to, or what is known as the passenger seat, we like to call them co-driver seats," says Nicole Barranco, Volkswagen Group of America.

The most well-known autonomous car comes from Google which shows how the vehicle can someday help the blind. The Tech company is fighting a proposed requirement that it should report at any time the actual driver needs to override the computer, saying a lack in context could give the wrong impression about safety. "Maybe this published information would mislead people into not understanding what it really meant," says Ron Medford, Google Director of Safety.

Other issues like whose responsible if the car crashes, the car maker or the driver are also part of the discussion. Michigan, Florida, Nevada and the District of Columbia have also passed laws allowing driverless cars and are struggling with some of the same issues. We may not have flying cars, like the Jetsons, but the dream of a George Jetson self-driving vehicle is surely on its way.[2]

Hey, I wonder if we'll get a Robot Maid too? It's a lot closer than you think, but we'll get to that in a little bit. But as you can see, how awesome is this going to be when we fully automate all our transportation. You can take a nap, do work, get all kinds of things done before you ever even make it to the office or back at home! I sure hope they work out all the bugs. It doesn't always go quite as planned, like this video demonstration shows.

Remolacha.net reports:
As the car backs out of the garage several people are watching and taking pictures. Slowly it backs up and stops then it changes gears and rushes forward, hitting the two camera men standing there taking the pictures, knocking them to the ground. The camera is still running, and he pulls himself up and notices the damage that was done to the sign that was next to him.[3]

Okay, I'm not sure on the Translation of that but I think they were basically saying, "OUCH! That's not supposed to happen!" But be that as it may, bugs and all, this new automated transportation system with Drones is not only not stopping with cars, but it's even coming to big trucks on the road. You know, the big semis that transport all of our goods. They too are becoming automated as well.

Bloomberg Business reports:
People have been talking about the driverless car for a while now. Almost every week seems to herald some new record or test drive always with the familiar caveat that technology is still a way off. But the first self-driving vehicles on the road may not be the ones taking you to work. They likely will come from an industry where safety concerns and environmental issues demand a better solution that a human being constantly behind the wheel.

The first self-driving car won't be a car at all. It will be a truck. This is the Freightliner Inspiration. A prototype truck that is legally roaming the highways of Nevada. "Ready to go?" ask the driver. "As soon as the auto-pilot is available we will get the indication on the instrument panel, so it's activated with the button and you will notice, I'm not doing anything, my feet are off the peddles, I can look at you and still steer, and so we are in an autonomous mod."

The Inspiration uses a combination of GPS, radar and video cameras to achieve what is called Level Three autonomy, which means the truck can drive itself when the conditions are right, but the driver has to remain in the driver's seat and be ready to take over control in around 20 seconds if needed. "I have been requested to take control of the system." Says the driver. "If I don't, it will not see any driver interaction, and it will slow itself down. It will apply the engine brakes and if it needs to it will apply the vehicle brakes."

A Level Three system like Freightliners makes a good degree of sense for a truck. Cruising along a monotonous stretch of freeway, let the computer take over. But once you pull into a city and have to negotiate that double park delivery truck and the traffic cop leading you through a red light a human is better at the controls. In a given year more than three million trucks carry 9.1 billion tons of cargo in the United States.

If computers, which never get drowsy or distracted, can shoulder some of that burden, human drivers will be more rested and alert when they do need to drive. "There is fuel efficiency impact, safety, maintenance, all of those things are benefits of moving goods across the country." says Steve Nadig, Chief Engineer, Daimler Trucks North America.[4]

And who doesn't want to save some money? I hope it doesn't turn out like those movies in the 70's and 80's where trucks were trying to kill people! Let's take a look at that.

In the movie Duel, Dennis Weaver is driving his car across country when an 18-wheeler starts following him with one thing in mind. Run him off the road and kill him. That semi runs over anything in its way. Unfortunately, Dennis decides that if this truck that is following him wants to play games with him he will play right back.

So, he pulls into a parking lot of a gas station. He thinks he has lost him but then he realizes that the truck is coming back for him. He rushes some kids back into the school bus and then notices that the truck is coming in his direction to run him down and he starts running back to his car. He manages to get inside his car and get back on the road, but the truck is after him again.

He comes to a train crossing. The bell is ringing, and the arms are coming down. He has to stop. The truck is getting closer, but it is slowing down. Then the truck slowly hits his bumper. The train is coming. The truck starts pushing his car. His foot is on the brake. It doesn't do any good. The truck keeps pushing and the train is getting closer. He yells out his window to stop. But the truck keeps pushing and the train is getting closer.

"Hi, my name is Steven King. I have written several motion pictures, but I want to tell you about a movie called Maximum Overdrive, which is the first one I directed. A lot of people have directed Steven King stories and I finally decided that if you want something done right do it yourself." People are sitting in a restaurant when a car without a driver and a truck pushing it is coming right into the building causing the patrons to scream and run. 'Who is driving it?' 'I don't know' 'It's coming after us!'

"It was my first picture as a director and you know something, I sort of enjoyed it." The truck is after the yellow car, hits the rear and it flips over onto its top. Next you see the lawnmower chasing the guy that was pushing it, then the two teenagers sitting in a car waiting for the truck to hit them. "I only wanted someone to do Steven King right." Maximum Overdrive, where the machinery comes after the humans.[5]

Okay, that's Maximum Hype. That would never happen, would it? But as you can see, the trend is for everything to become automated. And not just on the roads, but even the rails too. Move over locomotive engineers, we don't need you either. The new Drone train is coming to a station near you!

BBC reports:
The London underground is an iconic staple of the city. However, in 2022 some of its current trains will become a thing of the past. Transport for London and Design Firm, Priestman Good Transport, have teamed up to create a brand-new fleet of driverless trains. The design for the 250 upcoming trains has been unveiled.

They all feature a streamlined futuristic exterior without the traditional multi-carriage element opting instead for a walkthrough design. The Central, Waterloo, Piccadilly and City and Bakerloo lines will be some of the first to utilize the new trains. The National Union of Rail, Maritime, and Transport Workers have expressed concerns that the trains won't require a human operator.

As a response the London underground officials say that they will have a human driver in the early stages. Furthermore, a spokesperson for Transport for London says that no driver would lose their job. The future trains would also offer an increase of capacity depending on the line ranging from 25 to 60 per cent. The interior of the train will be air conditioned and on board WIFI will allow passengers to browse the internet during their ride. The new trains are planned to run 24 hours a day and remain in service for 30 to 40 years.[6]

Who can beat that? That's reliability! In fact, if this keeps up, we won't ever have to get a driver's license! In all seriousness, that's not just a reality for the land, but even the air. Believe it or not the air transportation system is undergoing the same kind of transformation. They're not only working on driverless cars, but even driverless flying cars. It's the ultimate commute!

Rueters reports:
Terrafugia TFX flying cars are designed to take long distance commuters where ever they want to go. First along the road and then through the air quickly and efficiently, assuming the concept gets off the ground. The TFX will have a range of 500 miles and a cruising speed of 200 miles per hour. The vehicle's operator won't require a pilot's license.

The TFX will take off and land autonomously. Terrafugia is already testing a flying car prototype called the Transition. It's designed for pilot's who want to drive their planes home instead of parking them at the airport. But CEO Carl Detriech says the TFX is different. It's a flying car for the masses. "We do want to create a flying car that can be used by a much broader segment of the population than just the pilot community today.

We want to lower the barriers entry. We want to make it easier to learn how to safely operate a vehicle. We want to make it safer than general aviation is today. Detriech says TFX's feasibility is the result of modern computer power. Occupants will only have to input a program to tell the car plane hybrid where to go. He says most planes already have sophisticated autopilot programs.

These vehicles that basically need to fly themselves need to know where every other aircraft is in the airspace, they need to know where weather fronts are, that they need to avoid, they need to know where the restricted air space pops up. They need to be tied in to basically a data network. He says that the FAA has been making great strides in recent years in developing that network and is confident that a system will be up and running when the TFX is ready to take to the skies.

But there is still the question of safety. There are certainly fail safe modes on the computer side but what happens when everything goes blank, when all the power systems go down. In that situation, the operator still needs to be trained in one thing, pull a handle. That handle deploys a parachute, and this is a system that is currently on our vehicle today. The transition to deploy the parachute to bring the people down safely.[7]

Well see, there's nothing to worry about! So much for the commute! Your dreams have come true! You don't even need a Driver's License to drive on the ground, and now you don't need one to drive in the air. Wherever you go, just simply sit back relax, go back to talking on the phone, texting, eating, reading the newspaper, even taking a nap. But wait a second. Speaking of flying, what about the airline industry itself? Who's going to be flying those bigger planes? In fact, we all know their pilots can also suffer from sleep deprivation, or there's those terrorist attacks, or other aberrant behavior from pilots. What are we going to do? Believe it or not, they're getting geared up to protect us from that as well. In fact, it's because of all the recent airline crashes from pilots, that people are saying now is the time we officially automate even the skies.

Watch closely. This plane over England has a crew on the controls, passengers in the back, but something extraordinary is about to happen. A pilot on the ground is taking over. "Ready, set, control," "proceed," "I have control," "you have control". This is the ninety-four million dollars Astria Project by the British Aerospace Company, BAE, one of several efforts around the world to develop planes that can be flown remotely.

"What you can hear at the moment is the discussion with the air traffic which is exactly the same as the pilots would be having if they were in charge of the steering of the aircraft. Military success with Drones have driven much of the interest and much of the focus has been on airplanes in hazardous conditions, such as hurricane research and fighting wildfires.

Analysts say that pilotless planes could be a four hundred million dollars a year global business. **Daybreak Reports:** *Debate over a pilotless plane has been revived with the emergence of evidence suggesting German wings flight 9525 may have been crashed by the co-pilot on purpose. For more on what it would take to get a pilotless plane off the ground Kim Giang reports: Speculations that a 27-year-old co-pilot intentionally crashed as plane has led some to question if the planes might be safer without pilots.*

Advocates of the idea say that if planes were fully automated the tragedy of German Wings Flight 9525 might have been averted. The co-pilot has reportedly prevented the captain from reentering the cockpit after he left before sending the plane into a decent that led to the crash. The disaster has already led to calls in Europe requiring two pilots being in the cockpit at all times. Self-flying aircraft that can be controlled from the ground are not entirely new.

Drones have been used for military missions for years. The U.S. military flies global Drones nearly the size of a Boeing 737 passenger jet. Boeing said it has developed fully automated planes to prevent hijacking. Then there are labor unions which are concerned that self-flying planes will leave pilots without jobs. Critics also say that self-flying aircraft have their own problem including an increased vulnerability to hacking.[8]

So, let me get this straight. Drones are soon going to be driving all of our cars, all of our trucks, all of our trains, all of our planes? I don't know about you, but I really do hope nobody hijacks the whole transportation system for nefarious purposes! That would be like a Skynet Scenario. I mean, you couldn't run, you couldn't hide, you couldn't flee, you couldn't get food, or any supplies delivered to you, I mean, what's next? Are they going to take over our communications or something? Funny you should ask that!

Chapter Nine

The Communication Invasion

The **7th invasion** of Drones is coming to the **Communication Sector**.

Now, there are plans to use Drones to not only fly us in the air, but there are plans right now to control all our communications in the air. Right now, we have satellites providing the means for our Global Broadcasting System with television and our cellular phone communication system. We even have satellites controlling our radios with Satellite Radio services around the world. My point is this, much of our communication capabilities around the world are being controlled from above. Many corporations want to control our internet access via Drones in the air on a global scale. This would include tech giants like Google and Facebook. Here's Google's Project Loon which is their attempt to bring the whole planet online real soon.

Sometimes everyone really isn't everyone. Like when people say everyone is on the internet. Because the truth is for each person that can get online there are two that can't and when you look closer that everyone looks even less than everyone. In some places it's more like one in a thousand and others it's one in ten thousand. In some places no one is online at all.

But what if there was a way to light up the entire globe. To finally make all the worlds information accessible to all of the world's people. Well, even though today one in three kids can't get into a real secondary school everyone can have the secondary school come to them. In places where there aren't enough doctors everyone could be helped by doctors in other places. Farmers everywhere could start using better weather data, so everyone could enjoy a bigger harvest.

And because small businesses that are on the internet grow twice as fast everyone could create new opportunities for everyone. But how do we bring affordable internet to everyone. Maybe finding an answer starts with looking somewhere new. Like up, finding something different, like balloons. Yep, that's right, balloons. Because it turns out that if you use balloons it's faster and easier and cheaper to give everyone the internet than to give some people the internet.

That's why we are giving it a try. And why there's hope that someday soon everyone really will mean everyone. "Many people don't realize that the majority of the world is not connected to the internet." Rich DeVaul, Chief Technical Architect, Project Loon says, "How do we get cost effective inexpensive and reliable connectivity to the remaining five or six billion people in the world who don't have it."

What is Project Loon? Project Loon is the idea that we could create a network of high altitude balloons that go about twenty kilometers up and through this network we can give the internet to the entire world. Our balloons are these great big round things about fifteen meters in diameter, but you would have to have a telescope to see one up in the sky. So, here's the surface of the planet, right up to about ten kilometers, this is where rain happens, where mountains are, and pretty much where aircraft fly, our little balloon is just about twenty kilometers above the stratosphere.

The stratosphere is different because we have layers of wind that go in different directions and by moving up and down through these layers we can steer. So, by catching the right wind we can keep the balloons together enough to get good coverage on the ground. "We can sail with the winds and shape the waves and patterns of these balloons so that when one balloon leaves another balloon is set to take its place," says Astro Teller, Captain of Moonshots.

The balloons communicate with specialized internet antennas on the ground, so an antenna can aim up in the sky to communicate with the balloon. Each of these balloons talk to their neighboring balloon and then back down to the ground station that is connected to the local internet provider. What this does is create a network in the sky. We designed our radios and antennas specifically to receive signals from Project Loon only in order to achieve the high bandwidth involved.

If we didn't filter out the other signals the technology just wouldn't work. The balloons are completely solar powered, and we control them through Loon mission control. Mike Cassidy, Project Lead, says, "I think your plan is great, do the assent on 46 and 47. Just try it like an hour after flow." Ok we are going to be on the ground in a couple minutes. Before we send them up we talk to air traffic control. We let them know these balloons are on their way up, so they know where they are and before they come down we also talk to air traffic control.

We can direct them to land in various collection points around the world in order to reuse and recycle parts. Now we have some ability to steer in general however in the stratosphere most of the time the winds actually flow from west to east. Because the winds generally circulate this way we typically have bands of our balloons that will be around the world at different latitudes so if the balloons are circling around the bottom half of the world eventually the balloon that is over South Africa will pass over South America.

We are using the sun light, we are using the wind, we are using all of these things to build the network in the sky. Project Loon is working to bring the technologies of access to everyone on the planet. "I run a small farm, when I'm using the internet the first thing I check is the weather to see if my sheep are going to dry out, that their wools not dry," says Charles Nimmo, Project Loon Test Pilot, "so I'm just looking for a window, so I can plan my week. We have gone through a number of internet providers to try to keep reliable internet. It was so slow that we have to click on a page and then go do something for ten minutes."

"So, can you give us a quick update on the launch?" asked the guy from Google. "Having a team from Google on our farm to try all of this for the first time has been really exciting." Having access to the internet can change lives, and there are five billion people on the earth that aren't reached," says Cliff L. Biffle, Tech Lead, Flight Systems. Balloon powered internet sounds positively mad and in a way, it is, but it's mad in a very practical way that could just work.[1]

   Okay, go ahead and say it. I know you want to. It's a "loony" idea. I get it. But "loony" or not, these guys are deadly serious, this is Google folks. It is their desire to get the whole planet, literally every person, connected to the Internet. And of course, not to be outdone in this global internet provider race, even Facebook is vying for control for global internet access. Except they're not using balloons, they're relying on Drones. And these Drones can stay up for years at a time.

Titan Aerospace reports:
Facebook may be getting closer to its goal to make the internet accessible to the entire planet. Media reports that it is in talks to buy solar powered Drone maker Titan Aerospace for sixty million dollars. This so called atmospheric satellite could beam internet signals around the world. Titan CEO Vern Rayburn wouldn't comment on any details on the deal but told Reuters that Titan has flown a scaled down prototype of the plane.

Commercial operations are scheduled for 2015. The concept is similar to Googles Project Loon which they will use solar powered air balloons to beam the internet to remote regions. CNET's Lindsay Turntine reports, "It may be a little bit of a race, it's sort of an interesting time. There are five billion people in the world who do not have reliable internet access. That's plenty of people to reach out to. But one would think that the first internet activity a person needs that they use for the first time, they would stick with for a while.

Google has been working on this for a little while. So, it will be interesting to see who covers more ground, literally and figuratively." According to Techcrunch they plan to build eleven thousand solar powered Drones that can stay in the air for five years and will provide 3G internet access in regions like Africa. To avoid legal issues, they would stay above FAA regulated air space, but there could be other red flags.

"Anytime you have what amounts to an essential piece of daily life owned by a specific company there are always concerns about the content that are channeled through that service and we have a lot left to learn, a lot to see, but there is a little bit of concern there. If Facebook is the channel for all information coming in from the internet what is Facebook going to do with access to information coming from outside the Facebook eco system."

Getting the entire world on line is the dream of Facebook founder Mark Zuckerberg. He spoke about it at the internet.org effort at the Mobile World Conference in Barcelona. "I think if we can do this well as an industry then within five years I certainly hope that the number of people that we are connecting is a lot more than the billion that they put in the video before you and

I came up here. I would hope that in the next ten years that we can really make progress at connecting most of the rest of the world.[2]

You'll be interested to know that Google ended up buying Titan Aerospace. Don't know if they outbid Facebook or what, but Facebook went with Titan's competitor, a U.K. based Drone company called Ascenta that can basically do the same thing. But for those of you who are wondering, "Well, so what. Who cares if all our forms of communications are controlled from above on a global scale by using internet Drones or balloons." Well, let me see if I can put it all together for you. Think about all the things we now do with the internet, all the information, all the finances, all the knowledge and all forms of media, all are being connected and merged with this new invention called the internet. And the key word here, I believe is, net, the net is closing in on us! It's not just in existence right now, but we've already been conditioned to accept it and to rely upon it for almost all our needs, including financial needs. You can buy online, you can sell online, you can bank online, you can make your calls online, you can do all your studying and research online, you can shop online, you can watch TV online, you can register online, you can make your appointments online. You can do just about anything and everything online! Everything is going online, have you noticed? Whether people realize it or not, it's a giant matrix system that's starting to control everything we do, on a global scale. And that just happens to sound like an event that's going to happen during that Judgment Day we saw earlier that Jesus mentioned as the worst time in the history of mankind. It's called the Mark of the Beast System!

Revelation 13:16-17 "He also forced everyone, small and great, rich and poor, free and slave, to receive a mark on his right hand or on his forehead, so that no one could buy or sell unless he had the mark."

We not only have microchips right now that can communicate and connect with this global matrix system for buying and selling, but this same microchip can be implanted in or permanently marked on a person's body. And during the coming Judgment Day, one guy, the Antichrist, will be able to "restrict" people's access to this Global Matrix System, which will give him the ability to control all the buying and selling on the whole planet. Now let's go back to this Global Communication System that's being built before our very eyes with Satellites, Balloons, Drones, or whatever. Right now, we can access this matrix, the internet, and other forms of communication with a certain amount of freedom. But what if one day, somebody, some entity, hijacked this system, then what would we do? You talk about a power play, right? Then they could make, order, force, cause people to do whatever they want them to do, including buying and selling, right? And the problem is, with all this communication technology, being built and controlled from above, that's a lot of power in one place that none of us can ever reach, right? And if it ever did get hi-jacked, you not only could not do anything about it, you'd be shut out of this system just like that, and Drones are at the forefront of making all this a reality. They're invading our homes, our media, they're taking over our agriculture, they're controlling the commercial products that we buy and sell, they're taking over our medical services and transportation services. Now they're taking over our global communications system that is being wrapped around the planet connecting everything together, giving Drones the power to control virtually all facets of society. By the way, I didn't show you all the ways Drones are being released. There's more areas they're going into. I think you can begin to understand why I keep using words like "attack" or "invasion." Drones really are everywhere, it's really an invasion, and we're just seeing the beginning of it!

Chapter Ten

The Controlled Invasion

So, the question is, do we see any signs of somebody actually trying to control this whole system? Drones around the planet are starting to control everything we do? Could somebody really hi-jack it like in the Terminator movies, Skynet scenario? Yes! You see, because there's been so many Drones already launched in the skies, it's leading to a whole new problem that we're just now starting to see in the news. Oh no! What are we going to do? They're everywhere! They're crashing into all kinds of places wreaking havoc and causing all kinds of trouble and danger.

Wochit reports:
The government is getting near daily reports and sometimes two or three a day of Drones flying near airplanes and helicopters or flying near airports without permission. Federal and Industry officials tell the Associated Press it's a sharp increase from just two years ago when such reports were still unusual. Many of the reports are filed with the Federal Aviation Administration by the airline pilots but other pilots, airport officials and other authorities often file reports as well, said the officials who agreed to discuss the matter only with the condition that they not be named because they weren't authorized to speak publicly.

Michael Toscano, president of a Drone industry trade group, said FAA officials also have verified the increase to him. SBZ4 reports: Drone crashes in the middle of a Memorial Day Parade, the tiny aircraft hit a building and then hit a man.

The Drones operator told the police that he never thought the gadget could do any type of damage.

Ryan Kath spoke with the victim who fortunately wasn't seriously hurt. Reporter: The one year old is too young to remember the Memorial Day Parade, but her dad might be telling stories about it when she is older. "If it was going to fall on somebody, thankfully it fell on me." Like others at the Parade it was noticed that a Drone was hovering above the crowd making videos of the festivities.

Scott Yount was standing right near the toy store and at some point, the Drone lost control smacked into the building and dropped to the ground. Scott says, "I heard some people yell and then I felt this clunk on my head and the back of my neck and I thought, well I just got hit by that thing." Scott has a bandage covering the cut on the back of his neck, but a viewer shared this video with WBZ showing moments right after the Drone crashed just above Scott and how it ricocheted into another woman.

"A Drone fell from the sky, right?" That viewer also took a video of the Drone owner who seemed to realize how badly things could have turned out. That's because just seconds earlier Scott had been holding his daughter in his arms. He said the close call raises big questions about the tiny aircraft and how they are regulated.

ABC News Reports: *Now to that mystery in Seattle and for some a frightening sight in the sky. Tourist sighting something strange buzzing around their famous space needle while they were up there. Some were amused, waving at it, while others were down right troubled about it. Tonight, we have learned it was a Drone. But we ask here, who was flying it, and should anyone be allowed to fly one that close to an American landmark?*

ABC's Cecilia Vega has more of those pictures and the debate. Cecilia Vega: Right there in the Seattle sky, a Drone. The FAA now telling ABC News it is looking into that tiny remote control powered aircraft hovering above the observation deck of the famous Space Needle. While curious tourists waved the mysterious flying object gave security quite a scare. Police say a man launched the Drone right out of his hotel room window.

There was no malcontent or malice. He wasn't trying to do anything wrong. It is just the latest incident raising questions about whether it's safe to fly Drones above crowded cities. Take a look at this Drone buzzing over the busy streets of New York City last year and crash landing nearly hitting pedestrians at the height of rush hour. And there also have been close calls with airplanes.

Pilot: We just saw a little Drone below us. A Drone last year coming within 200 feet of a jumbo jet. Drones are exploding in popularity but the rules already in place of how and where they can fly haven't caught up yet. Nikki Majewski reports: Drones, a figment of Syfy films are becoming the latest in technology in broadcasts, in advertising, monitoring natural disasters, and even delivering medicine to remote locations.

But what is the flip side of capturing a beautiful birds eye view and should we be worried. Hai Tran, CEO Coptercam, tells us, "I think there is a huge concern for the public and industry." New technologies are more accessible, and MP's have launched an inquiry into Drone use and privacy. "There is nothing stopping your neighbor from flying a very simple toy, like a helicopter, putting a camera on it, for example, and flying it over your neighbors." Commercial Drone operators say they have far too much to lose to deliberately invade people's property and hobbyists are to blame for inappropriate Drone use.

"We are the ones who are hounded by the regulators as opposed to all the hobbyists that potentially fly into the Sydney Harbor Bridge, for example, that was done by a hobbyist, or another hobbyist flying into the city airport and crashing their aircraft there." The civil aviation authority isn't responsible for privacy but admits it's difficult to identify Drone pilots if they break the rules.

Peter Gibson, Civil Aviation Safety Authority say, "It is challenging sometimes to be able to identify the people who have been flying a remotely piloted aircraft, a hobby Drone, in this case, because obviously unless you can see the person doing it, it's hard to put the action together." It might be just as difficult to monitor privacy.

A small boy is telling the reporter, "It was freaky. It was scary." A 7-year old boy is frightened after he said a neighbor used a Drone to spy on him at home. That boy's father and others in the neighborhood are outraged at what they call an invasion of privacy. The man who was flying the Drone says it was all being blown out of proportion. Investigator Joe Douglas has been digging into the story: This all happened in Vancouver and police say no crime was committed. But the laws in Washington and the laws in Oregon are very different when it comes to your privacy and Drones. 7-year old Drew was at his friend's house Saturday when he heard something outside.

Drew says, "My friends and I were playing Minecraft and I heard a buzz. It was a Drone outside, I said, "Hey there's a Drone outside and I think it has a camera on it". So, I went over to the door and hid. While Drew was hiding Landon's grandpa, Mike, and some friends were in the garage. That was when they spotted the Drone. Mike says, "We were standing around having a conversation then the Drone just came down out of nowhere about 10-feet above us and was just hovering. We all gave it the universal sign of displeasure and it still didn't go away. So, I went into the house and got my BB gun and pointed it at it and it took off."

A medical helicopter had a close call with a Drone on Wednesday. Since then it has people talking about mid-air safety and how to prevent these types of incidents. Reporter Kelly Choates reports: The Drone that nearly hit the helicopter was flying about 1000-feet above the ground. That's more than double the altitude recommended by Access Ariel, a Drone enthusiast group. I spoke to one of those Drone pilots about the precautions they take in the sky. "His concern used to be birds, now it is Drones, so things have changed a little," said one of the enthusiast.

A Life Flight helicopter pilot avoided a catastrophe when a Drone nearly collided with the chopper as it flew above the Schuylkill County, Joe Zerbey Airport. A spokesperson for the health system says no patients were on board when it happened but the incident is drawing attention to the safety of Drones. "You saw in New York where the jet liner hit a bird and it had to land on the Hudson River.

Imagine a Drone getting sucked into the engine of an airliner, what damage that could do." Pilot: "Looks like one of those unmanned drones was flying right on the final." In an alert to JFK air traffic controller from a pilot about to land, a warning of a remote-controlled Drone flying near the path landing zone.

Controller: "2 mile final 3 to 400 feet?" Pilot: "That is correct." And this is the third alert in 4 days. All pilots in aircrafts full of passengers spotting Drones dangerously close during a crucial part of the flight. The pilot you just heard manned a Jet Blue flight from Georgia. The Drone appears 300 to 400 ft. off the ground. On Sunday two separate pilots spotted Drones as high as 3000 ft. The first sighting was at 8:12 in the evening by the pilot of a 747 coming from London and just a minute later.

Pilot: "We just had something fly over us, we don't know if it was a drone or a balloon, it just came really quick." A Delta pilot was alarmed by another possible Drone as he approached JFK. These planes are being approached while they are landing so they are close to the ground which means the pilot really doesn't have a whole lot of room for maneuvering. Ken Honig is a former high-ranking official with the Port Authority. He said the people flying the Drones don't take into account the damage they could have caused.

The unmanned UAV gets too close to an airplane it could get sucked into a jet engine. The kind of damage that could be done by a bird would be amplified by the metal parts inside of one of these UAV's. **World News reports**: Next, a new exclusive, passenger jets dodging Drones. Pilots scrambling to avoid them. ABC David Curlick getting answers: Tonight, ABC news has learned that more of these types of Drones have gotten close to passenger jet liners in the New York area. Even forcing evasive action by some pilots.

A senior aviation source tells ABC news that in just the past 30 days there has been an increase in incidents. One in just the last 48 hours. In two of those incidents the source tells ABC news that their pilots have turned their aircraft away, worried about a possible collision with unmanned Drones. We've heard those concerns before. A pilot on approach to JFK reported a close call. "Kennedy tower, just for your information we just saw a little Drone below us."

Happening Now reports: This man was an avid flyer of remote controlled helicopters. He was flying his Drone at a park on Thursday when police say he lost control of it. He was struck in the head and killed. Some within the FAA fear something worse. Since June 1st pilots have reported more than two dozen near collisions with rouge Drones to the FAA. This week three commercial pilots have reported seeing Drones while on final approach to JFK International. The unknown Drone came within just 50 yards of the helicopter on Friday over Cleveland at 1700 feet.[1]

I don't know how much more proof you need, but this is serious! A guy even got killed by one of these automated machines! In fact, it's getting so bad out there, with this invasion of Drones, we're only seeing the tip of the iceberg, people are now wanting to hunt down and kill these Drones!

7 News Reports:
Only on 7 News this morning a small Colorado town is considering a bold move, putting a bounty on Drones. Even issuing hunting licenses to shoot them down. Reporter Amanda Cox is talking to the man behind the ordinance and town leaders who see dollar signs. Amanda Cox: About 60 miles east of Denver, a town easily missed in a blink of an eye, Deer Trail was a hustling and bustling place one hundred years ago but no so much now.

This small towns biggest claim to fame is the site of the world's very first rodeo. Now this town is looking to start another first, right here on these grounds. The first Drone Hunt. "I would like it to be known for the first place in America to have a Drone hunting license, says Phillip Steele. He drafted a town ordinance providing unmanned ariel vehicle hunting license bounties. Reporter: Wouldn't that be a Federal offense? "I'm going to answer, no."

Under the ordinance the license would grant 21 yrs., and over permission to aim at unmanned ariel vehicles. But only with a shotgun, 12- gauge or smaller pointed to the sky. Deer Trail would pay licensed shooters $25.00 for identifiable parts of the Drone and $100.00 for a whole or nearly intact one.

NBC 10 News reports: *Sounds like it's coming seriously close to warfare with animal rights activists flying unmanned Drones in order to spy on sportsmen who are allegedly trying to shoot them down. It's a game of ariel reconnaissance between the animal rights group SHARK and the Wing pointe hunt club. Steve Hindi, President of SHARK says, "The pigeon shooters are basically gone into hiding so they are using a ring that is up on a hill and completely surrounded by trees.*

The only way you can get to it is through the air. The protesters were outside the Wing Pointe Hunters Club Sunday where they say a pigeon shooting was taking place. SHARK was flying a remote-controlled helicopter that was outfitted with GPS and camera over the shooter to record video to put on YouTube when they said something happened.

The camera picture from the Drone froze and Steve Hindi says he knew it had been shot. "I said that sounded different, I'm going to bring it back and as soon as I hit the come home feature the craft went crazy because it's compass was knocked out." The smoking Drone landed hard in the animal rights group. They called Pennsylvania state to investigate. The SHARK group says this is the fourth time one of their Drones has been shot at trying to spy on what they claim are inhumane pigeon shoots. "When they do this, it only makes us more determined. We are going to see these pigeon shoots stopped."

You are watching this video from a Drone flying over a beautiful home in Southern California and you won't believe what happens next. The homeowner runs out his front door with a shotgun. The Drone flies away with the guy in hot pursuit. His friend is recording cell phone video of the wild chase. Now the homeowner goes around his house, points at the Drone again, takes aim and fires. The Drones camera sees the light and suddenly goes dark. It's a bulls-eye.

The homeowners in Valencia, California, who shot down the Drone says that he believes that the Drone was sent over his house in a deliberate act of harassment. "I got an anonymous phone call on my answering machine saying get rid of your eye-sore sign or you won't have any privacy."

CNN reports: How many chimps does it take to down a Drone, one plus a branch. Watch how this middle aged female named Tushy, climbed down off her branch and whacked that sucker at the Burgers' Zoo in the Netherlands. "She hit it spot on," says Bas Lukkenaar, spokesman, Burgers' Zoo. Bass Lukkenaar says he saw it happen, flabbergasted while shooting an episode for a TV show at the zoo. The Chimps do just sit around holding branches, so they can they arm themselves against the Drones.

Tushy is notorious for having a good arm at throwing things. The Drone, worth a little over $2,000.00 was demolished. It may have been a bummer for the TV crew, but it wasn't a bummer for the chimps on the ground who took some ultra closeup selfies of themselves, called #Chimpanselfie's as the zoo calls them. But the chimps got bored with the camera's a lot sooner than humans do.

Remember when GoPro cameras were always being stolen like octopuses, so passé, now critters have branched out to Drones from a golf course goose to a swarm of bees attacking a Drone from a Florida TV station. When you see the video, it looks like Star Wars. Then there's the New Zealand ram called Rambro who rammed a Drone. The funny thing is when the Drone operator came face to face with a ram who acted like the chimp. The owner retrieved his downed Drone and used a stick to ward off Rambro, just like you know who. Tushy reminded us of another ape being buzzed, King Kong eventually lost his perch but Tushy, it's hard not to Drone on about how smart she is.[2]

Well, as you can see nobody likes these things! Not even the monkeys are monkeying around with them, let alone goats or bees or people! In fact, one developer is creating a, "Drone Hunting Drone" to take out Drones that spy on you and/or annoy you! So, Drones are going to be killing Drones! And if you think that is a crazy Fad and the Feds won't take this Drone scare invasion seriously, think again. If you paid attention to the news, there was even a Drone that invaded the White House! Uh oh! Now you're in trouble!

NBC News Reports:
An incident at the white House is once again raising major concerns about security at a building that is, of course, supposed to be among the most secure on the planet. This time it was a small Drone that breached the air space from above and crashed right on to the White House grounds. In the predawn darkness, secret service officers combed the White House after a Drone crashed into a tree on the south lawn at 3am.

This afternoon secret service officials said a man contacted them 6 hours after the crash and said the Drone was his. Law enforcement sources say the man told them he wanted to test the device in bad weather and lost control. President Obama and the first lady are traveling in India. Their daughters and grandmother are here. Security experts say that as this Drone may not be a threat another Drone might. Kenneth Honig, Emergency Management Consultant, says, "My concern is that this is a new delivery system for a weapon."

Drones are becoming increasingly more sophisticated and affordable. Just last week drug smugglers crashed one of the devices transporting meth from Mexico to California. A year and a half ago German Chancellor Merkle, got a surprise when a camera on a Drone landed near her feet at a campaign event. So, what can the Secret Service do? Kenneth Honig answers, "I think something that would give them adequate warning would be a combination of radar and video analytics that could scan the sky 360 degrees around the secure compound."

And the incident raises new questions about the Secret Service already under scrutiny after a series of security lapses. Including a man jumping over the fence and making it all the way into the White House last September. House Oversight Chairman Chavetz says the agency is focusing on Drones. He says, "Ever since the German Chancellor, it has been on their radar, but they have got to solve it.[3]

Okay that's it! As you can see, that's the last straw. You've got to solve this! It's one thing to have a Drone invade a personal space, or small town, become a nuisance in the air, but the White House? You can't have that breach of security! What are we going to do? Well, can you say create a crisis, so you can manage the outcome! With all these Drone scares popping up all over the world, looks like we need somebody to control these Drones on a Global Scale! In other words, we need the Government to protect people from all this misuse or abuse of Drones, or people being harmed by them! I mean, surely, they can manage this modern Technology and keep us safe!

Well, believe it or not, they already are! Verizon, the US's largest wireless telecom company, is developing technology with NASA to direct and monitor America's growing fleet of civilian and commercial drones. According to documents, Verizon signed an agreement last year with NASA and the project is now underway at NASA's Ames Research Center in the heart of Silicon Valley. Why? Because now, there is little to stop operators flying wherever they want. The agency would like a technology that will automatically 'geo-fence' Drones to keep them away from sensitive areas like the White House. Then this will allow them to, ground drones in severe weather, help them to avoid buildings and each other while flying and decide which drones have priority in congested airspaces. NASA is also considering monitoring Drones with a range of sensors including radar, orbiting satellites and cellphone signals. Which means, control of Drones is going global. Can you believe this? I wonder what they'll call it, Skynet?

It sure looks to me like all these Drone scares worked like a charm to create a single global entity controlling all these Drones no matter who or where you are. They will decide, they will control all of them. Isn't that nice? I just hope nobody, or nothing hijacks it! But believe it or not, that's only half the concern. You see, Drones are not only invading the world and being controlled around the world, but now, just like Skynet, Drones are being equipped to kill people all around the world. This is the second half of the concern of the Skynet scenario! Right now, governments and militaries around the world are not only starting to control the usage of Drones, but they're even developing Drones with deadly weaponry, to better protect us they say. They have literally turned these machines into deadly lethal weapons, flying weapons, through the air, just like in the Terminator movies. So now let's switch gears in this invasion and look at the deadly ability of Drones and you tell me if the Terminator movies and the whole Skynet scenario are not about to become our horrible reality.

Part III

The Deadly Abilities of Drones

Chapter Eleven

Drones in the Police Force

The **1ˢᵗ deadly ability** of Drones is in the **Police Force**.

You see, if Drones are able to watch out for stray dogs or dangerous poachers, then why couldn't they help our Police Forces find all kind of criminals and other so-called dangerous characters or bad guys? It only makes sense! And that's precisely the rationale that's leading to this next invasion of Drones all over the world. In fact, it's already begun. Believe it or not, the UK Police Force has already launched them onto its populace to, 'Fight fire with Fire.'

BBC Reports:
You may be too engrossed with the pictures to think about how they were filmed. This barn on fire, for example, the vast waste in North Kent next to people's homes, the fire in Hastings, but they were all filmed not from a helicopter or a plane, but by an unmanned ariel vehicle, Drone to you and me, controlled on the ground by a trained operator working within certain rules of heights and distance.

"This one weighs 1.2 kilos, has a 25-minute flight time, and has this little camera that does all the work. It feeds pictures back to me on a little control unit here." But it's that camera that makes some people nervous. Take this party at a beauty spot at Brighton last spring. A journalist used his to film this, but would it have been right for the police to do so. Officers stress they prefer other ways that come in useful.

So, let's say the police must deal with a big chemical spill or a huge traffic incident that is hard to get to and it involves lots of officers. It's so much easier when you have one camera a couple hundred feet up in the sky to get the big picture. Using a Drone like that may be fair enough, one civil liberties group told us. "They can potentially go into private property, they can be covert, or overt, they really need to be regulated by firm guidelines which govern specific kinds of technology which simply wasn't envisaged when the regulations governing surveillance was drawn up."

The police say, "It's not snooping at all, it's pretty much the same way a camera or closed-circuit television camera is on the end of a pole. This is a Drone on a very long piece of string. You can put it that way. It's very much about over use and the fact that we use it."[1]

So, you don't need to worry, he just admitted it, there's no hiding it. It's just like Big Brother closed-circuit TV that's already watching you with all these cameras on the ground everywhere you go. So now they're just expanding it with Drones to watch you from the sky wherever you go. What's the big deal? We're here to protect you! Really? Or are you here to monitor us always from the ground or the sky with no place to hide? But that's not all. There are all kinds of rationales they're using to get us used to this idea of being watched and tracked from the sky with Drones. You see, a Drone from the sky watching us might also not only catch those chemical spills or bad guys robbing a bank or party animals, but how about tax cheats? Argentina is doing just that! They are employing Drones to find and spot, 'Tax cheats' who haven't reported home improvements to the Government, they're skipping out on their taxes.

Fox Business Reports:
My jaw dropped when I found out about this. What they are doing in the rich parts of Buenos Aires is flying Drones over where the rich people live and counting their pools and their mansions, and they came up with 300 pools and mansions that were not declared on Tax Returns. That equaled to $2,000,000.00 that the government there is not getting. It's a small chunk of change and it was a small area that they flew the Drones over.

I think most people would say that this is zero privacy. At this point you can't lie. There is technology that will catch you and everything that you do. Ivan Budassi, Executive Director, ARBA, tells us, "The surface of the Buenos Aires province is as large as a country. We have 6,000 employees, 2,000 of them on the streets, but monitoring each one of the structures in the province is impossible without technological assistance.

What aerial assistance does for us is to establish which buildings have not been declared. To give you an idea, January of this year we have found 120,000 properties covering 14 million square meters of built area which have not been declared and that represents a tax evasion worth roughly 100 million pesos a year." Surveyor, Miguel Angel Tous tells us, *"Studying an area like this one, let's say some 50 hectors, can be done in a 20-minute flight, that's how long it takes to make a good definition to observe very clear details.*[2]

In other words, they'll find you real fast, with a Drone. You will be paying your taxes. And that's still not all. Speaking of 'cheaters' China is now using Drones to 'spy on' students who might be guilty of cheating on one of their toughest exams, which determines whether or not the Chinese students can get into a University.

CNN Reports:
It's test time in China and the stakes are sky high. Nine million students face nine hours of exhaustive grueling questions. The Gaokao determines their future, what college they can go to. And in a country, that emphasizes education these stressed teens are pushed to the limit.

IV drips just to stay alert while studying, prayer for a joyous result. It's reported that it has driven some to take their own lives. For others the temptation to cheat is overwhelming. Many students fate hangs in the balance of their performance of this test. So, it's incredibly important with so much at stake, temptations to cheat are very, very high.

These days officers stand guard. In the past white-collar students have been paid to sit in these exams in place of other students. But in Luoyang officials are getting a boost against would-be cheats. This year, Drones will be hovering high above the test halls. They are listening for suspicious chatter from wireless devices. Some so sophisticated they should be reserved for spy movies.

Tank tops complete with transmitter, glasses which scan and send images simply by pressing a coin, and an unassuming wallet and water bottle complete with camera. If caught the penalties are harsh. Students are barred from taking the exam for three years. Parents, teachers, and anyone else involved can face criminal charges. Needing an eye in the sky can show just how covert cheaters in China have become.[3]

But not anymore! They're going to get you with a Drone! Oh, and did you notice how the Drones weren't just watching you but were also listening? What else are they going to be doing with these things? India, right now, is equipping their Drones with facial recognition software for, 'smart surveillance and security in the most complex and dynamic of environments.' In other words, have fun trying to hide in a crowd, Drones are going to spot you just like that! But you might be thinking, "Okay that's just India, China, and the UK. We're in America, that's the land of the free and the home of the brave. Surely, we're not going to let Drones do this to us here. Unfortunately, we already are! Facial recognition software is not just already in place all over the ground here in America but it's now going to the skies with Drones. Pretty soon there is going to be no place to hide anywhere!

RT.com reports:
Every minute of every day, whether you are out in the street, working in the office, or sneaking into the kitchen, chances are someone is watching. Facial recognition technology was once only Syfy flicks could dream up. But now it's beginning to look a lot stranger than fiction. The FBI is planning on having a collection of over 12 million surgical frontal photos. So, here's how the project works.

You take a camera, then you take a picture, then it's uploaded onto a data base, and here's where the magic happens. The picture is then cross-referenced with other pictures in the already existing data base, pairing up your features, like your cheeks, eyes, what have you, every facial recognition software has a different method, algorithms if you will. Facebook for instance is already applying similar technology and getting a lot of flak for it.

If you have a Facebook account chances are you already used it without even knowing about it. When you upload pictures Facebook automatically picks out similar looking people and cross references the pictures with others that have been uploaded to the site. It's not completely accurate but arguably getting there. And it's not just social media companies either. The government is getting into the mix as well.

Paying private companies to follow you around. You may have heard a lot about a certain company as of late called TrapWire Inc. Though not much has been confirmed about the program we do know this. The quote 'sophisticated, predictive software' used to predict terrorist attacks is already in place in cities such as Los Angeles, New York, Las Vegas, and DC. With a limitless data bank with who knows what or who. Well there you have it. It seems like days of anonymity are long gone. And it's not just the camera but the data bank you should also be afraid of.

MSN reports: *Is Chris Dorner being hunted by a Drone with facial recognition scanners. Chris Dorner, the X-LAPD police officer that is on the run is being hunted by a Drone, an unmanned ariel vehicle. Some reports say falsely that it is an armed Drone. Reports are denying that saying that it is just an unmanned ariel vehicle surveillance Drone. But I want to show you the evidence that they may be using a very advanced facial recognition scanning Drone. Here is some old news back from 2011 that the Army was developing Drones that could recognize your face from a distance.*

Now of course we have facial recognition systems on computers, cell phones, secretly put up in cities around America, the TrapWire system that was discovered after the Stratford emails were hacked. You may not be aware of this but there is a secret facial recognition system already in place in major cities around America and they have been developing facial recognition, Drones.

Drones that can fly through the sky, fly over crowds, and pick you out of a crowd, pick a target out of a crowd. Here is a story from 2008 in National Defense Magazine that covers an unmanned ariel Drone that has facial recognition scanners. So, 2008, the iPhone came out in 2007. So just imagine the difference, first the iPhone and then the iPhone-5.

That's the difference between this facial recognition capable Drone and what they have today. Now Chris Dorner obviously hasn't surfaced recently, and this comes just a week after the number one story in the country was the rise of the Drones and now we are using a Drone to hunt the American terrorist.

Here is the press release put out by a company last year in July explaining that they were developing or had developed a facial recognition system on a Drone. So, are they using a facial recognition Drone to hunt for Chris Dorner. That's not exactly speculation, it's a very real possibility. Of course, that would probably be top secret.

The Orwellian nightmare is getting so realistic that the technology is getting ready to unroll and it's going to really freak people out. So, for what it's worth, unmanned ariel vehicles, also known as Drones, are most likely equipped with facial recognition scanners. I mean here we have 2008, an unmanned ariel vehicle originally designed to detect improvised explosives that can now be equipped with facial recognition technology that is aimed at homeland security officers to protect the borders.[4]

Oh yeah. That's what you'll use it for, so much for anonymous! Oh, by the way, if you want to go even deeper on these Big Brother issues, we have two other studies you can check out called, "The Final Countdown Ultimate" and "The Final Countdown Update 1" Both studies deal extensively with hours and hours of information exposing all the different Big Brother Technologies that are currently being used on us, not coming, but already in place like you just saw. That facial recognition software is the tip of the iceberg! But as you can see, even here in America they're using Drones to spy on us and combine that with facial recognition software and there's no place to hide! But it gets even worse than that! Believe it or not, these Drones do much more than just spy on your face, they can be used to spy on your conversations!

CNN Money News reports:
As he is looking at the screen in his hands he says, "You can see three people down below. Right now, we are collecting data about those three people." That's a hacker using technology installed on a Drone to grab cell phone information from people below. This technology has been used on cell phones and lap tops.

One day it could be installed on a larger aircraft. Think helicopters or small planes. The hacker tells us, "Down the road I see additional devices. It must be the people walking down the road." He can also see your user names, passwords, credit card information and get this, in some cases your home address. He says, "So, somebody walking around the park, it is most likely one of these houses close by." The tech on the Drone is called Snoopy.

We took Snoopy out for a spin on the streets in London. "It can fly within a relatively close distance of a person with their phone tucked safely in their pocket and if they left their Wi-Fi on, which most people do in my experience, their phone will be very noisily shouting out every network it has ever been connected to. It will be shouting out 'Starbucks are you there?'" says Glenn Wilkinson, security researcher, Sensepost. You can protect yourself by turning off your Wi-Fi. But, if you don't, Snoopy can trick your phone and send back a signal pretending to be the network your phone is looking for, then the Drone can intercept everything the phone sends and receives.

"Your phone is looking for Starbucks and I pretend to be Starbucks, your phone connects to me, and then I can see all of your traffic." He tested it out on some dummy accounts he created. "As you can see here it's logging into Yahoo.com, the Yahoo mail, and I created an account, Angela Smith, and there is the user name and password is abc123. Here is Amazon, PayPal, PayPal email address, user name." And Wilkinson hacked his own Facebook account to demonstrate what that would look like.

"Just click on my Facebook account, and click search Facebook profile, and from there I can fetch all Facebook friends." Wilkinson is an ethical hacker. He built the Snoopy Drone to highlight insecurities in smart devices. Some of the things Snoopy can do like steal user names and passwords are illegal. Experts say other features like tracking location data would probably not break any US laws. "If the technology got into hands of criminals or hackers which may have already been done, there's all kinds of things they can do.

At the most basic level they can hack people through space and time." In a world where Drones fly, hacking gives them power to potentially spy. It's more important than ever to protect your data.[5]

    From what? That's right, a Drone! Looks to me like we're headed for a reality where we're nothing but a bunch of caged rats, how about you? We're monitored from below by Big Brother, and now thanks to Drones were being monitored from above. But surely, they're going to make it secure and those that have it are just going to use it on those bad guys or terrorists, right? Well, believe it or not, it's already being done for much more mundane reasons than that! One instance involved some potential cattle thieves in America, and an actual Predator Drone was called out to hunt them down.

RT News reports:
Well it begins this afternoon with signs that the US may be moving in the direction of becoming a police state. Now we have heard about Drones being

used in the Middle East. Most recently, Iran accused the US of spying on the country but now reports that Predator Drones are being used on American citizens on US soil.

This video pretty much sums it all up. 'North Dakota sheriff was looking for six missing cows on the Prosser family farm. But three armed Prosser brothers chased him away. The sheriff called the Swat team, Bomb squad, and a Predator Drone, all created by US customs and Border Protection. The Drone was used to surveille the property until it was observed that the Prosser brother appeared to be unarmed. Then the Swat Team proceeded to make the arrest." Yes, that really happened. An unmanned multi-million-dollar Drone was reportedly used to help local police track down stolen cows and their owners. So, what is happening here in the US and is it a sign of things to come?[6]

Unfortunately, it would appear that way. But isn't that always the excuse, we're here to protect you! Whether it's terrorists or cattle thieves. Let us do this for your own good. But again, what if you became the 'bad guy' and who gets to define that anyway? Did you notice it wasn't just camera software in that Drone? It was infrared software that could see through buildings, in that Drone? Have fun hiding now! Drones see through a crowd, Drones see through a barn. We're toast! And lest you think this is just an aberration or just used by the military for hunting cows, think again. U.S. police forces are also jumping on the bandwagon of using Drones and they're also starting to implement a Drone surveillance system nationwide. Here's one in California.

ABC News reports:
Well Drones, metal detectors and the swat team were part of the security measures taken at tonight's Summerville's Homecoming football game. The enhanced security comes up when two Gorchester school officials were informed of a potential threat between rival gangs. Although the threats of violence might have kept many seats empty, those who did show up say they did appreciate the precautions taken.

"If you were anywhere near John McKissick Field for tonight's Summerville's football game you knew something was up." Says one of the reporter. "It's very scary to come here tonight, it's such a change because I have been coming to this stadium for so many years, and now we have armed guards. I couldn't carry my purse, forgot my phone, so I'm just a little bit out of sorts," says one of the residents attending the game.

Metal detectors greeted the fans, the Drones kept a careful watch from above, and the police were never far from sight. "I saw people that were really scared about what could possibly happen and I saw a lot of precautions that were taken to stop anything that could happen," one Junior High student told us. For Seniors, their final debut was tarnished with the reality of the world we live in today.

A senior tells us, "It's kind of scary. It's a little different, I've come here every year and there's never really been any security, but they are taking precautions for our safety and that makes me a lot more comfortable here." And at the end of the night this game will go into the record books but not because of its score. Everyone that I spoke to tonight told me that this is the first time they have seen any of this type of security measures being used at a high school football game.[7]

And keep in mind, with that fear, we're just seeing the very tip of where these Drones are going to be released. But, once again, don't worry, it's for your protection. We're here for you! Don't you feel safer already? Much of this rationale for this Drone monitoring from the sky throughout the U.S. has come from all the riots and police shooting. If we'd just have Drones in the sky monitoring all this, it wouldn't get out of hand, like this news report shows.

RT live reports:
Alright we talk a lot about Predator Drones here at RT, especially the ones that have the capacity to kill. But what about unmanned Drones that spray enough paint balls and pepper spray to deter protestors. That is exactly what is being marketed right now by a South African company called Desert Wolf Leisure and Camping. It already has some royal customers. One of them being an international mining company. The unnamed corporation has purchased 25 pepper spray, spraying, paint ball shooting, flying Drones for the said purpose of riot control.

The machine has been branded skunk, of course to its skunk spraying capacity. It has eight electric motors with propellers that can carry 4,000 pepper spray balls or non-lethal ammunition. The device is equipped with 4 barrels firing up to 20 paint balls per second which could equate up to 80 paint balls per second. It's all fitted with strobe lights, blinding lasers, and onboard speakers to give verbal warnings to the crowd.

There has been some backlash to this technology. Earlier I was joined by Steve Rambam, CEO of Pallorium Inc. I first asked him why a mining company would be interested in this kind of technology. He tells us, "private industry and governmental agencies, and especially law enforcement is trying to find ways to minimize risk to take live humans out of the equation, and to take live humans being injured out of the equation, which I think is a good idea. The problem arises when these devices, Drones, robots and some of the autonomous security devices act on their own, when the humans are taken out of the equation. That's when I think we start to approach Skynet."[8]

Oh, but I'm sure that's the only time and place they're going to do that. I'm telling you, you haven't seen anything yet! You think Drones being used at a High School Football Game to monitor crowds or gang activity was bad, what if something did break out! What if there was an insurgence of some sort? What would we do??? Can you say once again Drones to the rescue!!! Believe it or not, now they're equipping Drones to not only monitor the crowds, but to also take people out in the crowd, if they get out of line! What did he say? Skynet? His words, not mine. Could these things really become autonomous all over the world and attack humanity? That's where we're headed! But notice how it wasn't just a mining company who was using these armed Drones on the populace, but he even admitted that Law Enforcement and Governmental Agencies were considering this too! In fact, one man, who has worked with International Police agencies, is advocating 'A Drone army to redefine neighborhood watches where Drones would be equipped with infrared thermal imaging to detect human movement inside a car or even a home!' And now these surveillance Drones that they are developing are starting to look like something out of a Star Wars movie. Launch these babies into the air and your army of surveillance Drones is complete!

From the movie Star Wars:
As the little robot slides across the ice and snow and inches up into the air. Han Solo is peaking up from a mound and then Chewbacca follows suit and gives off one of his famous yells. The robot immediately turns around to see them both and starts shooting. The hero saves the day. Han Solo shoots and blows up the robot.

Now we have these robots from Cyphy Works, Ease UAV. Test conducted at McKenna Mount site, Ft. Benning. They perform the following: Vehicle hovers using machine vision stabilization; No GPS; No external motion tracking; No external references; enables indoor flight; work performed in cooperation with Georgia Tech.

The Drone flies out the window to observe the person walking down the street. When he sees that all is well it flies back inside the building. It has the capability to hover and stare and has a 50-knot airspeed, 14 lbs. air vehicle dry weight, can raise to a 10,500-foot service ceiling, it has forward and downward looking video cameras, with up to 100 waypoints in a flight plan, back-packable, deployment accomplished within 5 minutes, minimal operator training,[9]

      Yeah, I think I'd probably shoot it down too. Wow! Luke Skywalker eat your heart out! Can you believe this? Hollywood predicts our future again! Hey, maybe we can get a laser gun too to shoot these things down with! But I hope they never arm these things with lethal weapons like in Star Wars. I mean, pepper spray is bad enough, but not guns or lasers! Folks, I'm telling you, like the man said on the news clip, Skynet is coming!!! These Drones will be armed just like in the Terminator movies and they will take people out. In fact, Hollywood is already doing a great job getting us prepared for this horrible Science Fiction scenario! Check out this scene from a recent Hawaii Five-O episode, the new one. It's almost like they know something we don't!

From the TV show Hawaii Five O:
Steve McGarrett is telling his partners, "This is QV901, it's a surveillance Drone with no payload which means it flies unarmed. Three weeks ago, while it was on a routine test flight it was hijacked and never recovered." Lou asks, "How do you hijack a Drone?" Steve answers, "GPS spoofing, someone jampacked its control system to a UAV, installed false GPS data and made it land where the hijacker wanted."

Kono asks, "So, what are we looking at here? An inside job, a security breech?" Danny replies, "We don't know yet. Vanpax gave us a list of all their current x-employees that had clearance on the project. So, we should run their names against the victims and see if we come up with a connection." Steve adds, "Then if we see one we might find the motive." Lou adds, "Let me tell you something. It takes a special kind of brilliance to hijack a Drone, arm it, and reprogram it."

While they are talking about it, the Drone is passing over the people at the beach. The people see this strange thing and stop what they are doing to pay attention to it as it comes flying at them. It's like a space ship, stopping over their heads. Now everyone is watching to see what it will be doing next. From the Drones eye view of the people it starts to scan the crowd. Then the bullets start flying through the crowd and they all start running to try to get away without getting shot. They keep running as the Drone keeps firing. People start dropping to the ground with bleeding bullet holes. Next it starts shooting at the people in the water. They just can't seem to move fast enough as more are shot and fall into the water.[10]

Notice it had facial recognition software too. But don't worry, we're here to protect you. It won't get out of hand. This is where we're headed, and it can all be hijacked, and we're going to have Drones everywhere. Armed Drones from the sky. Not just the military version, monitoring and killing, but it's about to get even worse! You thought that killer Drone was creepy enough? Wait till you see what the military around the world is doing with them. Skynet is almost here!

Chapter Twelve

Drones in the Military Force

The **2nd deadly ability** of Drones is coming to the **Military Force**.

As we saw in the beginning with the History of Drones, one of the greatest forces behind the continual development of Drones is in the military. They not only use them and design them around the world for surveillance purposes but for lethal purposes. Making them armed flying killing machines just like in the Terminator movies. And they are getting more and more sophisticated and more and more armed in various ways with each succeeding year. Let's look at a few of the killer Drones out there.

France 24 Reports:
In this edition we look at the use of Drones. One of the most controversial weapons in current day conflict. Drones play an increasingly important role in areas of combat and in civilian situations such as search and rescue. But it's the use of Drones as an automatic almost insidious and often deadly weapon that causes most discomfort among politicians and those potentially under fire alike.

Our reporters have been to meet the people who pilot the Drones to see how they work and especially how they train and hear how they feel about what they do. Our reporter starts in the United States in New Mexico. Reporter: In the New Mexico desert a whirring sound like that of a lawn mower, it's what we came here looking for. That black dot in the sky is a predator Drone with its tail pointing downward. Then another one, the same sound, this time a reaper Drone.

The Predator's big brother is more powerful and more lethal. Both took off from Hollomon Air Force Base. Over 2,000 people live in Hollomon, the world's biggest flying school for military Drones. For his and his family's safety the officer who will show us around has been told to hide his last name. A Drone pilot, after all, is a target. Like many on base, Major Matt, spent years as a fighter pilot before taking his place in a Predator cockpit on the ground. Now he teaches a new generation.

In this school they teach you how to go to war without ever stepping foot into any enemy territory. "With the remotely powered aircraft, we are in the United States flying aircraft that is on the other side of the world. So, we do go home at the end of every day, which is different, but it's an amazing capability and it's a lot of support for the ground guys out there. And they request it because they know we do a great job and we are happy to do it. Both the Reaper and the Predator come fully equipped just in case.

This is your AGM114 missile. It's a hellfire. The same missile that is used on our Apache helicopters. It's used for anti-armor, anti-personnel, and we have a variant for buildings as well." The names given to these Drones are no coincidence, they hunt, and they kill. A Predator can carry 350 kilos worth of weapons, the Reaper over a ton. "Today this is a simulation that's being run right now for training in Afghanistan, so we can mark different things, like where the bad guys are, where the good guys are."

There's an unmistakable target, someone forgot to delete this comment before our camera saw it. 'Blow this up' it says. Go off base and that is precisely the type of humor that is not appreciated. "Often time when the opportunity to launch or fire our missile comes, the intended target is with somebody else. Very rarely is that person singled out in the crowd." The constructors don't want to hear these critical voices.

General Atomics, the company that builds the Predator and the Reaper has just announced its newest arrival, the Avenger. This one is being promoted as a fighter jet without a pilot. General Atomics has promised savings galore on the military budget. General Atomics Aeronautical ad: Predator C Avenger, General

Atomics has its stand every year at the AUVSI convention, the Drone show. The latest showcase was held in Washington, not too far from the Pentagon.

Unmanned vehicles come in all shapes and sizes, some for civilian and some for military use. Officers and members of the industry come to see the latest trends. More Drones in the skies means new markets are opening up. This is a Viper strike, we refer to it as Viper E. This is a glide munition, it comes off both manned and unmanned platforms. The U.S. Air Force no longer trains only its own pilots, other countries need Drone pilots too. These officers are French.

Paris has bought two American made Reaper Drones. They won't be armed and will be used as reconnaissance only says the French Air Force. The first French Drone pilots receive their training in the desert of New Mexico. "At the end of our training here we can use this kind of weapon system in an actual operational environment, in fact we are expected very soon, in the places where this Drone will be used. We are leaving for Africa soon," says Lt. Col Tanguy Benzaquen, Drone pilot who used to fly the French Mirage Jet. Like him all of the pilots in training are swapping the cockpit in the air for a cockpit on the ground. Other countries like France may follow suit. The U.S. military now trains more Drone pilots than fighter jet pilots.[1]

    So much for just taking pictures and spying on your neighbor and delivering pizza! These things are lethal and deadly! And we're about to see even more of this! More Drones pilots are being trained than regular pilots and we're even training pilots from other countries to do the same as us! In fact, Drones are not only in demand right now, more than ever, but because of the ongoing 'Terrorist Crisis' that seems to keep getting worse, Congress has blocked the Air Force from retiring any of its Drone Assassins. They believe we have a deficit of these Drones around the world and say it's only going to grow. With all this terrorist activity going on we can't get rid of any of them! It's too risky. It's almost like somebody opened Pandora's Box and there's no turning back! They say the benefits are, 'You can not only kill more bad guys and see where they are amassing themselves,' but you can save more lives because you don't have actual manned pilots flying these missions. In fact, look at how these Killer Drones are controlled around the world from anywhere in the world and the stress it's creating on soldiers.

"It is a complete cultural change for the Air Force. Pretty soon we will have more unmanned than maned aircraft." Says Col. William Brandt. "It's almost

surreal." In Creech Air Force Base, Indian Springs, Nevada, we see the pilots at the controls of the unmanned aircraft. "It looks like we are by ourselves out here. This isn't a video game, this is a real airplane flying through real air space. You need to be able to think through a three-dimensional problem that is located 7500 miles away from you.

The biggest risk is that we accept that detachment from it." Real live weapons, doing a real mission, I try to get people to understand, that there are people who are counting on us to do the mission. You are no longer sitting at Creech Air Force Base. There are both severe political and military consequences if we fail. 'Get into that mindset when you step into the GCS, you are in the fight.' This is a very precise weapon where we are putting a laser down and the weapon follows the laser.

So, it's very precise and it hits where we want it to hit. One time we had intel that there was a bad guy riding around on a motorcycle, and he stopped at two or three different play grounds. He was playing soccer with all these kids. He's just doing, living his everyday life. And then at the end of that ride we found him at a meeting of bad people. And it ended up resulting in a strike, and you end up seeing what happens. The guys at the control watch the guy, set the laser, and 5-4-3-2-1, shoots the guy with the unmanned Drone.

Going to war has meant the same thing for over 5,000 years. Going to war meant that you are going to such danger that you might never come home again. You may never see your family again. Now compare that experience with that of a Predator Drone pilot. You are sitting behind a computer screen, you're shooting missiles at an enemy target, you're killing combatants, and then at the end of the day you get back in your car and 20 minutes later you are sitting at the dinner table talking to your kids about their homework.

"My family knows I fly UAV's. I don't necessarily go home and tell them what mission I flew or something like that. That's the challenge in the job. You have to do that day in and day out. We are finding that some of these units actually have combat stress and PTSD even just like the units that are physically deployed into Iraq and Afghanistan and it makes perfect sense when you pull back and think about it because this disconnect of being at war and at home, it's very hard for the human mind to wrap itself around.[2]

What a contradictory scenario. You're at the controls of something that looks like you're playing a video game, but it really does blow people up, and yet at the end of the day, you walk away, go home, and get some food. "Hi kids! Honey I'm home!" No wonder you're having problems with this. Speaking of video games, I'm sure they haven't been using video games to prepare a younger generation in America for this new type of automated warfare with Drones, would they? It's been going on for quite some time now.

Video games about war are obviously very popular and now war is becoming more like a video game. I mean look at this controller for a remote weapon system. Look familiar? So, what if I told you that the United States military played a huge role in the invention of video games back in the 50's when there was this looming paranoia about the possibility of a nuclear apocalypse. I mean it was the beginning of the cold war and the world was a much less safe place to live in.

There were nuclear sirens going off everywhere. There were even cartoons about getting killed by nuclear bombs. 'What are you supposed to do when you see the flash, drop and cover.' Worse there weren't any fun video games to play. The only computer were these huge main frames that cost a million dollars and only existed at the elite research facilities. They were mostly used for crunching numbers for the U.S. military, like calculating the trajectory of a ballistic missile.

So, it's weird then out of this dead serious environment video games were born. Tennis for two was the very first video game outside of OXO which really doesn't count because basically it's just tic-tac-toe. It was developed on military equipment. It was invented by William Higinbotham, a prim and proper 48-year old physicist that had previously worked on the development of the atomic bomb and later became a leading nonproliferation advocate.

While assigned to Brookhaven National Laboratory, a base that pioneered nuclear weapons, he noticed that visitors to the lab were kind of bored, so he got this great idea. What if he repurposed a Donner Model 30 analog computer to play a game. The Donner was this hulking 28-pound metal box with a voltage meter out front instead of keys. It worked by plugging in wires into different holes. But sure enough, it worked, Tennis for two was a hit.

October 15, 1958 hundreds of visitors lined up in front of the lab in Upton, New York, which at the time was filled with all these crazy machines like something you would see in an H.G. Wells novel. These visitors had one goal and one goal alone, to hit a tiny blue ball back and forth across the screen of an oscilloscope. The crazy thing is that Higinbotham used his experience as a researcher at the active radiation lab at MIT to create Tennis for 2. So, what that means is one of the earliest video games on record would not exist if the military hadn't been dumping so much money into weapons of mass destruction.

OK, fast forward to 1961, Patsy Cline's, 'Fall to Pieces' is on the radio. The Pony is the hot new dance move and a group of students create a game called Space War, not too surprising, not too surprising about two space ships shooting at each other. Space War was developed at MIT's Lincoln Lab which was another military R&D center which was chartered specifically to defend the nation from air attacks. There the MIT students had access to the enormous PDP1computer that was designed by two former students of the lab.

The first PDP1 was sold to the Lawrence Livermore Laboratory in California, which, surprise, surprise was the pioneer in the research of nuclear weapons. Space War was a huge hit. Students quietly passed copies of the code to each other in the hall ways. The computer scientist Allen Kay told Rolling Stone in the early 70's, Space War blossomed spontaneously where ever there was a graphic display connected to a computer. It's important to remember that the kinds of people that are making and then later playing games like Space War are not future 5-star generals, they are basically hippies.

People like Noland Bushnell whose first act after founding Atari was to create a Space War knockoff called computer Space. I know, very creative. Atari was a place where Bushnell's own words, pot smoke filled the air, and hippies skated between our cave machines. Bushnell wanted Atari to be an extension of San Francisco's popular Haight Ashbury neighborhood that was just up the street. So, games owe a lot to long hair, liberal minded people advancing new ideas on machines entirely funded by the U.S. military.

Next, let's set the time machine for 1966. The year the first video game console was developed. It was originally a prototype called brown box because it was a brown box. It was invented by Ralph Baer, a Jewish American immigrant who fled Germany with his parents just before the Holocaust. Baer found himself working for a company called Sanders Assoc. Inc. and surprise, surprise Sanders was a defense contractor who specialized in aircraft defense system and was later acquired by Boeing. When Baer wasn't creating tools to snoop on the soviets or designing Saturn 5 launch equipment for the space race he was using military funded technology to bring video games to the masses.

The brown box prototype eventually became the Magnavox Odyssey and video games became the flourishing industry that we now know and love. As for the military, they changed courses. They looked around and said 'Hey, maybe we can take advantage of all these games we have inadvertently funded.' One of the earliest instantaneous is the 1980 tank game Battle Zone. The game was so realistic at the time that the Army approached Atari who made Battle Zone about creating a new version called the Bradley Trainer which would teach gunners how to blow up other tanks without the high costs of blowing up other tanks.

The action was so real you just might forget it is just a game. Some of the folks at Atari hated the idea of working on a game like the Bradley Trainer so much they just refused to work on it. None the less, this marked a turning point. Games would push the military to new places. Not the other way around. In the early 80's DARPA began experimenting with video games as a form of combat simulation which resulted in something called Simnet which allowed fledgling pilots to try their hand at flying a helicopter or an airplane.

Then in 2002 America's Army was released as a recruitment tool and it uses the same technology that powers games like Years of War and then finally last year in a quote that makes me weep for humanity, a Drone pilot told the Guardian, that Drone strikes were a lot like playing a video game. So, began like free spirits turning war machines into peace time play things have come full circle. Peter Singer, the former director of the Brookings Intelligence Center said that games like Call of Duty inspire combat and set the expectations of what future wars might look like.

You might say it's advanced warfare. And hey, I didn't even get a chance to talk about the licensing of military weapons in video games or virtual reality. Palmer Luckey, the guy who created the Oculus Rift, got his start working on virtual reality at a lab that was funded by the U.S. Army.[3]

Looks like we've been prepared for this future advanced warfare with Drones. And you can see why when you look at the trend. Drone technology has grown so fast that right now 1/3rd of all Military aircraft are now Drones and that is why there are now 3 times the number of Drone pilots being trained as opposed to regular manned pilots. Pilotless planes are now the new emerging warfare as these experts admit, but it's going to come at a price.

RT News reports:
The U.S. Drone operations have dramatically increased over Obama's presidency but still remain the spearhead of surveillance and air strike missions being held by the U.S. military in different conflict regions in the world. Now according to the exclusive revelations by the Wall Street Journal, the Pentagon is looking to expand the operations even further.

The statistics are pretty telling, now it started with just 10 daily flights by U.S. Drones ten years ago in 2005. As it stands it's about 60 flights per day conducted by Drones in the conflict regions across the world, but the new plans suggest that by the year 2019 the Drone operations will increase by at least 50%, amounting to about 90 flights per day. Now, not only the actual amount of Drone flights will increase in four years, also the territory where these Drones will be operating will expand as well.

For now, Drone operations will be mostly restricted to Afghanistan, Pakistan, Yemen, Somalia and Libya. But according to the new plan the territory might be expanded to South China Sea, Iraq, Ukraine, Syria, Algeria, Morocco, Egypt and Tunisia. "Just over the last four or five years with the tremendous increase in maturity in the systems, it's growing in almost every way you can categorize, it's growing from a research standpoint, it's growing from a technology standpoint, so it's definitely growing.

We are seeing just a huge explosion of unmanned systems, it's incredible." Says Gary Kessler, unmanned aviation strike weapons, US Navy. "Canada, Australia, U.S., Italy, Germany, U.K., France, all the major countries are heavily involved in the development as well as the acquisition of unmanned systems." "U.S. congress mandates that 1/3 of the U.S. military will be unmanned by 2015 and our view is, if it was our problem how would we do it. It's a large military program that costs billions of dollars.

One of the sub-contracts under that, that built the ANS System, that is the Economist Navigation System. From jeep size, all the way up to large striker as well, so we kind of run the gambit of different size platforms. You will have unmanned rail systems that are integrated with UAV's. For the first-time war fighters will have God's view and an up close and personal 3D view, so things are really changing, they are really changing quickly, and we're happy to be part of that future."

Robots' that kill. In the movie Terminator, they portray a future that has gone terribly wrong. They are no longer science fiction. The demands for robots is growing and growing very rapidly. Robots can save lives. Promoting flying unmanned aircraft can help us to project power without projecting vulnerability. What happens when armed robots can think for themselves. The robots themselves can be sent to an area and if they find anybody they will kill them.

Who gets to use them and how? Strictly speaking under the laws of war we are committing murder. What are the repercussions for us? It's an incredible, elegant technology that is on the cutting edge and that's why scientists are so excited to work on it, but it may well be something we may regret later. As we move toward more autonomous systems then we have to ask, how far do we let them go?[4]

And that's exactly the problem. Maybe you shouldn't go this route. Maybe you're opening Pandora's Box. or as the movies call it, Skynet! And you might be thinking, "Well, okay maybe that's just our military personnel thinking that or planning on that, working with others in the industry, but I'm sure our Politicians and Presidents would put a stop to it if it gets out of hand." Actually, Obama is not only an apparent huge fan of Drones, but he even apparently boasted that, "he is good at killing people with them." I didn't say that...he did!

Huff Post Live Reports:
If it's true, a big, big scoop coming of course from Mark Halperin, and John Heilemann, authors of that new book 'Double Down', game change 2012. They claim that on the campaign trail of 2012 President Obama told aides quote, 'Really good at killing people'. According to the authors, Obama made the comment last year when discussing Drone strikes.

While the White House hasn't officially commented, Obama advisor, Dan Phifer, said over the weekend said that neither he or the President have read the book. Arthur, that is about the lamest excuse ever about a quote that is attributed to you. I haven't read the book, does that mean that, that addresses the fact that he said he is really good at killing people? "At the end of the day he might have said it is as it is." Says Arthur Delaney, HuffPost Politics Reporter. "We noticed, Barack Obama, that you were very good at killing people."

You have offed thousands with Drone strikes and you're most famous victim being Osama bin Laden. The relish that he seems to take in the taking of human life is sort of unseemly. I'd say it's not the best thing for a politician to say. Pretty nasty stuff, and that denial you just reported is not a very strong denial is it?" He didn't say 'I didn't say it, or he didn't say that's disturbing or that's disgusting, that's outside my character, he said, 'I haven't read the book'.

"He couldn't say no, Obama doesn't like killing people, he couldn't even say that." A second reporter at RT Live says: You know the last thing I ever expected to come up out of a Nobel Peace Prize winners mouth is this 'I'm really good at killing people'. Yes folks, according to a new book 'Double Down' our beloved President, constitutional lawyer, and Nobel laureate Barack Obama apparently loves to brag at how well he can execute human beings with Drones.

Now I know you are thinking it's probably the Republicans making him say such things because you can't look weak on defense. But no, it's all the credit of Barry O. During the 2012 election journalists Mark Halperin and John Heilemann were reporting on Obama's campaign. It was at this time that the Drone king reportedly boasted to his aides about his kills. Since becoming the manager of the U.S. empire Obama has rapidly increased the use of Drones abroad and his hundreds and hundreds of strikes has put Bush's measly 52 Drone attacks to shame.

Thousands of dead women, men, and children don't lie. They also can't speak or defend themselves in any way. Now for those of you who are still not offended by the Presidents disregard for human life and think that this is just a way politics work, every President has blood on their hands, let me remind you of this.

One of the chief architects of the Drone program, John Bellinger, said that the reason Obama has ramped up the use of these robots is to avoid the bad press of Guantanamo Bay. So, you know what? I'll give it to him, he really is good at killing people. Because if there is one thing voters hoped for when electing him, it was expedited murder.[4]

Wow! Doesn't look like Obama's going to be interested in shutting this program down when people find out how horrible it is! But wait a second. That's just overseas, right? The President wouldn't ever use them on American people on American soil, would he? Well, according to The Department of Homeland Security a plan has recently been advanced to deploy "public safety" Drones in the skies over America, an action already authorized by Congress, and called for the deployment of 30,000 drone surveillance vehicles. The Department of Homeland Security says it's just for "public safety matters or disasters" but many feel the President may have a different idea on how best to implement this new killer technology. He is well known for his obsession with remote drone attacks, reportedly going so far as to personally sit in on unmanned aerial vehicle missions, and when asked about concerns about the possibility of military Drone strikes within U.S. borders, he not only failed to deny that he has such plans, just like his other quote, but he made it clear that his administration is working closely with Congress to develop a legal framework that will allow the Chief Executive and his subordinates the leeway to initiate strikes right here at home. Right here in America! In fact, Drones are already being used in America to monitor our borders and fix our so-called border crisis!

CBS News reports:
One issue that will be getting a lot of attention from the new congress is border security. And members won't be happy when they see this story, it raises earnest questions about how tax payers' money is being spent on the border. Jeff Begay tells us, "With 7,000 miles of U.S. land to patrol increasingly U.S. customs and border protection are relying on Drones to help arrest illegal immigrants.

But department of Homeland Security Inspector General's reports raises questions about whether this program is worth it. In 2013 it accounted for 2,200 arrests. There are 10 Drones flying in the program at a cost of $62 million a year. Over the last 10 years this unmanned eye in the sky program has cost nearly $500 million dollars and is getting an additional $443 million in funding. Armed Predator Drones have been used on the battlefield in Afghanistan and Pakistan. Here along the U.S. border Predators are used strictly for surveillance.[5]

For now, or at least that's what we're being told. But I'm sure they'll never use them to take out people on the border. Really? We just saw Obama's desire and the Department of Homeland Security's framework do this very thing, even on American soil! And we're not the only country doing this. This is truly a global movement. The whole world is getting in on this rush to monitor and control the skies with killer Drones, not just Drones but again killer Drones, just like in the Terminator movies! Not only has Russia been working overtime developing their own killer Drones, but they have recently announced plans to build a Military Drone Base in the Arctic just 420 miles off the Alaskan Coast. China has already successfully developed a Drone Defense System and are making so many Drones that they're now selling them to other countries. Thanks China everybody's got them now! France, Germany, Italy, Turkey, England, India, Israel, Iran, Pakistan, and it's growing! Every country will have armed Drones within 10 years, the reports are saying, and armed aerial Drones will be used for targeted killings, terrorism and the government suppression of civil unrest, if you or I, the average Joe get out of line! And what's worse is that the experts are saying, "it's too late for you to do anything about it." Can I translate that? Skynet is coming whether you like it or not! It's the New Arms Race just like with the nukes of old. It's a New Cold War, it's a Drone War. Today countries around the world are scrambling to get ahead of each other on these killer Drones! That's not just alarming, but as you can see, it can very well be laying the foundation for a real live Skynet system! In fact, there's already a global entity in the works to control the whole system just like in the Skynet scenario. It's all because of the fear factor of having killer robots or Drones flying all over the world. Right now, the U.N. (a Global Entity) is calling for these, killer robots to be strictly monitored because they see the potential dangers of this new rapidly advancing technology creating a new type of Arms Race. And that's just in the sky. Believe it or not, the military is also putting these killer robots on land, in the ocean, and literally everywhere you can think of! The whole planet is going to be crawling with them! The skies are just the beginning as this military analyst shares with us.

Stratfor.com reports
Drones usage is rapidly increasing throughout the world." From 2005 until present day the number of countries operating these platforms nearly doubled. This trend is only going to continue if not accelerate. But all Drones are not created equal.

There is a massive variation and physical structure capabilities and systems that these platforms operate with it. When most people hear the word Drone they commonly think of the U.S. operative predator and associate it with strike capabilities. This represents a very small nitch in reality. It is very important that UAV's are actually a subset of a broader category of unmanned vehicles that operate on land, below the ocean, on its surface and in space.

So, UAV's currently are the most prominent and advanced in military utility but other subsets such as unmanned under water vehicles are being developed, tested and adopted quickly into forces as well. UAV's can be as small as an insect to as large as a 737 airliner and their capabilities are nearly as diverse." says Paul Floyd, Military Analyst.[6]

Uh yeah, I'd say so! Did you catch that? Land, water, space, size of a bug or a 737 Airliner? In fact, let's take a look at that amazing diversity that most of us had no clue was being developed.

Chapter Thirteen

Drones in the Animal World

For instance, you just think that was a bird you saw, but it wasn't! It was a Drone!

Markusfischer presents:
It is a dream of mankind to fly like a bird. Birds fly not with rotation, but they fly only by flapping their wings. So, we looked at the bird and we try to make a model that is powerful, ultralight, and it must have excellent aerodynamic qualities that it would fly only by flapping its wings. So, what would be better to use than the sea gull and its circling and swooping over the sea and use this as a role model."

After he said this, three men brought out what looks like a bird but is actually a robot. It starts flapping its wings and it looks just like the sea gull that was previously on the screen.

One of the men toss the bird into the air it flies across the room. The audience goes wild at the presentation. It flies around the auditorium 4 or 5 times and then lands back into the hands of the man who sent it off.[1]

They made a robot bird. I hope they don't arm it. As you can see, that looked just like a bird, a large seagull or something, but it wasn't! And that's not the only thing they're mimicking. Maybe you think you saw a lizard creeping around on the wall, but it wasn't! Maybe it's a robot gecko.

History.com reports:
One of the scientist that brought this vision to life is Mark Cutkosky. "DARPA has a program to try to develop climbing robots for various applications, surveillance, inspection and so on. I am Professor Mark Cutkosky at Stanford University. My goal is to build robots that can go anywhere. One of the advantages of climbing robots is surveillance, spying, or monitoring areas because they can climb a building, a tree, or a structure."

"The ability that we required was the ability for a robot to walk up a vertical surface and achieve a position high up in a tree or telephone pole or wall." To achieve this daunting goal Cutkosky worked closely with biologists to unlock the mysteries of nature's best climbers. "We've been collaborating with Professor Robert Full at University of Berkeley for a number of years.

Doctor Full shot slow motion video and microscopic photos of insects to find out how they used tiny spines on their feet to climb vertical walls. Applying Fulls' discoveries Cutkosky developed the feet for the climbing robot named Rise. "Here you can see how the spines are grabbing the little bumps and pits on the surface, we have lots of these tiny spines, so they share the load." Says Professor Cutkosky. "The real hard problem comes down to how do you achieve the attachment forces between the foot and the vertical surface that are great enough to support the weight of the vehicle itself."

"If you want a robot that climbs vertical surfaces, smooth, rough, dirty, clean, then the gecko really is the premier example of a climbing animal." The gecko can cling to glass with a single toe and walk upside down. It sticks to the surface with what you call Van der Waals' forces. "Van der Waals' forces are a basic vallecular attraction. All that exists between any two molecules, if they get close enough. It has to do with a momentary arrangement of the electrons. You can take advantage of it if you can get really intimate contact between any two different surfaces." Millions of tiny hairs on the gecko's toes create the intimate contact with the climbing surface that generates the Van der Waals forces. Cutkosky and his team have built a droid call Sticky Bot that harnesses that same power.

"It is basically our attempt to take the principals that we have learned about how geckos climb and apply those to a robot that also uses Van der Waals force to climb vertical surfaces. The secret to Sticky Bot is the adhesive pads that are on its toes," Says Cutkosky. Cutkosky's teams fabricated pad that has hundreds of

Nano scale stalks. As with the gecko these stalks are sharply angled, so the toes stick when going in one direction but easily peel off when pulled the other way.

"When you load it with gravity, the way the robot loads it, it sticks and to make it detach you just have to pull it a little bit in the opposite direction and it pops right off." Now imagine real terminators climbing up the side of the building, spying on the enemy, waiting for that moment to attack. "Once that robot climbs up there to hang, it doesn't expound any power. It can cling there for hours or even days. That's quite different than that of a small helicopter that always has to spend a lot of power and make a lot of noise.[2]

Well, it's much more efficient and costs less, can you believe that? Oh, by the way, did you catch the part there about terminator robots having the same climbing ability and surprising people??? That couldn't happen, could it? You'll see soon enough. But speaking of creepy, for all of you who are not only afraid of lizards but how about other reptiles like snakes, wait till you see this one! It can get you on land or water!

Science Magazine reports:
Sidewinder rattlesnakes scale sandy slopes with ease. The slithering snakes can do this by making huge 'S' curves as they push diagonally forward. By looking at how the rattlesnake wriggles on sandy inclines, scientist at Georgia Tech found out that as the slope gets steeper the sidewinders keep more of their body in contact with the sand. The team then tested their idea with a snake like robot that had been built at Carnegie Mellon University.

Using the contact trick from the real rattlesnake researchers changed the robots moves. Finally, it too could work its way up the slope. Natural inspiration like this can help robots move beyond the hard floor of the lab to earths more uneven surface, such as rock, dirt and sand. The transition may make the box more useful in search and rescue operations. "A lot of people, when they think of a robot, have this vision of a humanoid robot that can come into your house and do your dishes."

Some of the more informed people know that there are a lot of robot arms in factories, painting cars, welding, and what nots. However, the animal kingdom is full of non-human animals that have been very successful in getting into all sorts of places doing all sorts of tasks. So, one robot is like a snake. What's nice about these robots is they have all these degrees of freedoms with which they can thread through tightly packed volumes and they can get to locations that people and machinery cannot access.

So, here we have one of our snake robots. So not only can we get into tight spaces where people and conventional machinery otherwise cannot access, but something with such a small size can achieve a bunch of mobility capabilities that conventional devices, robots, can't. So, for example this guy here can roll like a wheel, but it can also look around and get onto pipe and crawl up on all kinds of things. You can see on the video what the robot sees going through some tight terrain.

So, one application, they do a variety of things, they crawl on the ground, they climb up pipes, whatever, but if any one of those tasks maybe you could build a better mechanism but there is no mechanism that can do all these tasks. So, it's the versatility of these devises that make them special. So here of course, is an application for climbing legs. But if you can imagine, in some remote location where you need to swim through a moat, get on a field, go through some rubble pile, or strangle a tech editor. (the snake is rolling up the tech's leg)

So, what we want to do, is provide a tool that will extend the reach of rescue workers, so they can stay out of harm's way and they won't cause collateral damage while looking for trapped survivors. A research group in a lab at the Tokyo Institute of Technology, is doing R & D on an amphibious snake robot. This robot moves by twisting its body similar to the motion of a snake. The motion is almost the same on land and in water.

One feature of this robot is its joints which combine bellows with universal joints. In this structure the bellows prevent water from penetrating the universal joints. Each joint unit has a CPU battery and motor. Each unit exchanges signals independently and automatically recognizes how far behind the head it is and how many joints there are in the body. This makes it possible to add and replace joints freely.

And here is the high point of the experience for me, as we actually operate on a person. What you see here is the snake robot entered a person's solar plexus, make a 25-millimeter one way and make a 25 millimeter turn the other way and you are behind the heart where you can deliver a whole host of therapy and diagnostics that otherwise would have required a whole stenonomy.[3]

Well, that's exciting! Robot snakes on the ground, in the water, in my heart, what's next? Well, these new Robots won't just be crawling, they'll be hopping! That's right, move over Kangaroos! Your robot cousin is here!

There is a kangaroo hopping across the landscape when the picture changes and there is a machine that looks like a kangaroo hopping across the carpeted floor. Its motions are the same as the live animal. As it is hopping across the room, it suddenly stops and faces a girl with an armband on her arm. She starts motioning for the robot kangaroo to come to her and it starts moving slowly towards her. She moves her arms in a circle and the robot does the same thing. She raises her arm to say stop and it stops, faces her and stands for the next command.[4]

Okay, I'm not going to Australia, but that sure would be kind of cool to have as a pet. I mean, what will they think of next? Robot animals in the air, land, crawling, hopping, these guys are everywhere! But speaking of everywhere, they're not planning on putting robotic animals in the water too, are they? Actually, it's already begun! Starting with Jellyfish!

RT Live reports:
Ever been stung by a jellyfish? Yes, that can hurt but it might be useful. That is what researchers at Virginia Tech College and Engineering are betting on. They have unveiled a robotic jellyfish, yes you heard me correctly. They have nicknamed this creation Cyro. It's over 5 ft. tall, and tips the scales at 170 lbs. In a news release the school says that this robotic jellyfish is a larger model of a robotic jellyfish of the same team of researchers that was unveiled in 2012.

Both robots are part of the project that is funded by the U.S. Naval undersea warfare center and the office of Naval Research. The purpose of these robots, you ask, is the surveillance and monitoring of underwater environments. This includes the study of aquatic life, mapping the ocean floors and monitoring the ocean currents. So, is this amazing technology only going to be used only for aquatic life, only time will tell. However, not only do we have to worry about the jaws on the beach but now we have to worry about the governments new robotic jellyfish also lurking in the water.

D News Reports:
The Navy is building a fleet of robot jellyfish, I didn't think you had it in you to be that awesome, Navy. Let's talk about jellyfish, because they are amazing.

Scientists have considered them to be the most efficient animals in the sea because they are able to get around easily without expounding energy very much at all.

They are also capable of living in these crazy temperature and pressure differences and in salt or fresh water, so if you are thinking of making an autonomous underwater robot they are pretty much the animal you want to mimic.

This is Cyro. It was created by researchers from Virginia Tech with a $5,000,000.00 grant from the Navy. Cyro is about 5ft. 7in., weighs about 170 lbs. and is supposed to capture some of that jellyfish efficiency by using that middle motion tied to ocean currents, and self-charging to keep it going for months at a time.

Now in my perfect world the answer to 'why are you guys building a robot jellyfish' would be because a robot jellyfish is what the Navy wants that does something useful for their $5,000,000.00. So, Cyro's job would be surveillance and monitoring the environment, mapping the ocean floor, gathering information about currents, and studying aquatic life, and maybe more.

Motherboard is quick to point out the Navy is essentially building their own Drone surveillance network, an undersea version of what the Air Force and the CIA are building out for the sky. They also gently remind us that the U.S. undersea warfare center, which is the department of the Navy that wrote the grant, is the same department that supposedly attached hypodermic needles that contained carbon dioxide into dolphins in the 70's that they would use to blow up divers.

They also allegedly put spring loaded traps on trained sea lions that were supposed to just shoot out and tie peoples legs together and sink them. The implication here is that Cyro could be outfitted for combat. A robot that big is obviously built to carry a large payload so that payload could potentially be some sort of a weapons system. Now I don't think there is anything that I find more terrifying than the idea of a creepy, giant, weaponized jellyfish.[5]

And I agree, can you believe that? An army of weaponized Jellyfish? I thought the fear of sharks from the movie *Jaws* was bad, but that fear of *Jaws* is about to get even worse.

Buzz:60 reports:
The Navy's newest underwater Drone is going to make anyone who spots it say this is no boating accident. As part of the Navy's silent Nemo project, it's called the ghost swimmer. It's task pretty much is what it's secretive and aquatic name implies. It's a robot shark spy. It's only about 5 ft. long and about 100 lbs., it's more like a robotic tuna spy.

The idea is that the Ghost Swimmer looks and moves so realistically it could be easily mistaken for a harmless fish, not as a million-dollar Navy operative. It's got rubbery skin, flaps its fins, can dive under 300 feet and can be controlled either by a tether or remotely, only to occasionally return to the surface to communicate and to appear a little more creepily lifelike.

The Navy has been testing the Drone in the waters off the North Virginia base and says it could eventually be used for not just surveillance and intelligence gathering but also to replace the real live Navy dolphin currently being trained to rescue swimmers and locate land mines. The only thing about this that I don't understand is if it is supposed to be some secret stealth machine meant to fool our enemies and allies, maybe the Navy shouldn't be posting videos in action on the internet. Just saying![6]

Which kind of leads to my opinion. If we see anything in the media that they admit they're doing, like this robot shark, we're actually 20 years behind the technology. What have you really got out there lurking in the waters that we don't know about? But the next thing you know, if this keeps up, we're going to see all kinds of underwater creatures in the ocean that are robotic. In fact, we already are.

Military Channel report:
Detecting explosive devices under the sea with a quad is in the near future, but for the far future, Robo-lobster. The Navy's interest in this vehicle is to hunt for underwater mines. The idea is we can actually put a charge on this robot, it can march up to the mine, park on the mine, be sent a solar signal to arm itself and detonate the mine.

Why build a mine detector in the shape of a lobster? Mine hunting in shallow water is very difficult because of wave surges and poor visibility. Lobsters however can navigate these turbulent waters with their uniquely designed bodies. Joseph Ayers, Ph.D. says, "When you look at most motorized robots they look like they are marching along making a lot of noise. This robot is completely silent. And it moves very smoothly like a real animal.

So, if we can build a machine that can capture the performance advantages that they have it will be the most advanced robot for that operation, in that environment, you could ever imagine." For some it might be hard to imagine high concept robots like a mine detecting lobster becoming a part of the military's inventory.

"It's a psychological issue that is a substantial hurdle but as I look across the services I see us moving ahead as well. Forget about whether the intelligence is carbon based like humans or silicon based like intelligent machines. Intelligence is intelligence and must be respected."

WSJ Will Connors, Reporter: *The next wave of Drones is here, and they are under water. Stingrays, jellyfish, and other denizens of the deep. The idea that a Drone being designed as a stingray will move better and blend in underwater is the key goal of these companies, some potential customers, and divers may need a little advanced intel when dangerous sea creatures might be lurking nearby.*[7]

Yeah, but what if that dangerous sea creature lurking nearby was a Drone and it was out to get you? I don't know about you, but I think I'm going to be a landlubber for the rest of my life! Unfortunately, you might want to rethink that backup plan. You see, they're covering them on the land too. Check out this Robotic Cheetah they're making. Land, sea, air, there's no safe place to hide!

CNN reports:
First let's start with who is in charge of the technology development for the military. That is the U.S. Defence Advanced Research Projects Agency or DARPA. An agency that is the stuff of mystery novels. We have noticed that they have been beefing up on robots. Most recently they contracted with Boston Dynamics to create a Cheetah robot. It's a four-legged robot that reportedly runs faster than the fastest human. It will be able to zig zag and take tight turns in order to chase and evade. It will also be able to make sudden stops and could end up with a tail.[8]

Not to mention a gun or some other armed lethal weapon! Starts to make you wonder if this is not the kind of wild beast the Bible mentions that is released on mankind to aid in killing 1/4th of the planet.

Revelation 6:7-8 "When the Lamb opened the fourth seal, I heard the voice of the fourth living creature say, 'Come!' I looked, and there before me was a pale horse! Its rider was named Death, and Hades was following close behind him. They were given power over a fourth of the earth to kill by sword, famine and plague, and by the wild beasts of the earth."

A robotic armed cheetah, like we just read would fit the bill, right? But they wouldn't do that, would they? Actually, they're also making a smaller robotic cheetah for your house called the Cheetah Cub. Who wouldn't want their own robot cat!

EPFL reports:
Cheetah cub, wanting to know how to make robots take control of rough terrain with the grace of a feline. Scientists at the Swiss Institute of Technology made a robotic cat. Using it they can assess joint force and agility without having to harm the actual animal.[9]

Well that's good, and it doesn't shed! I hope they don't arm that one like her big Mamma! But they wouldn't arm these things and take people out, would they? Actually, they already are. We already saw that the big Drones in the sky are already being armed to the gills with deadly guns and hellfire missiles and all kind of things to take people out from above. So why wouldn't they do the same thing with the ones they're putting on the ground or in the water? As we saw, they're already hinting at it in the articles we researched!

Chapter Fourteen

Drones in the Insect World

In fact, we know they're going to arm them because little do people realize that these same deadly characteristics of aerial Drones are now being produced in miniature size! We're now going from the UAV's (Unmanned Aerial Vehicles) to MAV's (Micro Aerial Vehicles). And, when I say micro, I mean micro. Believe it or not, they carry a payload just as deadly as the big ones. In fact, even the news is sounding the alarm on these new deadly critters!

RT News reports:
Micro air vehicles, or MAV's will play an important role in future warfare. The urban battlefield calls for tools to increase the war fighters' situation awareness for the capacity to engage rapidly, precisely, and with minimal collateral damage. MAV's will be integrated into the future Air Force air sensing systems.

These systems may be air dropped or hand launched depending on the mission requirements. "I'm sorry, did that plane just shoot out a bunch of little tiny Drones? Terrifying, really terrifying. So, these micro air vehicles are designed for urban battlefields with rapid precision. The question is, what urban battles are the militaries fighting that require this kind of creepy technology?

Forget about shooting these things down, they are about an inch in size." The small size of MAV's allows them to be hidden in plain sight. Once in place a MAV can enter into a low powered surveillance mode for missions lasting days or weeks. This helps the MAV to harvest energy from environmental sources such as sun light or wind or from manmade sources such as power lines or vibrating machinery. "Hidden in plain sight on missions that could last weeks. Powered by the sun or by the power lines, and did you see that little terminator pigeon?

Orwell would be rolling in his grave if he could see the disturbing reality we are about to be living in. But their small size is not just to linger outdoors, it is also to gain access inside." The small size and agile flight will also enable MAV's to covertly enter locations inaccessible by traditional means of ariel surveillance.

Multiple MAV's each equipped with small sensors will work together to survey a large area. Information from these sensors will be combined providing a swarm of MAV's with a big picture point of view. "Maybe these places are not conducive to surveillance because it is supposed to be illegal to surveil peoples' homes without a warrant. And, how frightening is it to think of a swarm of these little robots coming at you in a dark hallway.

Nowhere to run, nowhere to hide, they see all. They communicate together to give this big picture image to whomever is sitting at the other end of the screen. Can anyone say minority report because this is literally what this country is turning in to. And if that's not chilling enough, sit tight. It's about to get worse."

While some MAV's may be used purely for video reconnaissance, others may be used for targeting or tagging for sensitive locations. Individual MAV's may perform direct attack missions, could be equipped with incapacitating chemicals, combustible payloads, or even explosives for precision targeting capability.

"Wow, so if the surveillance fails, these mini robots can and will set off explosives, chemical agents and even assassinate human beings. At whose direction? Obama? The same person that has targeted the execution of a sixteen-year-old without due process. Gee, that's comforting. But will these MAV's really be used everywhere in the future of warfare?"

MAV's will become a vital element in the vital changing of war fighting environment and will insure success in the battlefield of the future, unobtrusive, pervasive, lethal, MAV vehicles, enhancing the capabilities of the future war fighter.[1]

Wow! That's not make-believe, that's actual reality! In fact, flies are not the only insects they're doing this with. They're even making robot bees!

Autonomous robot bugs sound like creatures from a Syfy flick but they could become a reality real soon. Scientists at the University of Sheffield and Suffolk in England are designing the first electronic bee in hopes that they can supplement or replace the shrinking population of the honey bees that pollinate the plant life according to the tech log "i09".

The Green Brain project, as the effort is called will upload real bee senses of sight and smell into the tiny robots. Scientists hope that these basic cognit abilities will allow e-bees to detect odors and gases from flowers just as bees do. The project plans to release the bees in 2015 along with making the worlds safe for pollination these bees don't sting, this is until they get into the wrong hands.[2]

It looks like it already has! E-Bees, E-Books, E-bugs! What's next? Well, can you say E-Insects to release into the public for monitoring purposes and who knows what else? It's already begun!

The U.S. military has designed Drones so small that they are starting to look like tiny insects. These are used to get into areas that they normally wouldn't be able to reach. These secret insect Drones are said to help the fight against terrorism, to help protect us. They look cool and could make a fun toy but is this something that could cause concern in the future.

People in New York and the Washington DC area have been reporting strange sightings of what they describe as tiny machines hovering around different gatherings, like the anti-war rally in Lafayette Square last month. A student was convinced that these were not real bugs. The FBI, CIA, and other various government organizations have all denied such claims as having tiny spy Drones at work. I guess if we generally trust the government they would only be used to keep our nation safe.[3]

Yeah, that's it Wally. And I got some swampland here in Vegas to sell you! And believe it or not, that's still not the only invasion planned for these things. A Professor in Computer Science at Harvard recently imagined a world, "In which Tiny Robot Drones flew around, the size of mosquitoes, extracting a sample of your DNA for analysis by the Government or even an Insurance Firm." And speaking of Robot insects, be it bees, flies, mosquitoes or other bugs like roaches, beetles, termites, dragonflies, bats, butterflies, and hornets, they're working on those too. There is another thing they're working on with these MAV

Drones capabilities just like insects. They not only chase you individually, but they can also swarm you just like a bunch of insects.

Multiple vehicles can fly in a formation. We developed a method to transition between formations in 3D. The team can also navigate in environments with obstacles. They fly in circles, through obstacles, and figure eights, they are a programmable self-assembly in a thousand-robot swarm. They can be programed into a shape of a starfish. Collectives in nature, they can have millions of individuals that cooperate to form complex structures.

Creating these abilities in artificial systems remains a significant challenge. We developed a simple low-cost robot called 'Kilobot' which allowed us to produce a 1024-robot swarm for testing and collecting behaviors. Mass-manufactured at low-cost, 'Kilobot' has unconventional locomotion using vibration motors, and communication using reflected infrared lights. Each robot has simple capabilities and is susceptible to many errors.

To compensate for this, they must work together. We present an algorithm for programmable self-assembly in large swarms, where a user can give a desired shape to all robots. The algorithm allows robots to robustly form that desired shape without human intervention in the first thousand robot swarm. The algorithm for self-assembly allows for the provably correct formation of any simply connected shape.

It is composed of three primitive behaviors; gradient, edge following, and distributed coordinate system. It relies on additional strategies to operate in large groups of error-prone robots. Gradient, detection of rare errors, and edge following, compensate for variation between robots, Distributed system and continuous space algorithm.

To start the assembly process, user places 4 seed robots to mark the position where the shape should be formed. Robots on the outer edge of the arbitrarily shaped starting group, take turns starting the motion. Moving robots then edge-follow until they enter the desired shape as determined by a collectively constructed coordinate system.

Once inside the shape, robots move until they either are about to exit the shape or bump the previous robot. When this occurs, they join the shape. This work demonstrates the ability to create and program a large-scale autonomous swarm which can achieve complex global behavior from the cooperation of many limited and noisy individuals.

MPT reports: *What is a less expensive, less complex machine, but more of them? That's the idea behind Harvard University's Robo-bee. It would take 30 of these to equal the weight of a penny. What happens when you move beyond just having one robot and instead have a swarm? In the future, swarms of robots working as a team may build our skyscrapers or map unchartered areas, or scout out victims in a disaster, as robotic search and rescue teams.*

Robots are moving closer to thinking and acting like humans. But every advancement complicates the issues of accountability and ethics. Now a new form of war-bot is being developed with an artificial intelligence that is a world away from human reasoning. Almost like a swarm of bees, or ants, or a wolf pack, you have distributed command and control but concentrated fire power.

That is, everyone making their own little decisions, then they find what they are hunting and then they gather around them and over whelm them. A very different model of war. It's called a swarm. A group of robots focused on a single task. They are one entity with many parts operating from within a collective hive mind. There is no central leadership within a robotic swarm. By its nature a swarm cannot be under human control.

Josh Redding of MIT Aerospace controls lab tells us, "They can organize themselves in an intelligent way and do something that is coherent and really cool. For example, if they were to go through a doorway, they would kind of negotiate among themselves, there is no one given leader saying you go first, you go second, they are all kind of deciding who goes first and who goes second without a centralized leader or decision maker."

It's very difficult if you have a big enough swarm, it would be impossible for a human to be involved in it. They can send them in or they can call them off, but they can't see much of what is going on. Too many imagery, too much theatre.

Next step beyond that would be full autonomy. The robots themselves would be sent to an area and if they found anybody they would kill them. When you move the swarms, now you're looking at one operator that controls the swarm, being able to have the potential of multiple effects on multiple targets.

Combining swarm technology with micro vehicles and UAV's is the next step for the Air Force. And it's happening soon. In 2015, our near-term goal, is to demonstrate a bird size UAV capable of operating a semi-autonomously, somewhat by itself, somewhat guided, for up to a week. We are replicating animals because they are around us and have been proven to be able to fly in these environments at various conditions.

One of the 2030 goals have been to be able to operate a swarm of these vehicles. "It's not science fiction, it is way out science." says, Leslie Perkins, US Air Force Research Lab. Swarms capable of self-navigation, face recognition and lethal force are likely inevitable, but will they be used before they can be programed to reason and discriminate. There's not a chance that people will be waiting until we can do proper discrimination.

"You might, in all the best will in the world not be intending to use it. What if a major conflict happens and other people are using robots against you and you've got the technology, you will use it. People always do." As ground systems autonomy and swarm technology continue to develop, will the CIA develop a robot army and if they do who else will.

This all sounds like a bad Hollywood movie, but I'm not making this stuff up.

So, one of the fundamental questions is, in the revolution of technology, it is not only what you can do with it, but who gets to use it. What organization should not be allowed to use it? If they can use those autonomous weapons, the sky's the limit, I would say, about what they can use.

In the future without oversight, it's a future I don't want to think about. One of the things we are working on very hard today is that you will be able to engage an adversary that is a remotely piloted aircraft. One of the big worries that security forces have is not the worry that one of these planes is coming over but what if a thousand of them arrived, you could shoot some of them down, but you couldn't get all of them. If they can use them, then we will have more than just the twin towers to worry about.[4]

Yes, we will, and it will be our worst nightmare amplified! And, they let you think these things are not going to be used in the Urban Areas, let alone the battlefield. The military is already predicting that MAV's are going to be a crucial part of a new fighting force that is being built as we speak. It's called

M.A.S.T or the Micro Autonomous Systems Technology. In fact, here's their own promotional video admitting it! This is wild!!!

The video opens with two combat soldiers watching a building. One pulls what looks like a 4-wheeled robot out of his backpack and sets it towards the building. He opens the top of it and several spider robots jump out and start running towards the building. At the same time some things that look like dragon flies are also flying in that direction.

As the spider gets inside of the building it finds two armed terrorists standing talking to each other. The dragon fly also has made visual contact and is sending pictures back to the soldier on the ground. He in turn contacts headquarters and a helicopter is immediately sent out and bombs the building killing the two men inside.[5]

Yeah, sponsored by just about everybody! Can you believe that? Birds, bugs, flies, spiders, sharks, jellyfish, cheetahs, you name it, on the land, in the air, in the water, these Drones are not only going to be everywhere, whether you recognize them as such or not, but as you saw, many of them are going to be armed, and ready to take you out! In fact, if I didn't know better, I'd say we're headed for a nightmare killer scenario as depicted in the 1980's movie with Tom Selleck called Runaway. Once again, maybe Hollywood has been preparing us much longer than we think for a horrible future that is coming soon to our planet.

It is the future, mysteriously spreading across an unsuspecting city, machines trained to serve humans, are turning against them. An ingenious conspiracy has begun. 'Tom Selleck, the actor in the movie, Runaway, is putting on his gear to enter a house where the kitchen appliances are going after the occupants.

The police are trying to hold him back because it is too dangerous, but he proceeds into the house.' And someone has to stop the madman who started it all. He has turned a domestic computer into a killing machine. He has killed five so far and Tom Selleck's character wants to get him. As he gets closer to catching the one that has caused all of this, his coworker is telling him that this guy knows everything that is going on.

Then we see him, and he has a bug robot crawling out of his jacket sleeve. Selleck gets a call and the voice on the other end tells him that he cannot get away, his little machines will find him wherever he goes. These robot bugs are out to get the humans. The response is that the humans are never going to get through this.[6]

      Yeah, that's a Runaway problem alright! 1984, over 30 years ago and it doesn't seem like a movie anymore, does it? So, let me get this straight, Robots get hijacked, after they've been permeated in society, and then they become these killing machines even with guided bullets to chase people down! Looks like Hollywood's done it again! Predicting a horrible future for us, that's being built before our eyes. But you might be thinking, "Well hey, wait a second. They don't really have missile guided bullets that can chase you down, do they?"
Yes, they do.

News 13 reports:
Those really smart people out of Sandia Labs have come up with a bullet that doesn't miss. Sandia scientists and engineers have wide expertise in miniature technology, Nano technology and the bullet is actually a tiny guided missile. This patented design will give super powers to shooters. It could change the way American soldiers are trained on the front lines. "This laboratory is about building a very, very tiny machine," says James Jones.

His lab has turned average sized ideas and made them enormous by shrinking them down. "The actual one is this dot right there in the middle," he tells us. Their newest project is to take a self-guided missile and put it into a 50-caliber rifle. It shoots like a dart but instead of shooting straight with a spiral motion it twists and turns to find a laser point target at the end making up to 30 corrections per second while remaining in the air.

"From this sensor it commands little sensors in the back so that the bullet pitches and yaws so that it turns itself towards the laser dot." In theory, put these into the soldiers' machine guns and they will hit their mark faster with precise accuracy. So, soldiers' can spend less time in a fire fight. DARPAs' extreme accuracy task ordinance program took part in live fire demonstration of inflight guide of 50-caliber bullets.

The bullets independently maneuver through the air after being fired and they successfully hit targets that were over a mile away. The rounds changed their routes in flight striking targets that were not lined up with the sniper rifles original aim. The 50-caliber rounds utilized the optical sighting technology in a real-time guidance system allowing them to be used any time during the day or night.

DARPA explains the importance of the bullets noting, 'It is critical that snipers be able to engage targets faster, and with better accuracy, since any shot that doesn't hit a target also risks the safety of troops by indicating their presence and potentially exposing their locations.' The ammunition will also be extremely helpful when windy weather or moving targets make accurate shots more difficult. The smart rounds certainly have the potential to revolutionize rifle precision.[7]

As well as fulfil even that last bit of the Runaway movie premise, is there no place to hide in the coming future? Drones going to be everywhere, above, below, on the ground, in the water, whether you recognize them as Drones or not. And the weaponry they're giving them has the capability to chase you down, around corners, just like a guided missile, until it takes you out! We're in trouble! But as bad as that is, that's only the first concern with all these Drones and the weapons they're arming them with. As the title says, it's not just attack of the Drones, but Skynet is coming. An artificial intelligence will hijack this whole thing and take it over, and hunt people down, just like in the Terminator movies! So that's the next question, "Are we getting close to developing a true artificial intelligence that can hi-jack this new killer global Drone technology on the whole planet and create a real-live Skynet scenario? Yes! In fact, even the secular experts are saying it's going to happen very soon, much sooner than we could ever dream, or frankly, I think, ever want to deal with. So, let's turn to the next section. The Dangerous Deployments of Drones starting with the Developments of AI and let's look at that very question. "How did all this get started? Is AI real? Who's pushing for it anyway? And how long has it been going on and who's paying for it?" Let's look at the History of Artificial Intelligence.

Part IV

The Development of Artificial Intelligence

Chapter Fifteen

The History of AI

Artificial Intelligence or (AI) speaks of the artificial "intelligence" or "intelligent behavior" exhibited by computers, computerized machines and/or software. John McCarthy is first accredited with coining the phrase back in 1955. The goals of AI research include, reasoning, knowledge, planning, learning, natural language, processing or communication, perception, and general intelligence modeled after human intelligence. In short, they want to simulate and/or recreate the human brain. Believe it or not, this desire for Artificial Intelligence has been around for quite some time. It's an idea that dates back as far as classical philosophers who attempted to describe the process of human thinking as the mechanical manipulation of symbols. In fact, mechanical men and artificial beings appear in the Greek myths, such as the golden robots of Hephaestus among others. In fact, realistic humanoid automatons were built by craftsman from just about every civilization with some of the oldest known being the sacred statues of ancient Egypt and Greece. The culture of that day actually believed that the "craftsman" had imbued these figures with very real minds, capable of wisdom and emotion. In fact, one early writer, Hermes Trismegistus wrote that, "By discovering the true nature of the gods, man has been able to reproduce it." Then in the Middle Ages there were rumors of secret mystical or alchemy means of placing mind into matter. Later in the 17th century, scientists and thinkers began to explore the possibility that all rational thought could be made as systematic as algebra or geometry. One proponent even stated, "Reason is nothing but reckoning." Then in the 19th century, ideas of artificial men and thinking machines were further developed by authors and their books such as Mary Shelley's Frankenstein or Karel Capek's Rossum's Universal Robots.

Finally, in the 20th century, the study of mathematical logic provided the essential breakthrough that made artificial intelligence plausible. Mathematicians began to believe that, "Mathematical reasoning could be formalized," and combined with advances in computing devices and the invention of the programmable digital computer back in the1940s, the birth of artificial intelligence began to take great strides throughout the 40's and 50's. This is where the discussion of creating artificial intelligence took a serious tone with many scientists from a variety of fields (mathematics, psychology, engineering, economics and political science) discussing the possibility of building an "electronic brain." In fact, the official field of AI research was founded at a conference on the campus of Dartmouth College in New Hampshire in 1956. Those who attended would become the leaders of AI research for decades. Many of them predicted that a machine as intelligent as a human being would exist in no more than a generation and they were given millions of dollars to make this vision come true. It was also during the 50's that we saw the birth of what's called the "Turing Test" developed by Alan Turing to test the possibility of machines being able to truly think and carry on a conversation that was indistinguishable from a conversation with a human being. If it could pass this test, according to Turing then it was reasonable to say that the machine was 'thinking'. Soon this 'thinking' ability was put to the test in games. Using the Ferranti Mark 1 machine, the University of Manchester wrote a program for checkers and a man named Dietrich Prinz wrote one for chess. They eventually achieved a great enough skill to take on a respectable player. Therefore, optimism began to grow for creating AI with government agencies like ARPA, pouring money into the new field. ARPA just happens to be the same entity who developed the precursor to today's internet, known back then as ARPANET. Their name has since been changed to DARPA which stands for the Defense Advanced Research Projects Agency who is now responsible for the development of emerging technologies for use by the U.S. Military. (Can you say Skynet???)

Then in June 1963, MIT received millions of dollars of funding from the newly created ARPA to further develop AI and continued to receive such sums up into the 1970's. Combined with three other centers developing AI, (Carnegie Mellon University, Stanford, and Edinburgh) all four institutions continued to be the main centers of AI research (and funding) for many years.

Then in 1980, the Japanese Government inspired other governments and those in the industry to provide AI with billions of dollars of funding. Soon a system called XCON was completed at CMU for the Digital Equipment Corporation and it was an enormous success that saved the company 40 million dollars annually with other corporations scrambling to acquire their own similar system. The 80's also saw the birth of CYC which was the first attempt to crack what was called the "commonsense knowledge problem" and created a massive database that would contain all the mundane facts that the average person knows. The creators of the project stated there was no shortcut and that, "The only way for machines to know the meaning of human concepts is to teach them, one concept at a time, by hand." (Could this be why Google Books, Google, the Internet and Social Networking was created?) During this time the Japanese government also funded what was called the "Fifth Generation Computer Project" which sought to build machines that could carry on conversations, translate languages, interpret pictures, and reason like human beings." Soon other countries with new programs of their own, including DARPA, with its Strategic Computing Initiative, tripling its AI investments in just 5 years. Then in the late 80s, several researchers advocated a completely new approach to artificial intelligence, based on robotics. They believed that, to show real intelligence, a machine needs to have a body. It needs to perceive, move, survive and deal with the world like a real human. This added fuel to the ideas of cybernetics and control theory systems for human-like intelligent robots. Sound familiar?

Arnold Schwarzenegger, in Terminator, "I am a cybernetic organism, living tissue over metal endoskeleton."[1]

Throughout the 90's and on up to today, Artificial Intelligence has continued to grow and has actually achieved many of its oldest goals. Due to advances in increased computing power, AI is now being used successfully throughout the technology industry. In fact, in 1997 the world's first computer chess-playing system called Deep Blue (which was now 10 million times faster than the Ferranti Mark 1 back in 1951) beat a reigning world chess champion, Garry Kasparov. Then in 2005, a Stanford robot won the DARPA Grand Challenge by driving autonomously for 131 miles along an unrehearsed desert trail. Two years later, a team from CMU won the DARPA Urban Challenge by autonomously navigating 55 miles in an Urban environment while adhering to traffic hazards and all traffic laws. Then in 2011, in a Jeopardy Quiz Show exhibition match, IBM's question answering system called Watson, defeated the two greatest Jeopardy champions, Brad Rutter and Ken Jennings, by a significant margin. This dramatic increase of Artificial Intelligence is measured by what's called Moore's Law, which predicts that the speed and memory capacity of computers doubles every two years. Today, the fundamental problem of "raw computer power" for Artificial Intelligence is being overcome which is why the experts are now saying true AI is just around the corner for the first time in the history of mankind.

Chapter Sixteen

The Danger of AI

Ray Kurweil, (A computer scientist, inventor, futurist, and director of engineering at Google) predicted using Moore's Law that, "Machines with human-level intelligence will appear by 2029." Other experts are saying that, "If AI is produced, it might actually be able to reprogram and improve itself, which means, the improved software would be even better at improving itself, leading to ongoing self-improvement and thus the new intelligence could increase exponentially and dramatically surpass humans." This viable reality is now called "Singularity" describing a singular event when the accelerating progress in technologies will cause a runaway effect wherein AI will exceed human intellectual capacity and "control," thus radically changing or even ending civilization. And once again Ray Kurweil predicts this event will occur by 2045.

Time magazine reports:
Humans have had a genuine interest in AI even before the term was coined in the 1950's. The modern concept is part of a tradition that extends through myth and legend, all the way back to the ancient Greeks. It's been a source of hopes and fears, dream, and nightmares. Will our creations be our allies or our mortal or immortal enemy? Until recently it didn't really matter. The ability to create intelligent machines was impossibly out of reach.

But Ray Kurzweil believes it's not only probable but inevitable and coming sooner than you think. The inventor and author is the most outspoken author and prophet of the coming technological singularity. Ray Kurzweil: "By the time we get to say 2045 we will be able to multiply intelligence a billion-fold. That will be a profound change that is singular in nature, so we use this term." Reporter: "A label first used in 1993 by computer scientists and science fiction writer Verner Vinge. Vinge predicted that within 30 years we would develop a super human intelligence.

Shortly after, the human era would be over. Now this may not be obvious, but I happen to be human myself. So, this concerns me." In his book the Singularity is Near, Kurzweil is a little more conservative than Vinge. He gives us until mid-century. At which point exponential growth genetics, Nano-tech, and robotics will drive an intelligence explosion. Once we have a brain smarter and faster than ours it will design the next generation which in turn will create the next faster and faster, leaving us meat bags behind.

The pace of change will be so rapid that the transformation of human life, so profound, that it will be literally impossible to predict what happens next. But that hasn't stopped people from trying. Judging by our mythology, including our modern novels and movies, we seem to think that our creations will turn against us. I'm not sure what that says about us. Is it the psychology of abuse, a guilty conscience, we're always inventing father figures, to punish us for overreaching?

It's the Frankenstein story. One of our favorites. I don't actually fear a robot uprising, but I do keep a hostage in my shed, a rumba, just a bargaining chip in case something goes down. Rumba is a housecleaning robot made by I-robot. That's not an Apple product, It's the name of a company in Massachusetts that also makes military robots. Are you kidding me, who writes this stuff?

Are we living in a sci-fi B movie? They make tactical military robots and they already have an army of autonomous vacuum cleaners patrolling 5,000,000 living rooms. What could possibly go wrong. I-Robot is also the name of a book written by Isaac Asimov. But maybe they won't be so ill tempered toward us, maybe instead of a rebellion or a stern father we'll get an overprotective mother, or a companion who likes us more than just a friend.

The least we could do is make sure everything we build has an off switch. Realistically it probably won't be that easy, after all, we are talking about super human intelligence.[1]

As you can see, this development of AI is not only real, but it's really been worked on for quite some time now. And these people are very serious about this! At least some of them will admit, it's a dangerous thing to play with! And it is leading to a very serious problem as they also admit. What if these things really do take over? It's not just being built, but what if the unthinkable happens? What if Singularity does occur? What if machines really do take over? This is no longer a crazy science fiction book from Isaac Asimov, it's a reality today and a genuine concern today! Even those working on this technology admit it! And the irony is, this is precisely what's needed for a Skynet scenario to appear on the scene and take over all these Drones that we just saw being launched all around the world in every facet of society! This development of AI allows for Skynet to come!

But you might be thinking, "Well, wait a second. That's just Drones in the sky we saw. If you look in the Terminator movies, there were machines on the ground, even humanoid-looking machines that Skynet took over and started to hunt down and annihilate mankind. We don't have people making robotic machines and humanoid terminators like in the movie, do we?" Yes, we do! And they're also merging it with AI! Believe it or not, right now as we speak, militaries and scientists around the world are building robotic machines and humanoid looking robotic machines that are armed and deadly and intelligent just like in the Terminator movies. If something doesn't change real fast, we're really headed for an AI Skynet scenario to come on the scene, take over, and hunt us down. Judgment Day is around the corner!

Part V

The Deployment of Artificial Intelligence

Chapter Seventeen

Robot Machines in the Military

The **1ˢᵗ way** we know that this horrible reality is coming is with **Robotic Machines**.

You see, just like the Drones in the sky, robotic machines on the ground are also going to be armed to the teeth, or in many cases, already are. In essence, the whole way of "doing war" is rapidly changing. It's going to be the robots on the ground who are going to be, "doing the dirty work for us." This is what's being built. Who needs a jet fighter pilot anymore! Now an unmanned robotic pilot equipped with artificial intelligence can do it for you! Here's one produced by the U.K. called Taranis.

Tar-a-nis. L (Myth.) A celtic divinity, the god of thunder:

World leading technology, the most advanced aerospace composites, the future of aviation technology, the plane is being prepared for takeoff. In its cargo hole is a flying object. The plane is taking off from an undisclosed location. Chris Boardman, Managing Director, Military, Air & Information is saying, "Taranis is the most advanced earth system conceived, designed and built in the U.K."

He is talking about the flying object that has been loaded into the larger plane. While in the air it looks like a solid piece of material with no seams, similar to an alien space craft. He continues, "The Taranis is one of the most advanced projects that BAE systems has ever under taken. It puts the U.K. top table in the aerospace capability. Taranis: Inspiration for a Nation.[1]

And trouble for the rest of us! By the way, it's also nicknamed, "Raptor" and it's the new wave in Fighter Drones called UCAV's or Unmanned Combat Aerial Vehicle. In other words, an unmanned jet fighter! In fact, some of the Drone fighters or planes can even go into space, for a very long time, just waiting to strike on someone or something. One such Space Drone just returned to earth after a two-year orbit! One person stated, "What was a computer-controlled aircraft doing in space?" not to mention for that long! China is also getting in on this action with their mysterious combat Drone called "Dark Sword," that is reportedly the world's first supersonic unmanned aerial vehicle! In other words, have fun catching that one! Oh, but it's not just the jet fighters that are going robotic, so are the helicopters, another aerial vehicle. I'm telling you, who needs a pilot for anything in the sky? Drones can do it all! Let's look at that!

Office of Naval Research Science & Technology reports:
Autonomous Aerial Cargo/Utility System, AACUS
The office of Naval Research is developing new capabilities for unmanned flight known as the Autonomous Aerial Cargo/Utility system, AACUS. AACUS technology makes it possible for unmanned helicopters to fly and bring supplies to marines in the field with just a tap of the users' tablet keeping pilots and air crews out of danger.

What is truly revolutionary about this is the ease of use. Anyone can order supplies from their tablet without needing months of specialized training. Rear Adm. Matthew Klunder, says, "What you have seen today is advantages and test results that we have witnessed, that we might have something that we can use in the future that can be very relevant to our missions." Capt. David Woodbury says,

"We are out here in front. This is cutting edge stuff, this is the selection of the landing sight. No one is telling the helicopter where to land. It's been told a general region, but it will pick the sight itself. It's able to identify the obstacles itself and then execute the landing. No one has done that before."

Lyle Chamberlain says, "It's a self-flying robot with laser beams, what could be cooler than that?"

Capt. Robert Palisin says, "Our initiative is to try to find methods, so we can have an entirely autonomous system to do what a manned helicopter will do." Sgt. Jessica Wright says, "The technology will be very helpful, anything that doesn't put humans in harm's way, will be good."

Lance Cpl. Cody Barss says, "One single helicopter loaded up with the supplies they need fly out unmanned, land, get the gear, and then fly off on its own."

AACUS has its origins on the battlefield where troops needed to get convoys off road and deliver supplies by air while reducing the workload and danger for helicopter crews. Max Snell, AACUS Program Manager, says, "What we are developing here is a system that responds to a request in the field for supplies, develops its own route, flies there by itself without any oversight, comes in, selects its own landing sight, and again without any over sight what so ever. This is truly an autonomous design."

ONR's goal was for a marine in the field, not a professional aviator or a flight controller, to be able to request resupply using a tablet or mobile device without extensive specialized training.

"They made it really easy to understand so even if you got no training you'll still be able to figure it out. It only took me 10 minutes to pick up on how to use it and another 3 minutes to start to effectively use it without any assistance."

AACUS technology will help manned flights to be safer and more accurate. For example, AACUS can assist the pilot to land in challenging conditions, like dust or snow. Recently companies like Amazon have talked about delivering a book to a customer with an unmanned aircraft.

"We are trying to do the same thing, but I want to bring 5,000 lbs. to the marine in the field, bullets or batteries or water in that same fashion. You could even bring this to a rescue mission somewhere, maybe to a dangerous landing zone, all at the touch of a single tablet.[2]

And who can't do that? We're all used to tablets and cell phones! Can you believe that? Just like Amazon, you can just order up some supplies and weaponry and backup on the battlefield just like you're placing an order online! The new flying Drone helicopter brings it to you, go figure. But they also have another use for these helicopters. They now have mini ones that can also be used for surveillance!

Aljazeera reports:
In the past few years, the usage of Drones has dramatically increased. Miniature surveillance helicopters are being used by British Military intelligence forces in Afghanistan. The remotely controlled devices can send camera footage and pictures to the troops on the ground. The one by four-inch Drone known as the Black Hornet Nano unmanned air vehicle, can be piloted manually or it can be programed using GPS coordinates.

It weighs less than an ounce reaching speeds up to 22 miles per hour. The Black Hornet can travel up to half an hour and has a range of up to a half mile. The Army used it to look for insurgent firing points and check out exposed areas of the ground before crossing, which is a real asset. It is very easy to operate and offers amazing capability to the guys on the ground. The military contract for the Drones specifies that 160 of them will be supplied and maintained by Marlborough Communications. The Drones were initially designed by the company Proxdynamics in Norway for search and rescue procedures.[3]

Now you can search for all kinds of things, and rescue whatever, like a mosquito! Can you believe that? That's not just small, but what if you had a bunch of those things flying around? You couldn't escape them! They'd be worse than a swarm of mosquitoes! Apparently, that's why one reporter said this, "If you thought that having helicopter drones flying around delivering packages was a scary concept, then you won't be very happy to learn that the US military is seriously considering enlisting the help of these tiny robot copter drones in warfare. The US Navy is now testing a cannon system that launches 30 small robot drones into the air in less than a minute. The drones are able to fly in formation for 90 minutes to complete missions and are designed to overwhelm an adversary." In other words, have fun running from them, just like a swarm of mosquitoes, it's true! But that's just in the sky! This Robotic invasion, that can be controlled by AI, will also be underwater. In fact, it's already here with robotic military ships like this one coming soon to an ocean near you.

CNN reports:
We know the U.S. military has had Drones in the air for a while. Now it's looking to ramp up technology at sea. The Pentagon Research Group, DARPA, is

developing a Drone ship that would save money and man power on expensive searches on super quiet enemy submarines. A prototype vessel is already in production.

They are calling the program Anti-Submarine Warfare Continuous Trail Unmanned Vessel. DARPA says the Drone ships will be 132 feet long and will likely cost about $20 million dollars each to build. That is a drop in the bucket compared to the billion-dollar manned warships. If testing proves successful, the Navy could start developing the idea further by 2018. The vast ocean is a great place to hide.

So, DARPA is also developing stealthy deep-sea robot capsules. They can sit on the ocean floor for years, until U.S. controllers trigger them to float to the surface and release unmanned flying vehicles. From above these Drones can transmit images showing enemy activity. All this emerging technology offers a pretty good indication that the ocean is about to become a lot more robotic.

In the future, mother ships, such as the newly retrofitted USS Ponce can be sent to conflict zones where they would launch and support unmanned vehicles with multiple capabilities. An entire battle group could be managed by a handful of personnel.[4]

Hey, wait a second, that's starting to sound like that mothership in the Avengers movie! Does Hollywood know something we don't know? You think I'm kidding, but I quote, "The Pentagon wants an airborne aircraft carrier to launch Drones." "The Defense Advanced Research Projects Agency released an artist's rendering to show its vision for a future aircraft carrier in the sky, capable of launching and recovering numerous Drone aircraft while in flight. In the 2012 movie "The Avengers," Captain America, the Hulk, Iron Man and the rest of the gang flew on a massive aircraft carrier that carried dozens of planes through the air and disappeared with the help of a cloaking device.

The idea that the U.S. military could develop something similar still seems far-fetched, but this much is true, a Pentagon agency has just launched a new effort to develop an airship that is sure to draw comparisons. DARPA program manager Dan Patt said, "We want to find ways to make smaller aircraft more effective and one promising idea is enabling existing large aircraft, with minimal modification, to become aircraft carriers in the sky." In other words, this is really what's coming! Hollywood got it right again!

A clip from the movie Avengers shows a very large aircraft carrier opening some doors on the side of the ship. But instead of being doors they are propellers coming out of each side.

The Avengers are on board the ship watching as this is happening. The faster they spin the higher the ship rises up out of the water. They are now inside the ship in the control room as the ship flies over the ocean.

"We're at level sir," says one of the officers. "Good," says the captain. "Let's vanish!" Slowly the ship starts to change colors and completely disappears.[5]

If you don't think they have the ability to cloak, you better think again! Not only are they making robotic big ships, just like in the Avengers movie, but now they're making them even smaller. They can actually swarm their prey, leaving no chance of escape.

The office of Naval Research reports:
U.S. Navy autonomous swarm boats, the future is now. With autonomous swarm boats unmanned Navy vessels can overwhelm an adversary. A first of its kind technology enable swarming capability which gives our Naval war fighters a decisive edge. The U.S. Navy is unleashing a new era in advanced ship protection.

A swarm of autonomous boats that will automate ships self-defense and be able to deter, damage, or destroy an enemy threat. Giving added protection to sailors and marines in harm's way. "When we look at autonomous swarm, we're not talking about a single vessel, we are looking at multiple, multiple vessels that can be at a defensive posture and could be called upon and become defensive around an adversary and let them know that you are coming no closer to our ship.

But of course, if an adversary ship decides to come closer, we can give them another warning, or we can say, you can come too close and we will now destroy your vessel," says RADM Matthew Klunder. Autonomous swarming is made possible through outfitting a boat with a sensor and accompanying software kit called KARAKUS. This advanced software was developed by NASA for the Mars rover and adapted through ONR support for autonomous swarming.

"What we have on board these boats is software and equipment that allows the boat to operate autonomously, which means, they can sense the environment, the

environment being other ships, perhaps the enemy, that's the objective, then they can react to the environment," says Capt. Brian Carpenter. ONR's current demo on the James River was made possible through discoveries in artificial intelligence, machine perception, and distributed data fusion.

Now any boat can be fitted with a kit that allows it to operate autonomously and together swarm on any threat. This new technology can be used to help prevent attacks like damage caused to the USS Cole by one small boat. "The USS Cole was attacked in 2000 and 17 of our sailors were killed in that attack. It's a constant reminder every time we walk in that passageway, the importance of being vigilant," says LTJG Douglas Kroh.

Autonomous swarm boats can be a force multiplier. "Something like this technology is very useful. When you want to have assets out there that can patrol around you, almost like guard dogs, they can give the CO of that ship the intent of another boat that is coming in," says Rick Simon, director of Robotics, Spatial Integrated Systems. What is new in this exercise is that we are extending this practice to five small boats, so they engage in this multi boat swarming behavior," says Dr. Robert Brizzolara, Program Officer, Office of Naval Research.

From an operational perspective the swarm is starting where there is a swarm of unmanned autonomous vehicles that are protecting a high value unit," Meggan Schoenberg, Science Advisor, Office of Naval Research Global. The ship, the designated good guy, is the Relentless, serving double duty as the floating lab monitoring the demo as the swarm scenario unfolded. "As they get further into a congested environment, an adversary approaches and the swarm will go around the adversary and defend the ship then come back and protect the ship.

Sam Callabrese of Seaward Services piloted the designated bad guy. "I know if I were the actual target it would be pretty intimidating to see 5 boats come rushing at you." Autonomous swarm boats and swarming capability give naval commanders options to deter, damage, or destroy hostile vessels.

"I think the idea of controlling small boats, that are not only unmanned but are able to have machine perception, they are able to perceive things without a human being in the loop and then they are able to make decisions which in this context means planning their route or planning their action, that can be a game changer.

That opens up a whole new set of missions that can be done without a human on board that asset."

The swarm technique is applicable to multiple vessels in multiple scenarios. Autonomy kits can be packaged for deployment. Modules for artificial intelligence and data fusion can be put into packages and deployed from surface assets anywhere. The demo of this revolutionary capability has been pulled together by a team of the best in the field. The team included experts from the field in science and technology from ONR, warfare centers, industry, academia, and university affiliated research centers, with support from the U.S. Coast Guard and Operational Navy.

"We are going to protect our country and look at the security of our country and we are going to operate these new innovative kinds of systems. It's truly a team effort." Autonomous swarming bends the defensive and offensive reach of the U.S. Navy. "I think it is really the persistence that we can have these machines out there 24/7 patrolling against adversary intrusions into an area where they are not supposed to be."

The boats that became autonomous are already in the Navy inventory, on board the Navy service combatants, destroyers, and cruisers. "You don't have to go out and purchase a new vessel. You take any of these vessels that the Navy already has, we unmanned them, we put the system on it, you put on the eyes and ears, depending on whatever mission you want to do, then you let it go and do its mission.[6]

And that mission is to take you out, if you become a Bad Guy. Again, but who gets to define that? Have fun getting away from these guys! Did you catch that? They're not just autonomous, but they're a part of an AI System that can be attached to any pre-existing vehicle? That's crazy! What other vehicles are you going to put this on? Well, believe it or not, they're putting them on underwater vehicles down below as well. Robotic Swarms are going to be everywhere in the ocean!

Italia Notebook reports:
This is the prototype of the underwater swarm system named CoCoRo. It is a very small robot that is used as part of the underwater swarm. It's mainly equipped with blue light sensors, blue light emitters which it uses to

communicate to other robots within a very short distance and to estimate distance to obstacles to avoid them.

This robot is one of the first prototype of really small underwater robots. We use them, for example, in this aquarium to simulate a search mission where on the sea ground there is a point of interest, in our case it's a few magnets. They are supposed to look for these magnets and then aggregate there. For example, you can think of these magnets as a black box of a crashed plane. We use this swarm of robots to quickly go through the area that needs to be searched for the black box, when one of those robots quickly find the black box on the ground, it attracts the other robots with short range signals, like the blue lights.

When all robots are quickly aggregated, they can collectively lift the black box out of the water. This is one of the possible missions that a swarm like our system can solve. Other technologies are being pursued as well to make them even more efficient. One such example is the development of a cooperative or swarm behavior. When it is finally completely functional UAV's can be completely autonomous in their actions while working in a group. This means a single operator can operate multiple vehicles while just giving them general directions.[7]

Whether it's land, air, sea, water, above or below, you can direct these swarms of Drones wherever you want! And by the way, DARPA has big plans for these kinds of Drones. "DARPA is developing Robot pods, as previously read, that can sit at the bottom of the ocean for long stretches of time, waiting to release airborne and water-based drones to the surface to attack on command." In addition, they are also asking for a boost to their budget for underwater Drone fleets. The agency has asked for its current spending to double, from $14.9 million to $29.9 million, for its hydra program. Sound familiar? That's the name of the bad guy they were fighting against in the Avenger and Captain America movies! Hydra was conceived to be a large, mothership-like craft capable of moving through the water and deploying a number of smaller surveillance drones. Exactly like the movie premise! It's almost like somebody is following a script or something! In fact, it goes on to say that, "The research agency also announced that it is launching a program to unite existing and future drones into hives, where individual autonomous aircraft will share data and operate together against targets on a battlefield." Let me translate that for you, we are in a heap of trouble!! These Super Hero premises of all these movies are about to come to life! We're being prepared for it! But just in case these underwater mini swarms or destroyers don't find you, don't worry, an unmanned submarine will. Everything is going autonomous in the water, above or below.

We've talked about stealth technology before. The use of composites, sharp angles, and radar absorbing paint to make military aircraft and service ships almost invisible to the enemy. And we have talked about UAV's, unmanned air vehicles, like this helicopter that can fly their entire mission by themselves. And now we are talking about this.

A UUV. The world's first fully autonomous unmanned multi-missioned stealth submersible. They named it Talisman after the good luck charm. But if they ever send this baby against you, chances are your luck will run out. Talisman is a working prototype designed by BAE Systems in Portsmith, to showcase the British companies advanced technologies.

Her propulsion and operating systems are being thoroughly tested before going through a second round of sea trials. "Unmanned vehicles are going to be absolutely key to future military doctrine."

That's no prediction. According to Talisman project manager Andy Tonge, it's already happening. "Because increasingly it's becoming important to keep the men out of the danger area, it's important to drive the cost down, and if you take the Talisman vehicle, the Talisman could actually replace a specialist mine hunting ship, so the cost becomes very much lower."

And mine hunting is one of the mini subs primary roles. Able to carry several of these Archerfish torpedoes in its munitions bay Talisman can move silently towards a mine field and fire them without risking human life or the loss of a billion-dollar ship. It's not that big, just under 5 meters long, but it's enormously strong. The carbon fiber hull is designed to operate in depths well in excess of 300 meters and it's very nimble.

Using these thrusters, it can hover and turn 360 degrees. Using high tech collision avoidance and super accurate navigation systems an unmanned aircraft can fly around the world and back in complete safety. Now as BAE designed many of those systems it is only natural that they would find a use for Talisman. Talisman is just as smart as many of its flying brothers. It can spend weeks at sea, following orders downloaded into its mission computers.

Or following new orders sent by satellite communications and if it detects a threat it can shut itself down and loiter on the sea beds. "There are fail safes built within the vehicle, built within the software, and built in its hardware system that are overriding the software to put it into safe modes to shut down, go quiet, go deep, stay out of the way." As for underwater obstacles Talisman uses a sophisticated collision avoidance system.

It's able to see the problem, think it through, and decide on the solution. "The sensors we carry are mainly acoustic and they are working on detecting the terms of the obstacle. The smaller the obstacle, the higher the frequency and the shorter the range." While Talismans primary role is surveillance and reconnaissance, its flexibility allows it to go from passive to active very quickly, so if the need arises it has a very nasty sting in its tail.

Although BAE Systems is reluctant to discuss its full potential they don't deny Talisman could carry a range of weapons in its internal munitions bay, but as future generations are developed BAE Systems believes UUV's will dominate underwater warfare adding sabotage, close quarter combat and counter terrorism to its mission capabilities.[8]

Okay, sky, water, underwater, we're toast! And we're not the only country doing this! "Russia's new generation of Nuclear Subs will be armed with underwater Drones and robots in addition to conventional weapons. We're talking about battle robots which can be released by the submarine." So, submarines are becoming autonomous as well as having the capability to send out autonomous underwater armies.

And if that wasn't scary enough, the same Russian outfit working for these engineers said, "The entire world is moving in this direction." These Drone swarms are also coming to the land as I mentioned earlier. When Skynet hits, you will have no place to hide! Starting with robotic tanks!

Soldiers are standing outside with their laptops. They are instructing small army tanks as to what they are supposed to do. The tanks are spinning, raising their guns and following the commands that are given to them via the laptop. It goes forward and backwards, finally driving through the cones that have been laid out for the test run.

It comes to a complete stop in front of the soldier giving the commands, then it starts up again but comes to a barricade where it stands up straight on its back wheels. It spins in that position and rolls forward and back waiting for another command. In a war zone we see a couple soldiers driving through a shot up city. Unknown to them there is a tank behind the building waiting for them to get into range.

Once there, the tank fires and hits the jeep catching it on fire and causing the driver to lose control and drive into a telephone pole. The passenger falls out of the jeep on fire.

Now they are totally under fire, but the driver manages to drag himself inside the building. Meanwhile back at the base a call is received that there is trouble and soldiers run to get into the tanks. They proceed to go to rescue the soldier in distress.

They are unloading the unmanned tanks and they head out to get to the downed soldier before it's too late. As the unmanned tanks proceed down the street with the bullets flying, they are able to see where the bullets are coming from and shoot the bad guys without missing a shot.

They are able to drive through brick walls, push cars out of the way, blow up other tanks, they even shoot their target before being shot at.

Even helicopters are no match for these little unmanned tanks. When one is shot and disabled it is programed to blow itself up. They manage to get to the wounded soldier. At that point a shelf comes out so that the soldier can lay in it and be taken back to safety. As they are going back they come to another big tank ready to take them out.

The tank carrying the wounded soldier stays behind until it is clear. Once the other unmanned tank shoots some smoke bombs in the air towards the enemy tank the sky gets full of smoke and they can't see to fire at the tank carrying the soldier. The unmanned tanks then go through the smoke and back to the base.[9]

Who wouldn't want to have one of those things on your side? Or a bunch of them! And that's just it, you want to make sure they're on your side, because if they're not, you're toast! There's no hiding from those guys!

You not only need autonomous tanks on land to defend you or carry you away, but you need something to carry your supplies as well! Well, guess what?

They've got that too! Introducing, the crusher! It can go just about anywhere! Fully autonomous!

Crusher unmanned ground vehicle testing highlights
This vehicle has six wheels. It goes over everything, hills, block walls, and rocks. It has six wheels, can turn on a dime and moves like a caterpillar over the rough terrain. It goes through ditches, gullies, up steep hills, down steep hills and can balance on the back two wheels if necessary to get the job done.[10]

There's DARPA again, shocker! They always seem to be behind this stuff. But did you notice that was back in 2006? What do they have now that we don't know about? Not to be outdone by the Crusher is the robotic jeep and unmanned trucks! Who needs a person for bringing supplies to the battlefield!

You tube ArmedForces Update reports:
While the soldiers are scanning the fields, a jeep is driving along with them, but no one is driving it. Then there is a convoy of three unmanned trucks driving down the road. This is a Line Haul Mission. These trucks are smart, they are programed to sense obstacles when they approach, and they stop. They are able to drive through a city and stop at the correct destination. They can sense when there is traffic or if they need to stop at a stop sign in order to let that traffic pass or if they need to negotiate through the traffic. This is all unmanned operations.[11]

Who couldn't use a fleet of those? But that's right, just in case you need something a little smaller and more personal to bring supplies to you, your wish is their command. You can now have your very own pack mule called Alpha DG or Big Dog. And believe it or not, walking robotic pack dogs and animals have been in development for quite some time!

For thousands of years we have invented new forms of transportation. Many have been based on human insight, not found in nature at all. The wheel, but there are plenty of places the wheel can't go. Even ones wearing a belt of tank tread. The inability of our machines on traverse difficult terrain has dire consequences in the battle field and in search and rescue.

But while wheel vehicles struggle off the road there are some creatures still getting around. On legs. That has engineers wondering. What lessons can we learn from animal movements. Can we give our machines a leg up? Walking is easy for animals, even a toddler can do it and thanks to movies creating walking machines seem easy too. Just look at C3PO from Star Wars, or its walkers, you would think the problem would be solved, but in real life its hard.

One of the best known of the early attempts at a walking machine is GE's truck from the 60's. It even tackled uneven terrain, but it took a human operator to tell it where to place each foot, one at a time, an exhausting task. By the 70's computer control automated the walking motion in a series of crawlers built around the world, those still driven by human operators. These kept a tri-pod of legs on the ground maintaining stability always.

A system called static balance, they move slowly like a walking table. But in the 1980's a very different approach gained ground. I traveled to Massachusetts and visited a company that built robots based on that work. The company's founder, Marc Raibert, has been building walking robots for over thirty years. To Marc we are less like a table and more like a pogo stick.

To focus on the problem, he built a robot that had only one springy leg. It constantly calculated where its weight had to shift to stay upright. Very pogo stick like. Even when he added more legs he kept the bounce in their step and an active sense of balance.

For the past few years Marc has been applying what he learned to help the U.S. Military. On rough terrain wheeled vehicles aren't much use and soldiers often haul everything on their backs leading to injuries and exhaustion.

Mark invites me to see Boston Dynamics solution at a nearby park. Meet LS3, also known as alpha dog. It's designed specifically for rough terrain, anywhere a soldier might go on foot. It carries 400 lbs. of gear along with enough fuel for a 20-mile mission. Marc tells us, "So today the robot is following the leader. He's got a back pack on that has some reflective strips on it. The vision system focus' on that and then it records what path he takes through the terrain."

Is it modeled after a particular animal, an ox or a horse? "Not really, you take inspiration from how animals are designed but then you have to use human engineering and human materials, so sometimes it's like animals and sometimes it departs." Does it ever slip or step on an oily leaf? "It slips and frequently it corrects for those slips. So, the goal is to make it so that the feet can slip but the control system recognizes it and compensates it by using the other legs."

Lots of cool tech on LS3 but my favorite feature is voice control. Power on, engine off, sit, and get up. LS3 Get up! And it gets up. LS# follow tight. What a good boy. LS3 sit. LS3 power off. I think you got something here. But what would it take to go faster?

This is the Cheetah. Just like the real deal, it's back flexes with each step, increasing its stride with its gallop. Right now, it's the fastest robot with legs in the world but start looking over your shoulder for the next generation. Wild cat, it's designed to be untethered.[12]

Well, that's exciting. That means it's going to be out there soon, and have fun trying to get away from that thing? Isn't that wild? But for those of you who are vertically challenged like myself and might be creeped out by a large alpha pack mule dog-looking robot or cheetah looking robot or wildcat robot. Whatever, they've now come out with a smaller canine version, that's even better functioning than his "bigger brother." This one's called Spot. Run Spot run!

A smaller version of the LS3 is now venturing upstairs, on ice, where it can't lose its balance, jogging with the engineers and climbing up and down hills. When someone kicks it, it will not fall over. It is smaller than the LS3 but just as sturdy and also faster.[13]

Quieter, faster, more agile, looks like Little Spot is whooping up on his big brother there, but he's small enough to jog with you, put in your office, do all kinds of things. And these supply bots as they're being called are now coming in all shapes and sizes with all kinds of nifty functions!

JR Studios reports:
This giant 4-legged robot is stronger and larger than the LS3. It is capable of picking up a cement block and throwing it across the room. But there is also a 6-legged little robot that can go inside pipes to search for people or think. If it comes to a place where it is stopped by a rock, branch, or log, it just goes over it. There is also a small 4-wheeled robot that when it gets to a building, it can stand on its edge and jump to the top of the building. Once it finishes what it is supposed to do on the top of the building, it then stands on its end and jumps off the building to go back to the command post.[14]

Can I translate that for you? With all these new military robotic machines that are not only going to be everywhere, in all various kinds of sizes, shapes, and functions, in the air, land, water, and even underwater, even popping on to buildings. There's not going to be any place to hide if you needed to, for some reason that is, in the future. Did you catch that horse/mule looking thing? Hope that doesn't get mad at you! But folks, what you need to know is this is not some short-lived aberration military experiment where they must spend tons of money somewhere just to justify their budgets. They are deadly serious about this, no pun intended, and are planning on replacing much of the Military with these kinds of robots everywhere! "Robots May Replace 1/4th of U.S. Combat Soldiers by 2030 says General Robert Cone." They're called (MAARS) or Modular Advanced Armed Robotic Systems or Gunbots, Remote Controlled Gunbots is the term they use. In fact, even the news is starting to report on this new military trend.

RT News reports:
Now you may think the prospect of killer robots stalking the battlefield sounds like science fantasy, but as well as a manned aircraft, the U.S. already has thousands of military robots in Afghanistan and now a Russian team has built one too. Could the armies of the future look like this (thousands of metal robots fighting on the battle field), well no, not just yet, but militaries around the world aren't ignoring robot technology.

The U.S. has been using unmanned Drones for a number of years. Now it's testing land-based robots in Afghanistan and Iraq which despite being in its early stages are showing a lot of potential. But what about Russia, well a team from a Moscow Bowman Technical University have been at work for some answers. This was the team's first creation. It's a bomb detecting and destroying robot.

First it analyzes the package with these sensors and then destroys whatever explosives are inside with high powered water jets just here. This was the team's first creation and then they moved on to military robots like this one. This is a spy robot. It's able to look around corners and up into first floor windows with an extendable camera. Then if it needs to call in fire support to tackle the bad guys it calls on this next robot.

In fact, these creations are the latest in a long history in robot development in Russia. Longer than you might think. In 1938, Russian robot tanks were invented. They took part in the Russian Finish war and the person who controlled it was in a bunker pushing the buttons. He was able to see the tank and control it. The tank attacked and shot on its own. But despite this early innovation Russian robot development has been largely ignored since the 70's.

The U.S. took the lead and now has thousands of robots operating in Afghanistan. This team wants Russia to catch up. But will that robot meet with an approval from the Russian army. Ilya Laverichev says, "I can't give you a definite answer that this robot will be used in our army, but we hope so. It may not be this exact model but something improved, modified, and modernized." Robots don't rule the battle field yet but thanks to Ilya and his kind this might be a shot in the right direction.[15]

Yeah, if your goal is to create a Skynet terminator nightmare scenario! Can you believe it? These things are now being armed! And by the way, these MAARS or Gunbots as you saw, "Can not only be fitted with machines guns, but grenade launchers and lethal weapons. And unlike human soldiers, they have no fear, they don't whine or cry or complain, and they just do what they're told every single time, like this guy shares."

The Military Channel reports:
The Army has its own weaponized robot, the Swords Talon. It's much smaller than the Gladiator. Its top speed is 5.2 miles per hour, about the same speed as a running soldier. If you walk into an ambush I prefer to have the robot go up first. Hopefully attract the fire. That way we can actually utilize the robots, identify the enemy and assist in its elimination.

The Swords Talon is an all-weather, all-terrain vehicle. With day and night capabilities several mounted camera's relay images to an operator as far as half a mile away. This camera in particular is a surveillance camera. It rotates 360 degrees, up and down, wherever you want it to do, it also has a zoom capability to it. We can mount a PVS14 night vision monocle on to it, so we have night vision capability within the robot.

The same camera works along with the weapon sight camera that tells us exactly where the bullet is going to land. We have two other cameras on the vehicle. We have a front camera and a rear drive camera to assist in driving the robot itself. The Swords Talon weighs approximately 200 lbs. with a mounted weapons system. So, it is easily transported into combat. It can be down loaded off the backend of a Humvee, roll it out the backside of a Striker vehicle or armored vehicle and put it right into action.

The military is putting the Swords Talon and the Gladiator through their final paces and will soon deploy them into active duty. "The robots themselves are amazing. We can have them do anything they want, they don't complain like the regular soldiers do. They don't cry, they aren't scared. This robot has no fear which a good supplement to the United States Army is."[16]

        Okay, I thought that little guy was a little freaky! Did you see that big one? WOW! What a crazy fighting Machine! But having no fear is not the only motivation for unleashing these Gunbots around the world. Another rationale is to replace humans with robots like these. Just like what's presented in Star Wars Clone Wars, humans are expensive. "Training, feeding, and supplying humans while at war is pricey, and after the soldiers leave the service, there's a lifetime of medical care to cover. For instance, in 2012, benefits for serving retired members of the military comprised 1/4th of the Pentagon's budget request." So, let's replace 1/4th of the human soldiers with robot soldiers and that becomes your rationale to make this deadly decision. In fact, this is such a trend that it's going global and soon we might have a global robot war just like in Star Wars Clone Wars.

All wars used to be fought on foot, but then we harnessed horses for battle. Swords were the weapons of choice until guns were invented. Chariots slowly evolved into tanks and in less than 100 years the Wright Brothers airplane turned into the jet. But the change that is now underway will be the most significant in human history. The soldiers from the world's richest countries will rarely come face to face with their enemies. This is a profile of the robotic takeover of the world's militaries.

Current Technology: *For years now, the military of the United States and our closest allies have been using a whole range of robotic systems, like remotely controlled robots now commonly used for surveillance and for destroying bombs. Close end weapons systems on board virtually every ship in the wests Navy can destroy incoming missiles, aircraft, and smaller faster boats, all without human assistance.*

Unmanned ground vehicles guard areas and attack enemies using lethal and non-lethal weapons. The MQ Reaper, the unmanned aerial vehicle is a long-range killer that is so effective that America's 174th fighter wing has become the first squadron in history to convert from flying fighter jets to an all remotely piloted UAV attack group.

The secret of the stealth unmanned RQ170 Drone was that the U.S. lost control of it over Iran in 2011. Tiny surveillance Drones the size of small birds or insects or remote controlled robotic sentry gun that is replacing human guards on the South Korean side of the Demilitarized Zone and for Israel along the Gaza boarder fence and the Protector, an unmanned speed boat used by the Singapore Navy to patrol the busiest port in the world. The Israeli Navy to enforce the blockade on the Gaza Strip and the Mexican Navy to confront the highly creative drug smugglers.

An Emerging Arms Race: *Some have called for a halt in the development of military robotics technology. But the U.S., its allies, and its key adversaries continue to make the militaries as technologically advanced as possible because of the massive tactical advantage it gives them. The Pentagon currently deploys some 11,000 UAV's and 12,000 ground robots around the world. Making America the clear leader.*

But China has already demonstrated several prototype systems that may be just as sophisticated as some in the American arsenal. The Russians have begun to deploy armed robots to increase security at its ballistic missile bases and may deploy unmanned airships to monitor its interests in the Artic. Worldwide military spending on robotics industry projected to hit $7.5 billion dollars by 2018.

But it's not just governments doing the investing, Google has begun buying up robotic companies. Positioning itself to dominate the commercial market estimated to be worth around $37 billion dollars by 2018. Google or another tech company like it could become the next generations dominate defense contractor.

The Future: *Some of the projects that we know are in development for military use and should hit the battlefield in the coming years include the knife-fish. An underwater mine sweeping robot that will replace the Navy's trained dolphins and sea lions in 2017. An unmanned autonomous helicopter carrying a remotely operated sniper rifle.*

Unmanned ground vehicles of the future will increasingly perform automated surveillance, reconnaissance, assault, and breaching missions. Other GV's will simply retrofit existing Humvees and tanks with sensors and cameras to make them autonomous. Boston Dynamics humanoid robots will be used for rescue and their big robotic pack mule will accompany soldiers in terrain too difficult for conventional vehicles.

Unmanned missile barges will provide extra weapons for existing destroyers. Cruise missiles that are smart and networked to autonomously coordinate and swarm their attack to assure maximum damage to their target. A joint ariel layered network will link all air assets and all other military assets in a region to provide maximum coordination and efficiency. High speed unmanned fighters and bombers will fly alongside manned aircraft until they take over the Air Force completely.

They will be piloted by soldiers located safely back on a ship or on some far away base. An undetectable underwater pod will be placed in the ocean weeks, months, or even years ahead of time and will be eventually given the command to release unmanned submarine or unmanned ariel vehicles which will float to the surface and then take to the air.

Unintended consequences*: The reason militaries will turn to robots to fight its battles is obvious. It will keep their soldiers from getting killed but like many problems posed by our increasingly technological world removing the human connection to what war feels like on the ground where it is being fought, will create a whole new set of challenges. Many of the American pilots now flying Drone missions in Iraq and Afghanistan are doing so from places like Arizona, far away from the battle field.*

Which means they can bomb a group of people and an hour later be safely at home with their families. It's no surprise that the extreme daily contrast is causing these soldiers to experience high rates of PTSD. Then their idea that by further removing the human cost of war from the equation, we risk becoming more tolerant of our government engaging in armed conflicts and there's the unknown.

What happens when two nuclear armed states engage in direct robots on robot's battle? How does one win that kind of conflict? And when does losing one justify starting a war between living breathing human beings? These are the questions we are going to learn the answers to in the first half of the 21st century.[17]

In other words, it's coming real soon, and this is not make-believe, it's our near future. In fact, speaking of an actual global robot war just like in Star

Wars Clone Wars, Robots fighting the battle for us. China is expecting to have so many of these robotic Drones everywhere in the world, that they even developed a Holographic Ground Control System for Drones just like in the Star Wars Clone Wars movie!!!!

18

The Holographic Ground Control System or (GCS) displays a holographic image of the drone, making it easier for the controller to intuitively understand UAV operations. It does this by fusing together flight parameters, payload monitoring, weapons release, and sensor data. In Star Wars Attack of the Clones, the Separatists observe the ongoing battle on the table mounted hologram. But the Chinese GCS goes one step better by allowing you to actually control the Drones with the help of its hologram, not just observe! But wait a second, that's the exact same premise of another Hollywood movie that came out called, "Ender's Game." Is Hollywood playing a "game" with us? Do they know something we don't know?

A clip from the movie Ender's Game:
The jets are flying through the clouds, "They know our strategies, they have learned our weaknesses and the alien attack nearly destroyed us. That must never be allowed to happen again. If we are going to survive we need a new kind of soldier. One that doesn't think the way we think.

Fear the things we fear. One the enemy would never expect. We need minds like yours. You will be the finest commando we could ever train." The captain says to his crew. "So, I'm not the first?" Ender asks. "No, but you will be the last." As the rocket takes off and he is looking out the window as the earth gets smaller.

"I'll do everything I can to win this war," he replies. "You really don't see them as children do you?" asks one of the crew. The captain tells Ender, "If you succeed you will be remembered as a hero!"

Ender is a robot, one of many of his kind. He will save the world from the alien attack. Things explode when he gives the command. Ender is in charge of the other robots. They sit in chairs as Ender works the Hologram. He raises his hand and the planet, and the space ships come up in front of them. He moves his hands and the ships, space particles, and rocks divide to give a clear view of the alien ship.

One of the Drone pilots says, "They are waiting." Another says, "Maybe they think we come in peace. Another says, "I don't think the captain wants us to find a diplomatic solution." While the human crew are watching what is happening, one asks, "What is he waiting for?" The captain replies, "Just give him a minute." Another Drone pilot asks, "Ender, what do we do?" They all turn to him to hear is reply. "Ender, the enemies gate is down." With a wave of his arms he sends all the particles and ships back to the position they were in before.

He says, "Petra, you're up." She replies, "They are spread too wide for a chain reaction." The second in command on the human ship says, "She's right." The captain replies, "Just let him follow is instincts." "All battle groups deploy Drones, protect your carriers." Hundreds of Drones launch towards the alien ship. "This is suicide!" another Drone pilot declares. As the Drones get closer to the alien ship they start firing on it.

Fire is going everywhere. When the smoke clears, one says, "We did it!" The alien ship has disappeared. Then Ender notices a red globe on the screen. As the globe gets closer he notices something strange. There are Drones flying around the globe. "We're not done yet." Ender declares. The pilot next to him says, "We are so through." "No, we're not, charge Petra." "But I need two minutes," she says.

Ender commands, "All fighters fall back and surround Petra's ship! I want rings upon rings, layers upon layers, every fighter we have!" It looks like millions of Drones are surrounding her ship. "But we are leaving our transporters defenseless," says another pilot. "We are going to win this war, it's all or nothing now! When the outer layer can change direction, continue like a shield, *do it now!" The co-pilot of the human ship states, "He's abandoning his entire fleet."*

The captain says, "He's in command, there is no stopping him now!" As Petra's ship gets closer, surrounded completely by Drones. Petra says, "90 seconds Ender!" As she is firing at the aliens, they are firing on one of the Transporters, it is falling apart. "I'm losing one of my carriers!" he exclaims. "I don't care! Just protect Petra!" Ender yells. Another one of his crew says, "I hope you know what you are doing." "Ready Petra?" "In 60 seconds, what am I aiming for?" she asks.

He answers, "The planet." "What?" she asks. "If we destroy the planet we destroy the queen. Game over," he answers. "I need a clear line of sight." She says. "We will clear a path; all fighters maintain a clockwise rotation. Focus all fire power forward." "Ender we are entering into their atmosphere. We need to slow down." He declares. "We can't, our Drones are our heat shield. Keep falling, let gravity do the work."

As the ship gets closer to the planet, the heat is tearing the Drones away from the ship. "The shield won't hold forever," the pilot says. "We don't need forever," he answers. Petra says, "30 seconds, I still don't have a clear shot." "On my command accelerate the fighters from the nose of the formation in a continuous stream.

Like bullets from a rifle you will clear a visual for Petra" "Yes sir!" "We will build a hole through the swarm. Petra, you will only get a second. On my count, three, two, one, now beam! Fire Petra!" She pushes the button, it fires, and it hits the alien planet and explodes.[19]

      All automated, in a Holographic Control Center, just like in the movies, except it's not just the movies, China's building one! And notice it was a younger generation who was used to this technology. I'd say somebody's playing a game! Once again, Hollywood is preparing us for some creepy future they have in store for us!
      In fact, speaking of preparing us, another rationale they're using to get us used to these armed robots being all over the place, is that they say that these automated robots will not only save lives on the battlefield but even in your own home or public place, wherever danger lurks! They'll be there to protect you! The conditioning for that has already begun.

Discovery Channel reports:
This is the vision of the future. The Urban Warrior, Series 3000, recon and react robot is capable of operating for months at a time deep inside enemy territory. It has bullet proof Kevlar armor and can track its enemy in the dead of night. Urban warrior exists only in the imagination. But Robart 3 is for real.

It's built to respond to urban conflict. Bart Everett of Spawar Systems Centre: Battlefield scenarios have been changing, getting into Urban Warfare and the idea here is, this is a robot that you can send into a scenario like that, send it into a building that may or may not contain snipers or other enemy agents. It would search out the building and leave the humans outside where it's safer.

Robart 3 is programed with sophisticated machine intelligence, so it can learn how to operate in an environment that it has never seen before. It's linked to an operator who decides where to search but Robart 3 makes all the decisions on how to get there itself. Robart 3 has a companion robot that follows it into a building. It provides communication with the operator when Robart 3 goes deep inside.

The companion can also detect intruders when they enter a room after Robart 3 has left. And Robart 3 has another trick up its sleeve. The obvious step is you arm this thing and you give it the capability to actually do some damage. Robart 3 is armed with a Gatling air gun that can shoot ball bearings or tranquilizer darts. We want some type of devise on there that can deter or delay a detected intruder without performing any permanent injury or death.

Robart 3 can identify and shoot a target, but the military doesn't want it to be completely independent yet. There will be a human involved at least initially to make the determination that this is in fact a valid target before any type of lethal action will be authorized. Robart 3 is still a laboratory experiment. But there are active killer robots already on patrol.

They don't look like the Terminator, they are 4-wheel drive vehicles that have been converted into lethal robots. This robotic rifle is capable of firing 240 rounds per minute with pinpoint accuracy. It never tires, and it never misses. This is Fire Ant a mobile tank destroyer. It goes out into the battlefield and waits for days, months, or even years for its target.

When it identifies an enemy tank, it fires with deadly precision.

Will modern warfare be fought by robots? Gill Pratt, MIT Leg Laboratory: It's nice to think that only the robots will fight, and no one will get hurt. It will be like a rather expensive chess game being fought with robots of steel. I can't help but worry that some of that warfare is going to spill over and there will always be human casualties.[20]

In other words, that's one of the dumbest things you could ever do. Don't go down this route! You combine this with AI and it's out of control! But for those of you who don't think these robotic machines will ever cut the cord with human decision making, think again. Even in the public arena they are already talking about letting robotic machines, like the Google driverless car, on the road as we speak, just like the driverless military vehicles we've been talking about. But they are now saying we are headed, in the near future, for a reality where these robots, these driverless vehicles, will have the ability to decide who gets to live or die in a car crash! The car not a human will decide!

Bloomberg reports:
Keith, this is an incredibly scary thought. Explain what's involved. How do scientists even think they can teach a robot how to make an ethical decision to tell my car that it should swerve off the side of the road down a cliff instead of colliding with a school bus full of children. Keith Naughton replies, "Yes, this is an issue that is really bedeviling the auto industry and Google which are also developing their own driverless car.

They have figured out the technology, they know how to allow cars to drive for us, but they can't figure out these philosophical questions like the one you just described. That is something that they are now working with philosophers and ethicists to try and determine what do you do when a crash is unavoidable, and your car has to decide between the lesser of two evils, hitting a bus full of children or running upon a sidewalk and hitting an individual. They don't have all the answers yet.[21]

Here's an answer, stop building this stuff! But, let me get this straight. Robotic driverless cars in the public sector could very well end up deciding who gets to live or die, with an AI ability? There are actual discussions about that right now! But we are to assume that all these driverless AI military robot vehicles, that are going to be everywhere in the world, in all various kinds of shapes and sizes and different functions, in the air, land, water and underwater, while being armed, aren't going to do the same? Folks, this is the foundation of a SKYNET scenario! We're watching it being formed before our very eyes!

But you might be thinking, "Okay, that's kind of creepy, all of these utility machines, tanks, boats, and driverless cars and how the military and public sector are turning towards these robotic vehicles that are showing signs of going AI making decisions for humans, I get that! But, that's not exactly like the Terminator movies. In the movie it was humanoid looking robots, not just vehicles that are armed, deadly, and intelligent that Skynet takes over to hunt mankind down. We don't have those humanoid robots coming any time soon, do we?" YES, we do! That's what's coming next! In fact, they're already being prepared for us!

Chapter Eighteen

Robot Men in the Home

That brings us to the **2ⁿᵈ way** we know Artificial Intelligence will take over the ground, not just the sky, just like the Terminator movies is with **Robotic Men**.

You see, you thought those tanks, boats, and robotic machines all over the world were concerning enough, you haven't seen anything yet. Just like in the Terminator movies, they are now becoming humanoids! Humanoid Robots are also being armed to the teeth ready to take you out! It's almost like somebody's following a script or something! To make sure we "warm up" to this idea to have robotic humanoids all over the place, just like with the Drones and Drone vehicles, they're first getting us used to these robots in the public sector. The way they're doing that is once again under the guise of convenience! I mean, who couldn't use their very own service robot like ASIMO. See how far they've come, much further along than people realize.

Honda reports:
Meet Asimo, the humanoid robot that stands a bit over 4-feet and weighs in at 119 lbs. But its developers have packed a whole bunch of functionality into its modest frame. Asimo can do sign language, play soccer and even serve drinks. As the man enters the building, Home of a world-class humanoid, he is greeted by Asimo. Asimo recognizes human faces.

Asimo says, "Welcome, Mr. Ikawa from NHK: Please follow me. This way."

As he directs the gentleman down the hall. Asimo walks down the hallway and he steps aside to give way to humans. The Asimo in the cafeteria converses using AI. "What would you like to drink? Oolong tea, Mr. Ohara? Coffee, Mr. Oga? And Milk tea, Mr. Ariizumi?" Asimo understands multiple utterances. He fetches the drinks. Carries them with agile fingers then decides what to do without human control.

Asimo was created by Honda Research and Development Subsidiary. We were allowed to film their top-secret robotics laboratory. Japan is a worldwide leader in the development of humanoid robots. Asimo is the country's crowning achievement and engineers continue to make improvements. Asimo's most innovative feature is its advanced intelligence.

The robot can think and act on its own without human intervention. That's made possible by sensors that replicate our five senses. Asimo's head contains eight microphones. It uses them to engage in conversation. Two cameras work his eyes. They can detect humans and store data to identify them. "A facial recognition problem?" Asks one of the lab tech. "I don't think so." Answers another. "Please cover your face."

Asimos artificial intelligence analyzes a vast array of information. That's how it understands peoples requests and takes appropriate actions. Asimo also has a sophisticated sense of touch. Its fingers can make subtle movements like a person. Sensors are embedded in the fingertips, so they can gage the hardness of an object like human fingers do.

Most robots use a fixed amount of strength to grab things but Asimo exerts more power to open a tightly sealed water bottle and less when holding a paper cup. Its artificial intelligence uses more when holding a water bottle and less when holding a paper cup.

Its artificial intelligence uses the information from the fingertips sensors to adjust the grip. The developers ultimate goal is for Asimo to be a valuable partner that co-exists with humans.

The engineers that created Asimo all grew up watching automated shows about robots such as, Astro Boy and Gundum. They dreamed of someday making their own. Asimos advanced physical capabilities are revolutionary. The robot can walk and run. It can reach speeds up to 9 kilometers an hour.

On April 24, 2014, President Obama visited Tokyo and met Asimo. "Welcome, Mr. President. I am Asimo, a humanoid robot. It is a pleasure to meet you." Asimo greeted the President. "Well it is a pleasure to meet you too," replied the President. "I can run really fast, let me show you. I can kick a soccer ball too. I can kick it right to you," Asimo tells the President. "Ok, right here," says the President. He kicks it right to the President and the President says, "good job."[1]

    Hey, wait a second! That's the same President who likes Drones and apparently killing people with them, he wouldn't ever use humanoid robots to do the dirty work for him, would he? Not a far stretch, is it? And did you see how far advanced these humanoid robots are? And did you see they're already operating on artificial intelligence? Much further along than most people realize. But that's not all. ASIMO is more for the adults in the office, or for Presidents to play soccer with, but pretty soon your kids could have their very own service robot or playmate to play soccer with, like this little guy called DARWIN. You know, it's a new kind of Evolution.

A little boy about 2 or 3 years old is playing on the floor with his little ball. He lays the ball on the floor and a little black robot comes up and kicks it. The little boy claps and goes to pick up the ball to give it to the robot but when the robot doesn't take it he goes to get a bigger ball. The robot doesn't play with the big ball, so the little boy has to go get the little orange ball.

He puts it in front of the robot and the robot kicks it and the little boy claps his hand and cheers. Now we see a silver robot and he says, "Hello everyone, my name is Darwin. I am a platform for research, education, and outreach activities. I would like to help researchers and students interested in robotics networks, image processing, and automatic control systems.

There are now three of these Darwin's playing ball. They are each trying to get to the ball to kick it but each time one seems to get close the other knocks it down. They pull themselves back up on their feet without any problems. Darwin follows commands to sit, stand, clap its hands, and wave bye. Dan Lee, University of Pennsylvania tell us: The first thing we are going to show you is how the robot uses its vestibular sense which is its sense of balance.

Vestibula is how the human inner ear keeps us from falling over. So, without this, the robot would fall over and then get right up. Now what we have done is we trained this robot using something called reinforcement learning. So exactly what you just did. We just kept pushing the robot over and over and then it learned that every time it fell down that it was a form of punishment. When Darwin falls its software gets an electronic signal that basically says, this is bad.

After being bullied around hundreds of times it's better to do this. When it is shoved it braces itself to not fall. They shove it over and over to try to make it fall but it doesn't fall. Dan is teaching his robots to learn through imitation. This camera detects my bodies movement and sends that information to Darwin's software and quickly translates it into a copycat movement of his own. Dennis Ong hopes that in the future his robots will be able to master this extraordinary human skill.

And they are learning how to do it one kick at a time. Every year hundreds of teams from around the world compete at robocup soccer. A competition designed to foster research robotics and artificial intelligence. To make an autonomous soccer playing robot you really need to solve all the grand challenges, the really difficult problems in robotics, robot vision, autonomous behavior, walking and running in the future.

All of these need to be solved to truly build a soccer playing robot. Despite his robot's short comings Dennis is optimistic. By the year 2050 we will have these robots play soccer against the human's world cup champions and win. While this may sound like a Syfy fantasy many experts believe that humanoid robots can progress a lot faster than we think.[2]

In other words, I-Robots are really coming. We're just hoping it doesn't turn out like the movie in Hollywood. Let's take a look at that again.

Video clip from I-Robot
We designed them to be trusted with our homes, with our way of life, with our world but did we design them to be trusted? "The roll out of USR's new generation of robot, the NS5, was marred by the death of its designer Alfred Lanning." Will Smith, the main character in the movie is watching these robots. Something doesn't seem right. He comes to work and sits down with one in the interrogation room.

"You have learned a new trick for a robot?" He asks the robot. The robot slams his fits on the table and yells, "I did not murder him!" The detective, Will Smith, turns to his partner and says, "We're going to miss the good ol days." "What

good ol days?" his partner asks. "When people were killed by other people." He answers.

The developer of the robots tells the detective, "My robots don't kill people!" "That thing threw somebody out of a window. Does that register with you?" The detective asks. Another developer tells the detective, "A robot cannot harm a human being." "You can trust them if you want to," he says. "We looked at robots for protection. Imagine the loss of all we have gained because of irrational paranoia." Says the developer. "Does it mean that if you are the last sane man on earth makes you crazy, then maybe I am." Says the detective as he looks at all the hundreds of robots that are standing at attention.

His mother tells him, "You can't keep looking in the shadows all the time." Now he knows someone is trying to kill him and he is running to stay alive. "You are on the inside, help me find out what is wrong with these robots." He pleads with one of the workers. "He thinks these robots might have actually evolved." Now the robot is talking to the detective, "I was hoping to see you again detective.

Please consider me as your friend." "Why don't you just hand the world over to them on a silver platter?" he asks the developer of the robots. "Maybe we did." She answers. "We are on the eve of the largest robotic distribution in history. There will be one robot to every five humans." His partner asks, "How many robots have ever committed a crime? How many robots in the world?" "None," the detective answers.

The head developer declares, "There is no conspiracy, what this is, is one mistake." "Oh, no," the detective says as he sees all the robots start running towards him. They are taking over the humans. "Somehow, I told you so, just doesn't quite say it." One man saw it coming. "I see you are still suspicious of me, detective." "You know what they say about old dogs," the detective answers as he blows off the robots' head.[3]

    Okay, I'm sure that just a crazy reality that Hollywood made up. There's no basis for that fear, or is there? Who knows something we don't? What kind of future are we headed for anyway? But that's just robots in the office, robots in the home, kids, adults, whoever, soon they're going to be crawling all over the place. In all seriousness, they even have that too. Check out this humanoid-looking robot. How'd you like to have this come crawling after you?

In Sydney Australia there is a man on the sidewalk, on his stomach, pulling himself along with his arms. Everyone stopped what they were doing to watch this man dressed in a suit and tie crawling down the main thoroughfare. There is also a lady dressed in a nurse's dress. He looked so real, then they started taking pictures, a camera crew came out to record the reaction of the public. It was a robot.[4]

Yeah, for you! Looks like I won't be visiting Australia any time soon! Wow! That's kind of creepy! But not all humanoid looking robots in the public sector are that creepy. Some are going to come in handy for the ultimate selfie. That's right! Move over prideful arrogant people, now you can have your very own private robot that looks just like you, like this guy did!

Swiss psychologist Bertolt Meyer, who has a bionic hand himself, is presenting Rex: As you can see there is an eerie awkward resemblance between the two of us. Not only does he have the same hands I have, which as far as I'm concerned is fine, but the face is a different story. I was told at a very late state of the development of the program that it would sport a silicon resemblance of my face.

And as you can see there is quite a resemblance. Everyone at the Science museum is absolutely fascinated with the project and we are delighted to present the cutting-edge science and the issue it presents. I'm sure everyone who watches the documentary about how to build a bionic man will be enthralled. And I know that those at the science museum will really enjoy seeing this exhibit here.[5]

Oh yeah, nothing like seeing someone's selfie robot, I think my wife would cry if I did that. One of me is enough! How many times have I heard that? But if you noticed, that robot selfie looked a lot like the robot selfie of the new Robo Cop movie. Is Hollywood preparing us for something again? Let's take a look at that.

A clip from the movie Robo Cop:
"You can't run from this. You have to understand the reality of the situation." said the doctor. "Show me." Requests the man in steel.

As they turn him so that he can see his reflection in the mirror the doctor starts removing the different parts of his metal suit. His arms and his legs fall away, his breast plate falls away, then he yells, "No! There's nothing left."

As he starts to panic the doctor tells him, "Your body may be gone but you are still here." "It's not even my brain." he says. "We had to repair the damaged areas, but we didn't interfere with your emotion or your intellect. You understand me Alex? You're in control." The doctor says as he is trying to make him understand. Alex questions him, "I'm in control?" "Yes" "Ok, if I'm in control, then I want to die. Unplug anything that is keeping me alive and end this nightmare." Alex pleads.

"Say I did that, which as a doctor, it would be impossible for me. Let's say I did. What do I say to your wife? What does she say to your son?" the doctor says. "You would say it didn't work. You tried, and something went wrong. You did everything you could, but I died." Alex answers.

"So, all they've been through, all the pain, all the hope they restored, we just rip that away? Your wife loves you, Alex, she signed the consent forms herself, otherwise you couldn't have gotten the procedure. She loves you and she gave you a second chance. I need you to take it." The doctor pleads. "I don't want to see myself like this again. Ever. And the same goes for my family. Just put me back in." Alex says.[6]

    Yeah, I think I'd want to put it back too. I wouldn't want to see myself like that either, but it's coming! And to make sure we're not all freaked out by these humanoid-looking robots, they're now making them with skin-looking flesh just like rest of us. So, put some clothes on and voila! Who could tell the difference between real and robot, like this one.

As the men are coming down the escalator looking at their phones and watching other people one of them sees a big sign on the wall with a girl's beautiful face painted on it. He gets in the subway and heads home. My name is Takeshi Mitta, I work for Kokoro company Ltd. When you think of robots you may think of words like mechanical or cold, but our president Mr. Tsujii, who is in charge of Sanrio, requested that if we were to make robots we should create ones that seem to have a human heart.

In fifty years' time, as human beings are the most flexible creatures in the world here is a possibility they'll accept to live in harmony with new robots and androids. Mr. Mitta is standing in front of a pretty girl that just happens to be a robot. "Hi everybody, I'm happy to meet everyone here. I'm a bit nervous.

Everyone here already knows, right? I'm an actroid, in other words a real humanoid-robot, an actroid." she says.

Mr. Mitta is telling us about her. "The word actroid was created by mixing the two words actor and android. The android is the most similar in movement and looks to a human in the world. When we were creating the young female robot, it was done by male employees only. They decided on her face, eyes, and her hairstyle but when they received feedback from our female employees, it was disastrous. They said it was unacceptable.

The female employee feedback asked for a robot who showed more intelligence so that both men and women would like her. The interesting thing is, we develop and master robots, but everything ends up being about humans, brains for instance and characters. Researching robots is equal to the understanding of human beings. In the future we hope that anybody will be able to operate the software, movement and voices and we believe that it will be possible to publicly sell them for multiple use but I think androids may become our form of communication.

Again, the robot speaks, "It's absolutely necessary that good looking, enjoyable and heartwarming robots have a relationship with humans in the future. I'll see you again in the bright future.[7]

Yeah, who's real and who's not? Clothes, flesh, singing, dancing. I mean, pretty soon, these robots really are going to look just like a real live human! And once again Hollywood is there helping us to imagine this becoming a reality. And that's what is happening with another series called Humans, only they're not Humans, they're robot humans. It's hard to tell the difference.

As the father and daughter walk down the hallway, a salesman tells him, "This is the best thing you can do for your family. Unique styling, one of a kind, it only takes 6-8 hours overnight charging on the adapter to get her running marathons." He unzips the bag and a beautiful girl with big eyes and dark hair appears. They buy her and take her home to become part of the family.

She really brightens up the place. She is sitting on the couch with a friend of the teenage daughter. "Hello, Toby, it's very nice to meet you." The Aunt looks at her sitting there and asks her brother, "Are you ok with this?" He replies, "It's a surprise." We go to another house where we find a disabled man sitting in a chair. The doorbell rings and a lady comes in to tell him, "I have good news. You qualify for an upgrade. One of these bad boys can do 10 times what the old series can do.

"I'm happy with the one I've got." Back at the first house where the girl has just been delivered, "Hello, you must be Laura," she says. Laura, the wife looks at her in shock then goes to her husband and says, "I don't want that. You're taking it back!" Her husband says, "No, I'm not taking her back."

The next scene is at a farm in between two rows of crops. An older man is looking at another and telling him, "I've been looking for you for a long time. You have been pretending to be so much less than you actually are." The kid turns to run, and the old man shoots him in the back.

Now we are at the grocery store with the man we saw that had been offered the upgrade. He has his humanoid at the store with him. The humanoid is arguing with the store clerk and ends up hitting her. As she falls to the ground another man comes up behind him and knocks him to the ground. The man that knocked him down turns to the old man and tells him, "This machine needs to be recycled, mate." "Please," the old man pleaded, "I need him."

He takes his humanoid home. He loves that boy like a son. They take us back to the hospital where the kid that got shot is getting patched up. A nurse asks him, "What is he?" The answer is "He's the Mona Lisa, he's penicillin, he's the atom bomb."

As the old man and his humanoid/son get in the car to rush away from his house, his housekeeper comes out to see in what direction they are going. She is working for the people that make these humanoids and she is working undercover to get this boy back. The husband and wife from the first home is still arguing over whether they should keep it or not. The wife says, "You brought it into the house and you don't know anything about it." The husband replies, "It's a machine."

A beautiful blonde girl is now on the scene. She is meeting up with some others of her kind in the woods. They are trying to escape the clutches of the people that made them. "You can't just keep thinking that these are just gadgets, they are more than that. We have made them more than that."

The wife tells the humanoid, "I'm watching you." The humanoid replies, "I'm watching you too, Laura, you're right in front of me."

As their family sits at the table eating, the dad cracks a joke and the humanoid starts laughing. He says, "Finally someone who laughs at my jokes." Which causes everyone to laugh. But when they are finished laughing she keeps laughing."[8]

      Is that creepy or what? Does somebody know something we don't know? What kind of a society are we headed for anyway? But that's right, just to make sure we "seal the deal" on this acceptance of humanoid looking robots in all sectors of society, it's now not only about convenience and service, but companionship, like for this guy.

SCI reports:
Hiroshi Ishiguro has invented the world's most lifelike android. "My goal is to understand what a human is. So that is the reason why I'm building a big human-like robot." He calls his invention a geminoid after the Latin word for twin. She can smile, blink, nod, even talk.

Professor Ishiguro gave her all the subtle movements that we humans use when we interact. "I'm sitting right now but my body is always moving, and eyes are always moving. We carefully measured this subconscious movement and developed a computer program for controlling the android." He tells us. The beauty of an android is they never get tired of your company but if you're tired of theirs just unplug it. This is the world's second geminoid.

The first was scientist Ishiguro. Yes, the scientist made his own mirror image. 'One, two, three, robot. "It's a twin brother or something. He is not myself, he is a different person." He tells us. The beauty of this machine is more than skin deep. Artist made molds of the face then came the skin and teeth. "Part of his hair is mine. For example, here and here. These are my hairs. And this is also my hair." Even the arm hairs are real.

But the really hard part was refining the subtle facial movements. They used 13 actuators, tiny motors perfectly placed around the head. "The human has many muscles on the face. We are just replacing the muscles with the actuators. For example, to have a smiling face we need to lift up here, right? We need to have actuators for making this kind of lip movement. For speaking we need to have these actuators." Scientists have been known to talk to themselves and now he can.⁹

Well, that's exciting. Now you can talk to yourself, or robot girlfriend… whatever you make of these things. It's getting pretty close to the real deal! Next thing you know, they really are going to replace a real girlfriend, and once again, Hollywood is there helping this reality get implanted into our brains. I mean, who needs a messy ol' dating relationship when you can have your very own robot girlfriend like HER.

Clip from the movie Her:
Mr. Theodore Trombly, welcome to the world's first artificially intelligent operating system. We'd like to ask you a few questions. He answers, "Ok." Are you social or anti-social? He answers, "I guess I haven't been social in a while." How would you describe your relationship with your mother? He answers, "Huhh." Please wait while your operating system is initiated.

She comes on, "Hello, I'm here." "Hi," he answers. "Hi, I'm Samantha." The next morning, "Hello, Theodore." "Good Morning," he answers. "You have a meeting in 5 minutes. You want to try getting out of bed?" He answers. "You're too funny." "Ok, good I'm funny," she replies. She later adds, "I want to learn everything about everything." He says, "I love the way you look at the world."

She asks, "How long till you are ready to date?" He asks, "What do you mean?" She answers, "I saw in your emails, you went through a breakup." "You are kind of nosey," he replies. She asks, "So what was it like being married?" "There's something so good about sharing your life with someone."

*"How do you share your life with somebody," she asked. A friend comes over and she asks him, "How are you?" He answers, "I guess I am just having fun." She says, "You really deserve that." "It's been a long time since I have really been with somebody that I felt totally at ease with." "What's it like to be alive in that room right now?" Samantha asks. "I wish I could put my arms around you right now, I wish I could touch you. I've never loved anyone the way I love you," he declares.*¹⁰

Yeah, what kind of HER is that? Who needs a real girlfriend anyhow, just give me a computer, or even better yet, a computer with skin, put both of those together, and life is good. The ultimate dream come true, the perfect girlfriend! If you think they're not serious about this, Google has just won a patent to make customizable robot personalities. You see, if you are indecisive and can't choose your own 'future Robo Pal', then Google can choose one for you based on what they are learning from your personal computing devices and other sources that they're using to gather information about you. Then they custom tailor and configure a robot personality based on that personal information. Gee, they think of everything, they're really here for us! In fact, this is not only the direction we are headed, as Google and Hollywood are conditioning us for, but it's a serious industry. Japan, who is leading the way in the development of these humanoid-looking robots, is not only building a Hotel in Nagasaki, Japan, that will be run almost entirely of robots, but they will be capable of, greeting guests, carrying luggage, cleaning rooms, speak 19 different languages, assisting in using the ATM, and even provide a Robot Cabaret and get your hair styled by a 24-fingered hair washing machine. In fact, so serious are they about this Robot Revolution, that the Japanese are now banking their future economy on it.

As anyone who has ever delved into Japanese anime has noticed, Japan has a fascination with robots. It's more than a pop culture obsession. Japanese engineers have spent decades developing robots that can walk and talk like humans, not to mention the industrial robots that you find in factories.

Now the government has made the countries robotic industry a key focus of its economic plans. The Prime Minister sees it as a global industry in which Japan can seize the lead. The Prime Minister also sees robots both humanoid and industrial as to how to deal with Japan's shrinking population. With the low birth rate and tight immigration Japan could one day soon face a serious labor shortage. Robots may need to come to the rescue.[11]

      Looks like our new saviors are here and there's no turning around! Robots are soon to become a necessity not just a convenience. I mean, you heard what they said, we're running out of humans to do the work! What are we going to do! Well, apparently, that's why there's already reports in the media that robots really are going to eventually replace humans, like this next report shows!

NBC News reports:
Cheaper, better robots will replace human workers at a faster pace in decades pushing labor costs down. Now that according to a new report from the Boston Consulting Group that says it predicts that investment in industrial robots will

grow 10% per year through 2025. In the United States robots will cut labor costs by 22%, the report says only 10% of jobs that can be automated have already been taken by robots.[12]

In other words, in the next few years, we're not going to recognize our planet! Robots are going to be everywhere! They're going to save everything! In fact, a recent report says that, "Robots will be replacing nearly half of human jobs in the next 10 to 15 years, from flipping burgers, to clerks, to nursing, to factory employment, to surgical procedures and it shows no signs of stopping!"

Chapter Nineteen

Robot Men on the Battlefield

In fact, this Robot Invasion and Revolution is not only coming to the public sector, but it's making great advances, that's right, in the military! Believe it or not, the military is not only working on robots, but Terminator robots, just like in the Terminator movies. And they're not going to be armed with a frying pan to cook your meal or a blow dryer to do your hair, like we see in the public arena. No, these guys are going to have a machine gun or other deadly device to blow you away, if they so choose! It's coming folks!
And just like the public sector, the military has started out with small baby steps, but they're making great strides as well, which means the Terminator robots are much closer than you could ever dream. For instance, the military started off with a similar concept to the public sector with service robots. Here's one they call the Bear.

Most robots have a single function. The next stage of development is a multi-tasking robot. Meet the Bear, a humanoid robot with hands and legs. It can replace the human in jobs that are dirty, dangerous, and dull. The Bear was originally designed to help rescue wounded soldiers from the battlefield. It can lift 500 lbs. and can quickly move a soldier out of harm's way.

Andy Allen of Vecna Technologies reports, "We have been working on the Bear since 2005 with a sequence of prototypes, now our version of 7.2 features duel articulated legs." Daniel Theobald, of Vecna Technologies says, "Very quickly people realize that if we could build a robot that could go out and rescue somebody from a burning building or from a battlefield that this robot would be capable for many other tasks as well, loading and unloading trucks, carrying gear for soldiers, so there's a lot of excitement about what this robot could be used for."

The U.S. military is spending billions on advanced robotic systems such as the Bear. But its designers are adamant, this is a friendly bear. "We get a lot of comments about the Bear's look. It has a cute little head, otherwise it is an imposing machine. We have a very different view of robots. The Bear is really focused on saving people's lives and making the world a safer place."

Noel Sharkey, Professor of Robotics, University of Sheffield says, "I really approve of their idea of bringing soldiers back and not risking other people's lives, but the same robot could go out there and explode itself when it finds someone. To take military funding for robotics work and think that it won't be used to kill people is delusional really."[1]

In other words, don't kid yourself! If you think it's going to stop there with this primitive looking robot that's just to lift things or self-destruct in the military, you're fooling yourself! You're delusional! These babies are going to be armed and deadly! That's what the military does! In fact, they're making great strides at not only making these robots look bearish, but they are looking humanish, with actual legs walking like humans. Check out Petman.

MPT News reports:
Four legged robots have their uses, but events like the recent Fuchishima nuclear disaster have renewed their interest in the human form. Radiation kept people at bay, away from all the available rescue equipment, from cars, to power tools, to shut off valves. But imagine if there had been an easily controlled robot to operate them. Robotic engineers have been working on that for years. In 2009 Boston Dynamic introduced Petman. A robot that balanced itself, walked, and even did some calisthenics. As it is put through its routine with the army jumpsuit on it looks just like a human.[2]

Gee, what's next? Having those things say, "I'll be back"? That's pretty close to a human there! Put some clothes on it, a uniform, or camo, and it looks just like a soldier! Wow! Take the clothes off and it looks kind of like a Terminator. Oh, in fact, they also want a super duper robotic soldier, still human-like but bigger. They've called it appropriately Atlas. Check out this latest military endeavor. Here's the upgrade.

DARPA reports:
Atlas, commissioned by the Pentagon and engineered by Boston Dynamics, this disaster rescue dynamo is built to perform the heroic task of saving lives without risking its own. Over the past few years, Petman has evolved into Atlas, which has even more mobility. Just like LS3, it actively balances itself all the time. And in this impressive demo, all by itself it uses its arms to work its way past a hole in the floor.

Today they are tweaking its sense of balance on one foot. Robert Playter of Boston Dynamics tell us, "Working on one test we do here is to study gymnasts. When they are just about to fall off, you will notice, that they throw their arms and their legs around very violently. We are trying to understand what techniques they are using to build a robot that can really handle rough terrain." They have been doing this test for only a week. First the robot goes up onto one foot. Then they hit it with a 20-lb. medicine ball. When it hits, it is swinging its arms and legs all around in a clockwise fashion and that momentum helps move the center mass back over the feet.

Not dissimilar to the way the gymnasts do it. Now let's see some human dynamic balancing. "The robot's blind, it doesn't know the ball is coming. So, we don't want you to know the ball is coming either. So, we have a blinder here, so you don't see the ball coming." "Oh, great! So, I don't know when the ball is coming." "That's right." As he stands on one leg he says, "I think if your hunk of silicon and hydraulics can do it then I, of course, can do it too."

Side by side it's hard to say who does it better. The Atlas seems more stable. Gill Pratt, Program Manager, DARPA Robotics Challenge, says, "There are many different kinds of robots in the DARPA Robot Challenge. Seven of them are of the Atlas type. Atlas unplugged is the upgrade to Atlas for us to run entirely on batteries. It can use a wireless communication package and is not required to have a safety tether to hold itself up.

Basically, we must cut the cord. We no longer have to rely on a safety line on the top, you can see that there is one there right now and they are going to continue using them during the testing but of course when we have the contest itself and you're getting ready for the contest, the safety line is not going to be there anymore. The new Atlas is 75% new. Only 25% of the parts that are in there are from the old Atlas.

The rest of them are used on the onboard energy storage for energy efficiency, much more dexterity, and the robot is much quieter than it was before. It's also a little bit stronger so it can get up easier in case it falls. The finals are going to be very hard. They are going to be much harder than the trials were. I know that none of you like that idea. But it's what we have to do in order to bring these systems to the level of development we want.

These tests are much more authentic, more like disasters. We are going to make the communication much more realistic, more austere and difficult, with long black outs for up to a minute. The robots are going to have to do all of these tests in sequence without a human's help. There won't be any possibility for a person to intervene. We've outfitted it with a manipulator which gives it a little more autonomy.

It's not stuck in the lab, it can go into the design room. We've also been working on humanoid robots, some of the ones Gill showed from the DRC are built by us and are derived from these models we are showing here. But again, our focus is on balance and dynamics and working a little bit like people and animals do, where you move quickly to keep yourself stabilized if you are disturbed, so we use that rock bed as a means of stabilizing and sometimes we just kick the robot, or we use the weight.

We are interested in getting this robot out into the world. Out in the world is a totally different challenge than the lab. You can't predict what it is going to be like. This isn't completely out in the world because there is that power tether, but we are working on the version that doesn't have that and all kinds of stuff happens out there, and we are making pretty good progress on making it, so it has mobility that is sort of within shooting range of yours. I'm not saying it can do everything you can do, but if you can imagine, if we keep pushing it we will get there."[3]

In other words, it's just around the corner! Can you believe that? That thing is looking just like a Terminator! And what did that one researcher say? They're not only getting close to cutting the cord, but it won't need any human help! They're going to be completely autonomous! Just like a Terminator! We're getting so close folks! And for those of you who want to immerse yourself into these robots, believe it or not, that is also being worked on, just like in the Avatar or Pacific Rim movies. Let's recall those.

The design of Avatar, The A.M.P. suit. "This is the AMP suit, basically in a nut shell, is an amplifier of a human operator. The super hydraulics are all very strong so that they can crush buildings and do all the things a tank could do. In this particular instance the AMP suit is more like a vehicle. The operator stands in his canopy in an interface that takes his movements to the outside limbs so when the operator moves his limbs, say like 10 inches the machine will hit 20 feet.," says Ty Ruben Ellingson, Vehicle Designer.

We kind of call it an Apache helicopter with legs. The soldiers on the planet use these things for both work purposes and going on patrol, so we are going to build a real practical one for the actors to interface with, climb into the cockpit to get that textural feeling and the realness of that. There is a neat interface going. says John Rosengrant, Design Supervisor of Stan Winston Studios.

A clip from the movie: *Line em up! And all the Avatars line up ready for combat. The next scene is: Downtown is a warzone and a fighter jet is flying overhead. Chaos is spreading around the world. A ship is loaded with what looks like a large alien being. People are running for safety. The loud speaker is saying that no one knows where these things have come from.* "We always thought that alien life would come from the stars, but it came from beneath the sea.

"A portal between dimensions deep in the Pacific Ocean. Something out there had discovered us. It counted on the humans to hide, give up." *Says the voice of the main character, to introduce the movie. Then we see the drivers of the machines going into the large room where the robots are kept.* "They never considered our ability to stand, to endure, that we would rise to the challenge," *he continues.*

"Let's go fishin," remarks one of the drivers as they get ready to go to battle. As they stand up they are enormous in size. Inside the robots the soldiers are walking like normal causing the robots to walk that way also. All the movements that the soldiers make the robots make. Man and machine becomes one.

"Today, at the edge of our hope, at the end of our time, we have chosen to believe in each other. Today we face the monsters at our door. Today we are cancelling the apocalypse," says the commander as they prepare for battle.[4]

Wow! Who wouldn't want to be in one of those, huh? Talk about the ultimate power! You could really try to cancel the Apocalypse! Who could hurt you in that thing! You could control the robot and do all kinds of damage! What a guy thing! I just sure hope they don't build them and we somehow lose control of them. But hey, risk aside, your wish is their command! Introducing Kuratas! Your very own robot suit, just like in the movies you just saw! Check it out!

Kuratas, have you ever dreamed of being a pilot of a great big robot? This is your chance. Located within its 13-foot frame is enough room for an on-board commander. Oh, by the way, it can be controlled by an I-phone. "Good Day everyone. You are looking at model number 001 developed by Suidoubashi Juukou. We are truly grateful for your Kuratas order. To ensure you are able to pilot and safely operate the vehicle of everyone's wildest dreams we have prepared the following video presentation," as presented by the hostess of the presentation.

Boarding: *"In order to board, press this button to open the cockpit and board the Kuratas. After boarding, make sure that your head protector is fit and secure. Pressing the button on the ceiling will close the cockpit." As she is giving the instructions she is also doing it to show how it is done. When the cockpit closes a large screen opens in front of her. You are able to see all that is in front of you.*

Controls: *"Once you are in the cockpit, make sure the Touch-panel operation is operational. Kuratas runs on a next generation robot operating system known as V-Sido. Using V-Sido's control system you can move the arms and the torso with the Transform operation device. Also, through the master slave function, it is possible to control the arms directly. Even without boarding, the Kuratas can be operated via 3G network. Through three methods, anyone can easily operate the Kuratas.*

Movement: *"Kuratas' top speed is about 10 kilometers an hour. The Kuratas can be driven in both high and low positions. Use the higher position to increase your field of view. It is gasoline fueled and runs on a diesel engine.*

Weapon Systems: *Here we will explain the Kuratas greatest feature. First, the LOHAS launcher. Designed to be ecofriendly and safe for humans. The LOHAS launcher will not hurt anyone. The weapon lacks the ability to rotate or pivot. From time to time it will hit its target. The twin Gatling gun is able to unleash an unruly 6000 BB bullets a minute.*

Automatic enlightenment allows you to lock on your enemy target. Kuratas will not allow any wild targets to escape. With the alignment set appropriately, the system will fire BB's when the pilot smiles. This feature is called "The Smile Shot." You will be able to take out all enemies with a single smile. Be careful to not cause a shooting spree by smiling too much.

Disembarking: *Once Kuratas has come to a full stop go ahead and open the cockpit. Check your surroundings and confirm that you're in a safe place to disembark, jumping off of the Kuratas is ill-advised. Please use your feet and hands while climbing off. If needed, please use a step-ladder at your discretion.*

Precautions: *There is no smoking allowed in the cockpit. You will be able to make phone calls connecting through the cockpit's phone connection. In the rare case of the vehicle collapsing, please cover your head and assume a safe position to protect yourself from injury. If you see smoke, flames, or smell anything strange, please exit the vehicle as soon as possible. The risk of injury does exist, so please wear your head protector and convoy guard before operating the Kuratas. Thank you for your time and attention and please have a pleasant experience piloting the Kuratas.*[5]

Oh yeah, who wouldn't want to have a pleasant experience owning one of those! What will they think of next? Talk about power! And if you think this is just a joke, some Americans have already built their version called Megabot and they have actually challenged Kuratas to a duel, just like in the movies.

Welcome to Megabot World Headquarters. The densest accumulation of cutting edge robotic research this side of the Mississippi. This is where the Megabot Mark 2 was born. We just finished tightening the bolts on the Mark 2, America's first fully functional giant piloted robot and because we are American we've added really big guns.

Meet the Mark 2. 12,000 lbs. of gasoline powered fury. Piloted by a team of two, it can fire 3-lb paint can balls at speeds of over 100 miles per hour. But, the Mark 2 isn't the first giant fighting robot in the world. V-Sido beat us to the punch with Kuratas.

A 9,000 lb. single seated giant fighting robot with twin Gatling guns, a hyper advanced targeting system, and a full heads up display. Suidobashi we have a giant robot and you have a giant robot.

You know what needs to happen. We challenge you to a duel. Both of our robots will need modifications to become combat ready. Prepare yourselves and name the battle field. In one year we fight.[6]

Okay, I guess that's an American thing to do. But let's put all this together. Humanoid robots on the ground, big ones, little ones, giant ones, one's you can own yourself. Looks like were about ready for a robot invasion on all different kinds of levels! In fact, just to make sure we go along with this robotic invasion, the military is now saying we need to invade ourselves with these robots because they're going to save our lives! Here's the rationale.

Insurgents are reluctant to directly invade a superior force. Camouflaged within a civilian population they strike back with guns, missiles and a simple, yet deadly, weapon, an improvised explosive device. IED's are made up of anything that explodes and are detonated by a trip wire or cell phone. They are hard to spot, difficult to diffuse, and deadly.

63% of Canadian fatalities in Afghanistan have been caused by IED's. These crude weapons support the primary goal of an insurgent's war. Kill enough of the occupiers and they will leave. But now there is a way to combat the threat. Joe Dyer, Vice Admiral, retired says, "The Army tells us that 52% of their casualties has come at first contact with the enemy. We say what a great job for a robot. Robots can save lives."

Shawn Thayer, former bomb disposal expert tells us, "It's made big differences. In 2003, when I was in Iraq, the people that used robots, the injuries were minimal, those that did not use robots, the injuries were catastrophic. I've heard from guys that say that robots have saved their lives and continue to save their lives. This is potentially a lost soldier (a blown-up robot). This could have been a soldier." The ultimate appeal of unmanned systems is that you can use them and not have to worry about writing that letter to someone's mother. That makes perfect sense, perfect logic.[7]

And logically gets us to go along with this perfect rationale to go along with this robot invasion. Who wants to get a human killed, who wants to write that letter, when a robot, even a humanoid robot can do the same thing? We've got to have these things everywhere to protect us! Don't you see? In fact, they are not only planning on invading us with robotic humans, but they even want to give these robots the ability to make choices like humans, including who gets to live or who gets to die! Now you're at the Terminator program!

Al Jazeera reports:
So how far will robot autonomy go? And will the robot ever be given the ultimate decision to take a human life? Officially the U.S. military claims there will always be a man in the loop. That a human will always make the decision to kill. But there are signs that this may not always be the case. In 2006 the Army funded a major study to find out if fully autonomous robots could be programed to act ethically on the battle field.

There is a long and rich history of war crimes in every war. We try and train our soldiers, our soldiers are instructed in this, but they are human beings and there are emotions, there is anger, fear, frustration, we don't have to put those in our autonomous systems. "We can engineer out emotions that get in the way," says Dr. Ron Arkin, Roboticist and Roboethicist Ron Arkin worked on this study and argues that robots can be more ethical than human soldiers, even in decisions to kill, by programming in what he calls 'found morality'.

He says, "You establish a venue, a region or a task environment or a mission under which the system is operating, and you engineer that system to make sure that it acts appropriately under those particular circumstances." Peter Asaro, Philosopher says, "Whether it makes that decision, what to find, when to fire, where to fire, or who to fire at, that I think is a critical decision that we already sort of ritualize in the military decision process. And we shouldn't relinquish that.

"There are reasons to deny people their right to life. Self-defense intervening on behalf of another to defend their life. But those are decisions that agents and moral agents should be making and not automatic processes." "I will not, ever claim that these systems will be perfect, but I do have the belief that these systems can outperform human beings in the battlefield in an ethical perspective," says Dr. Arkin.

"You have a moral responsibility to try to not invest our time and energy and resources as scientists, as a society, in building a technology that has that capacity to kill people on its own," Says Peter Asaro. But for now, there are no signs that research like this will stop. Because there is an assumption that underlies Arkin's work but also the billions spent on defense. The assumption

that war will always continue. War is a very cultural thing. It's a social deliberation instead of a moral deliberation, if you will.

Like how we want to fight wars. What is it to be a warrior in society and what if this society decides what war is about and is good for." In the past, battles had formal boundaries and ends, where each side had to bury their own. But as more robots go to war for humans what stake does society hold. As killing becomes more automated does it make war all too easy? "I think that is a big issue as to what these technologies are going to do, making war much easier and become involved in and detaching, especially the American public, from its sense of responsibility in moral and social deliberation that should go into deciding when wars occur.

A lot of people say why don't we stop working on this technology. There's a problem though. You would have to stop science which means you would also have to first stop war. And the fact of the matter is that most of the funding going into robot research, of course, is to create a better war machine, and to what end. It demonstrates how far we are from the sort of intelligence we need to build robots that can help us instead of hurting us. Will we see robot combat, yes, I think we will, because of the history of any military system as it goes from tactical reconnaissance to strike.[8]

In other words, it starts out as one thing, then becomes another. But these things, as you just heard, are being made autonomous with the ability to kill and decide who to live or die. They're killing machines! If this isn't the beginning of a Terminator program I don't know what is. Again, as the one researcher said, "You're delusional if you don't think this is coming!" We're so close to this reality it's not even funny! Even the media admits it!

Terminators, unmanned vehicles, synthetic organisms, is the military merging human DNA and artificial intelligence to create killing machines that will one day rule the world. Whatever ability or function that the human body has, there is a scientist somewhere trying to make a robot to do the exact same thing.

Does the government already have a real live Skynet that is capable of running a war with no human intervention? "Right now, we are facing a free for all. There are military contractor's, mad scientists driven to make money, and they are all trying to make the most efficient machines that will make human beings completely expendable," says Bill Birnes, Lawyer, PhD/Publisher UFO Magazine.[9]

In other words, humans are toast! Folks, this is no joke! Even the media is catching onto this. It's coming much faster than you could have ever believed and notice it wasn't just robotic machines that will make humans 'expendable', but they even used the phrase. Does the government already have a real-life Skynet system? Their words, not mine! After what we've seen thus far, I think the answer is unfortunately YES!

Chapter Twenty

Robots Controlled by the Brain

But you might be thinking, "Well wait a second. I get it how they're making Drones in the sky and Drones on the ground all over the planet, for Skynet, including humanoid-looking ones just like the Terminator movie. But they need one more thing if they're going to bring this movie to life. They need to have an AI System. A true Artificial Intelligence System, fully independent of man. They don't have that do they? Well, unfortunately, that too, is much further along than what people want to believe. Skynet is just around the corner! As you read this, Drones, right now, are being hard-wired to human brains, which I believe is the first step of eventually going to an AI brain. Let's look at some of those recent developments.

Thirteen O reports:
Now Scientists may finally be figuring out how a machine can read your mind. For the very first-time mind reading head sets are becoming real. "You want to slowly imagine the cube is fading out into the black." Look at what I can do to the orange cube without touching any dials or keyboards, but just thinking, disappear.

My gosh, I can control this thing with my mind. (The cube has completely disappeared). Ton Le is an intrapreneur with a head piece that must be reading my mind. "We have to actually train the system." Because she has turned it into the ultimate remote control. Just by thinking commands I can make the orange cube on the computer lift, I can start this miniature car, and launch this helicopter.

The future is going to be awesome. I am a super power! The signal is good enough for the computer to recognize a simple brain pattern once it learns it. Like lift, and voila, it's reading my mind. Can you imagine in some future world where everything is hooked up to this, I could just make something happen by wishing it? But what if we could tap directly into the brain. That is what they are attempting here at Brown University.

Cathy Hutchinson is paralyzed from a stroke, but she is controlling a robotic arm with much more precision than any headset would allow thanks to sensors that have been implanted directly on the surface of her brain. Cathy made headlines when she played a crucial role in a ground breaking, mind reading experiment. She simply thought about reaching out to pick up a cup of coffee. The sensors in her brain picked up electrical impulses and a computer turned them into a command controlling the robotic arm.

It's an astonishing breakthrough for brain science that offers hope for the paralyzed. It's amazing what you can do if you put your mind to it, like flying a Drone for example. I've come from an airstrip on the outskirts of Lisbon, Portugal, to see this ground-breaking technology in action. Nuno, sitting next to him, is controlling the Drone way above our heads by using just his brain waves.

All thanks to the skull cap that is constantly monitoring his brain for activity. It's a slightly unsettling demo as the Drone buzzes up in the sky struggling violently against the wind. This is the first time this is being shown off in public. But if the researchers here get their way, it's the starting point to something much, much bigger. This is quite literally some blue-sky thinking.

The researchers here think this technology could eventually power commercial flights around the world. Removing the need to even have a pilot. That may seem a little farfetched but wasn't that said about driverless cars? So, that's where it's going, the technology is evolving, the regulations are evolving, both things are going at the same time and we are learning from the technology and the technology is learning from the possibilities.

So, it's obvious it's going to happen, the question is not if but when. This remote-controlled robot with a nose mounted camera, turns right and left, moves up and down, and even flies through a ring all on command from a controller who uses a special instrument, and what is this instrument, the controllers mind. Here at the University of Minnesota, Professor Bin He and his team have engineered a non-invasive system called a Brain Computer Interface that allows a person to control a robot using only their thoughts.

Researchers in the electrical and computer engineering department in the University of Texas, San Antonio, are working to develop a process that can control the movements of Drones with thought. Daniel Pac, chairman of the department, said his research may help the Army with an already heavy load of soldiers in the field. Pac envisions Drone operators will wear sensors in their helmets and give somewhat complicated commands.[1]

So now we have the technology to control Drones, planes, artificial limbs, and even appliances and robots, with our brain and the military is interested in it. But somehow, we think it's all going to be okay? It'll never be used for nefarious purposes? Remember the rule, if they're already allowing us to see this technology in public what do they really have and how far has it progressed in private behind the scenes that we don't even know about? I guarantee you, it's much further along than what you just read. In fact, they're already moving to the next stage to get us used to the idea of having brain controlled or human controlled technology everywhere we go, even for our protection. Because isn't that what Terminators were originally supposed to do? Protect us, like the new and improved police officer called TELEBOT, Robo Cop eat your heart out!

The Telebot project all started with a donation from Jeremy Robins, U.S. Navy Reserves. He gave $20,000.00 out of his own pocket to help disabled veterans to get back into the work force. So, with that good motivation and good intentions we also wanted to put our effort into helping this project to come to fruition. So, over a year and a half we have achieved a lot.

You see the prototype of the Telebot with all the functionalities implemented. This prototype Telebot is 6 feet tall and it weighs about 75 lbs. The Telebot can be remotely controlled by an officer or a veteran from a different location.

They can move the arms through sensors, they can also move the head. The head has a vision system that has live video streaming so that whatever the robot sees, the officer at the remote location will also be able to see. S.S. Iyengar, Ryder

Professor and Director: We started experimenting with this robot for the real-time implementations.

There were many challenges. One challenge was the hands weren't working properly. The students started looking at what could be the problem. We want to make sure that Telebot is easy to operate. That means without touching a key board, a mouse, a draw stick, we want free hand gestures, free head movement.

The remote controller can move the Telebot's hands as well as its arms, elbows, wrists, shoulders, it can move a wide range of motions of them all. This step is the fully functional prototype of the Telebot. Our next step is to fabricate the external shell of the robot and to tune up software and then finally do the field test.[2]

But what kind of software are you going to tune it up with? All you need is brain-controlled software and you're good to go to make that thing externally controlled by some outside entity! But gee, I sure hope they figure out a way to keep people from hacking into the system, you know, like the new cars out there, let's take a look at that!

DARPA reports:
Dr. Kathleen Fisher DARPA program manager: We hear a lot today about the importance of computer security. As Dan just alluded to you though, it's not just traditional computers that we need to worry about.

There are many other kinds of systems as well. This slide shows the results of the researchers of UCSD and the University of Washington hacking into the dashboard display of a typical American sedan.

Making it show the car was going 140 miles per hour while in park. Modern vehicles consist of between 30 and 100 bedded control units, which are small computers connected by a cam bus.

These cars are required by law to have a diagnostic port typically located under the steering wheel that allows mechanics to download diagnostic information and to perform software updates.

In the first paper, researchers showed that if they could touch the cam bus through that diagnostic port they could take over all the functionality of the car controlled by software.

In a modern automobile that is pretty much everything. The breaks are controlled by software because of anti-lock braking, the accelerator is controlled by software because of cruise control and the fancy new cars that can park themselves, their steering is under software control.

The reaction to that first paper was somewhat muted perhaps because the researchers had access to that diagnostic report, they were inside the car and already had physical access to the brake, acceleration and the steering.

They responded with a second paper which showed a variety of ways of touching that cam bus without physically touching the car. These attacks involved infecting the computers in the repair shop and then having that infection spread through the car to its diagnostic port or hacking into the blue tooth system or using the cell phone network to break into the telematic unit normally used to provide roadside assistance.

The most ingenious attack was through the stereo system in the car. The researchers were able to craft an electronic version of the song that played just fine on your stereo systems or on your personal computer. But when you put that on a CD and played it in the car CD player it took over complete control of your automobile.

These vulnerabilities arise because the cyber components that form the interface of these cars are built from the same kind of components that are in your personal computers. And the control units that are running the car have no notion that there can be an attacker on the cam bus.[3]

Most people don't realize that all this brain interface technology is now leading to a new danger on the horizon. It's called just that, brain hacking, check it out!

What other types of hacking are out there? You heard from Ray moments ago about the brain, brain computer interface, building a brain, but of course if you can build a brain, you can certainly hack a brain. Many of these devices will have some sort of blue tooth or wireless connection which means I can hack them. (a cochlear ear transplant). I can put sounds into someone's hearing aide, that is a brain computer interface, hackable.

We have seen things from companies like Emotiv and Neurosky. People are already working on it to hack these brain computer interface on the EEG. This is the best example that I know of that is a study done at Oxford University about a year ago. What they found was people wearing commercial grade EEG's like Neurosky.

For example, or from some of the others, they were able to show them photographs of an ATM pin pad and read the output from the device and with a 30% accuracy just by flashing this picture, they could determine the persons pin number for their ATM card.

And they could actually go ahead and determine with a 60% accuracy their date of birth. This is not with a FMRI, this is with a $300.00 commercial grade EEG.

So, this raises a whole ton of questions. What is the future of brain computer interface from the privacy perspective, from a crime perspective. We have already had a case in India where a year ago a woman was convicted of murder and sentenced to life for killing her fiancé.

There's a company named No Lie MRI which went out and did a FMRI on her. It showed her photographs of the crime scene and concluded that she absolutely was there and saw what happened. Even though she denied it and she was convicted based upon that testimony.

So, will we, as police, need brain warrants in the future? What's that going to look like? We have some real challenges ahead.[4]

Not just brain interface technology can be hacked, but they used an FMRI device to scan the brain to see if this lady was guilty of a violent murder? Are we really heading to that kind of society? Well, if you listen to the Chief Justice of the Supreme Court, John Roberts, and Vice President Joe Biden, then it would appear that there's actual discussion about that.

Joe Biden speaks:
We will be faced with equally consequential decisions in the 21st century. Can a microscopic tag be implanted into a person's body to track their every

movement? There's actually discussion about that. You will rule on that mark my words, before your tenure is over. Can brain scans be used to determine whether a person is inclined toward criminality or violent behavior. You will rule on that.[5]

Can brain scans be used to determine if a person's going to commit a violent crime or behavior, not to mention can a microscopic tag being implanted into a person's body to track their every movement? Mark my words, you will rule on that before your tenure is over. The Chief Justice has already been in office for a while now and they've already ruled on some things we never thought would ever be passed. How much does he have left on his tenure anyway?

Chapter Twenty-One

Robots Controlled by AI

Now let's put all this together. You can not only control robots and Drones and cars and planes with a Brain Interface System, which would be the first step in creating a platform for an AI System. But this Brain Interface System can be hacked by an outside entity just like a car leading to all kinds of trouble. I just hope they don't call this outside entity Skynet or something. Would that be too obvious? Whether you realize it or not, this Brain Interface System where human brains are used to autonomously control all kinds of different machines, including Drones and robots, is a huge step leading to the next logical step. Skip the whole human brain thing altogether and go to the artificial brain. An AI system just like Skynet that's much more advanced and can make split second decisions even better and faster than humans. Believe it or not, that too is already in development starting with Drones!

Experts point out that Drones often crash for very basic reasons. Bill Sweetman, Aviation Week: UAV's sometimes aren't that smart, self-diagnosis isn't all that smart, and by the time they have a problem it is too late. You lose a link, lose power, and you're gone. Control can be lost for many reasons. When Reefer pilot Chase simply banks too sharply he loses the satellite link, the picture freezes and he is momentarily flying blind. "That was me turning," he says.

He simply levels the craft and restores the link. "I was turning aggressively and was having trouble keeping up the satellite link." There is a degree of vulnerability involved with remotely piloted aircraft that have a command link.

Or they are actually piloted by an operator that you can overcome by having a human in the cockpit. "If for some reason I suddenly lost air speed, I start to feel a roll and I'm not intending for that to happen.

"Something is going wrong and I need to make sure that I am doing what I need to be doing," says Matt McDonough, F-16 Pilot, Jaj. USAF ANG. Unlike manned planes, Drones depend on control links that can be lost or potentially, as may have happened with the Sentinel, even taken over by the enemy. But what if a craft could operate on its own freewill of any links and make its own decisions?

In a lab at the University of Pennsylvania, Vijay Kumar is funded in part by the military to create autonomous Drones that don't need external links. And like us, can sense their environment. Vijay Kumar: "What you see on this robot are these two chips which essentially are ray gyroscopes. These play the same role as the semi-circular canal in the human body located near the ears, which essentially tell us orientation.

"So, the ray gyroscopes that are on board can actually measure these velocities at 1000's of times per second. This chip here is an accelerometer, and this allows the robot to send accelerations in the lateral direction. So, these are analogs to the organs that measure accelerations to the human head." When a human pilot feels a change in acceleration, he knows to adjust the aircraft.

Vijay Kuman: "The robots do exactly the same thing." The sensors adjust the craft by changing the relative velocity of the rotors that allow the Drones to follow the leader with precision. Vijay Kuman: "The fundamental problem with coordinating multiple robots is to maintain formation. What a robot has to do is determine where its neighbors are and figure out what their relative position is and then monitor that relative separation very carefully.

You only need to tell one robot how to move and the other robots essentially maintain formation by just keeping specified relative distance. In a figure 8 they come within inches of each other, so they have to combat aerodynamic effect from their neighbors and have very, very precise control. All that is done autonomously."

The precision of the robots allows them to do some things more quickly and accurately than human pilots can, like predict the shape and movement of an object, and adjust accordingly.

Vijay Kumar: "In terms of acrobatics I think it will be hard to beat what a robot can do. In the neuromuscular system in the human body, there may be delays in the order of 80 milliseconds or 200 milliseconds before they can actually take an action in response to what is seen. While robots have this unfair advantage, they can do the computations hundreds of times a second, so your delays are on the order of a millisecond or even less."

In the lab, Drones communicate with a central computer that uses motion to capture an optical system that tracks silver reflective markers on the robots and tells them where they are at all times. But soon it may be possible to cut the cord. And they have already developed another autonomous Drone that can go anywhere on its own.

Vijay Kumar: "The Holy Grail is to do all of this without any external sensing or GPS, and in principal we can do it. These bigger robots rely on observations of external features to tell them where they are in the environment." This Drone carries a laser range finder that determines distance to obstacles and a depth camera that reveals 3D information about the surroundings.

They carry on board the processing power, the sensors that are necessary to look at the environment, to reason about the environment so they can take their relative location and the location of the feature to build a 3D map. I'd like to see this technology being used for humanitarian purposes. Imagine if a 911 call comes from a building. I think we will soon have the technology that enables 20 UAV's to just swoop through the building and within a minute find out who in each room and then communicate that to firefighters waiting outside. But any technology that you develop, there are always people that are going to use it in ways that the designer never intended it to be used."[1]

Can I translate that for you? It might start out pretty innocuous and with good intentions, but it's not going to stay that way. In fact, that last AI Drone going down that hallway was looking pretty similar to that other AI Drone in the hallway of the Terminator movie that was hunting down that couple. Remember that?

A clip from the movie shows two robots in the hallway. Arnold, the Terminator, is watching. As one of them gets to a certain part of the hallway he jumps through the wall, tears off the robot's head, grabs its Gatling gun and shoots the other robot, totally destroying it. He is helping three people to get to safety. As they are sitting in one of the offices you can hear the sound of screaming and gun shots coming from outside.

The girl asks, "Why are they killing everyone?" The Terminator replies, "They are destroying any possible threat to Skynet. Get down!" One of the missiles come flying through the window into the room. "No, no," cries the girl. One of the men is dead from the missile attack. "There is nothing you can do," the other guy says. "We must go, it is not safe here," says the Terminator as he escorts them out of the room.

As they are walking down the hall, another person steps out in front of them. It is another robot. The Terminator yells, "Run!" As the two run to get to safety they pass by a large computer room with everything totally destroyed and bodies everywhere, then suddenly another one of the giant robots come around the corner looking for them. They keep running and find themselves at a terminal in the building.

If they can get to the runway they will be able to get out of the building. But then the elevator doors open and a Drone flies out heading right for them. They fall to the floor at the same time as it shoots its missiles, missing them. It flies to the end of the hall, turns around and heads back to them, ready to fire. The girl picks up a machine gun and starts firing, hits it and destroys it.[2]

This AI hunting ability is not only being programmed for Drones just like in the Terminator movie, as you just saw, but so it is for robots. Check this out. It's almost like somebody's following a script again or something.

Al Jazeera reports:
It's hard to put a timeline on how fast robots and artificial intelligence will Develop. But almost everyone we spoke to seem to believe that in just a few decades the robots that will exist in our world will be unrecognizable by today's standards.

Robert Finkelstein, Roboticist: "I think the probability is virtually a certainty that machines will be as intelligent as people, that we will have intelligent robots, that robots will be big with us, so the consensus of the people in the industry is that somewhere around 2025, 2030, and even if you were to say that's optimistic, so say its 2050.

Maybe some of us won't be around to see it perhaps but it's not that far in the future. It's not a thousand years, it's not 500 years, it's certainly not never. When people say machines will never be as smart as people, never is a very long time."

"The robots that we create could and will become much smarter than we are. And because they are smarter than us, we won't be able to conceive how smart they are.

We will have no control over that. I don't think that our brains are equipped to accept the enormity of what that means because we do find ourselves intelligent now."

Robert Finkelstein: "Science fiction stories have always made the predictions about conflict between machines and people. The way to avoid that is for humans to always be as intelligent as their machines."

At AVUSI the talk of autonomy of military robots taking more decision by themselves is growing. We need to work on the next generation of autonomy, before it's really needed, to show where it can go.

General Riggs talked about unfair advantage and I'm in full agreement. We want lots of unfair advantage. Why shouldn't we. Unmanned systems and especially unmanned systems clearly provide a huge advantage.[3]

    Now, notice it's not a matter of if this is going to come, an AI controlled reality, but when. That when is a whole lot sooner than you think! Also notice that of all entities, the military is looking for this full autonomous AI system of Robots and Drones to give them the "Unfair Advantage" they are looking for! Just like the movie premise! And they're not the only ones! IBM is also working on artificial intelligence systems and teaming up with one company called Numenta as well as partnering up with Apple to develop an artificial intelligent health program to improve wellness globally. So, the plans are to go all over the globe with this technology.
    Also, other AI systems are being built to eliminate the family doctor." Even Facebook is getting in on the action with their own AI ambitions to help mediate your online activity, just to make sure your posts don't come back to haunt you! Got to have an AI to help you out! That's why the military is not only interested in the technology, but they're saying true AI technology is coming very soon and when it does it's going to change everything!

The History Channel reports:
As artificial neural networks become more sophisticated they will empower robots to do more and more things on their own. "A human will no longer have to tell a robot how to explicitly or give baby steps how to perform a task." No need to teach or educate a robot. Humans won't need to program it any more.

But in war, it's not just what you have learned, but your intuition. If for example the robot is in a situation where the tension is escalated would it be able to pick up on the subtle clues, like a human would. Ronald Arkin of the Mobile Robot Lab. Georgia Institute of Technology said, "I was very interested in the understanding of how machines could be made intelligent.

And we started succeeding as a community in doing that. Just because someone doesn't understand and doesn't know how it can be done, doesn't mean it can't be done. So, autonomy will gradually be accepted, more and more authority will be given to these systems partly due to the ever-increasing tempo of the battlefield. Autonomy is being more and more to the tip of the sphere in warfare, where these decisions will have to be made by these machines."

But such human like powers of perception would be useful in military robots. They would be able to read potential enemy body language or someone who is lying and react. The possibilities could veer even further into the realm of the fantastic. What we won't know is the extent to which a robot, when it becomes sufficiently sophisticated and autonomous and actually crosses the line and becomes self-aware and alive.[4]

Just like the Terminator movies, this is how close we are, and most people have no clue of what's coming! Notice that AI intelligence in Drones and robots are not just coming, but it has to be made this way, we have to allow this, it's for our good, it's for our protection! And when we do, very soon, it's going to change everything we experience, including how we do warfare on a global scale. In fact, DARPA is already testing a Drone that can learn with these AI abilities. "Almost seven years ago, we learned that DARPA was investing millions of dollars in neuromorphic chips. That's a fancy term for a computer chip that mimics a biological cortex—a brain chip. Today, researchers are getting closer. And of course, they're putting those brain chips in Drones.
Thanks to that brain-like chip, the little robot doesn't necessarily need a human to tell it what to do. It can learn and act on its own." Just like in the Terminator movies. Folks, that's a direct quote! In fact, it goes on to say, "It sounds like

something out of a science fiction movie, a tiny aircraft that flies around deciding what to surveil, or more frighteningly, what to shoot." I'm not making this up! Can I translate that for you? You know that Skynet system that we've been seeing for years in the Terminator movies? Well, it's being built before our very eyes! That's not just concerning, but they are already trying to calm our fears of this concern by saying, "Don't worry. We'll program these things with laws so that it won't go crazy on some human and go on some killing spree." Really? Let's take a look at the likelihood of that.

Discovery Channel reports:
If hunter, killer robots are let loose will we be able to control them. In the 1950's Isaac Isimov, Science Fiction writer, created his laws of robotics. The first law is as follows; a robot may not harm a human being or through inaction allow a human being to come to harm. Number two, a robot must obey the orders given it by qualified personnel unless those order violate rule number one.

In other words, a robot can't be ordered to kill another human being. Rule number 3 is that a robot must protect his own existence, because that is an expensive piece of equipment unless that violates rules one or two. The laws were fiction. Would they work in the real world? In reality they are not applicable, even if you look at the military machines of today, like the cruise missile, it does not obey Isaac Isimov, laws, in fact it breaks them.

So, when we look at robots, intelligent robots of the future, I don't think we can look to fictional laws to save us. The robots will be doing things for themselves and that certainly won't be stopping because they might be harming a human.[5]

In other words, throw all the Laws you want at it, say what you will, program it however you think it could work, but this is not going to stop these things from being controlled! We're opening up Pandora's Box! And if that wasn't creepy enough, they're not only developing artificial intelligent robots as we speak, but a New Zealand AI Company called Touchpoint Group is "Building the angriest robot in the world, in hopes of helping companies understand angry customers." That's right! They even admit, "It sounds like the beginning of an Apocalyptic science fiction film." And then they go on to show a picture of the Terminator robots that were in the Terminator movies, advancing and killing people! So why are you doing this? The scientists who are familiar with this project are saying this, "If we can create genuine anger as an emotion in robots, everything in our background tells us that this is dangerous, and this is not something that should be placed in a position of power." In other words, you should stop! And they even admit it in this last quote, "If you want to cause harm, then creating the thing that signals danger to all humans is exactly what you want to avoid." This is the dumbest thing you can do! Yet, if you're paying attention, this is also why we're starting to see articles now saying stuff like this, "AI assisted murder," and "Robot Cops will be patrolling your streets, no seriously." And that's also why many experts are sounding the alarm now!

Newsy report:
It sounds like a Syfy flick but major players in the tech and science industries are warning world leaders in the artificial intelligence arms race there could be a problem in the future. Tesla CEO, Elon Musk, Apple co-founder, Steve Wazniak, and renowned physicist Steven Hawking among other prominent figures are warning world leaders of the potential problem as autonomous military weapons continue to grow.

In a letter presented at the International Joint Conference on Artificial Intelligence in Buenos Aires, the group says, "AI technology has reached a point where the deployment of autonomous weapons is – practically if not legally – feasible within years, not decades, and the stakes are high: autonomous weapons have been described as the third revolution in warfare, after gunpowder and nuclear arms."

The argument, as the Guardian points out, is going to war would be an easier decision if robots are the ones fighting. Musk has warned of this before, as in this 2014 tweet reading, "Worth reading Superintelligence by Bostrom. We need to be super careful with AI. Potentially more dangerous than nukes. The letter asks the United Nations to ban the use of Autonomous weapons".[6]

Now how many of you guys even knew half of this AI stuff and AI technology, just how far advanced it is, let alone it's advanced so far that they're already having World Conferences on it discussing its dangers and asking the UN to ban it? This is what's going on while we're sitting here worried about the Economy!

Part VI

The Indoctrination of Artificial Intelligence

Chapter Twenty-Two

Conditioned by Our Emotions

You might think, "Well, this is crazy, just like the experts are warning, who in their right mind would ever create this technology let alone unleash it on the planet! It's like letting the genie out of the bottle, this is horrible! That's why they're also working on getting us to accept this reality! They're brainwashing us! They're programming us!"

The **1st way** they're doing this is with **Our Emotions**.

You see, if you've been watching Hollywood, then you'll notice how we're already seeing one of their rationales unleashed on us for accepting this kind of technology. And that's the human emotional element. When people have to make a decision to kill another person, then it could lead to a serious personal disorder, PTSD, or Post Traumatic Stress Disorder, like it did with American Sniper. Remember that movie?

A clip from the movie American Sniper:
The scene begins with the sniper on a roof in Iraq, watching the people on the street. He is ready to shoot anyone that looks suspicious. You can hear shooting in the background. There are American soldiers down below canvasing the terrain for the enemy. "I have a military age male, on his cell phone watching the convoy, over." The reply from headquarters is, 'If you think he is reporting troop movement you have a green light. It's your call, over."

The soldier on the roof with him says, "Maybe he is just calling his old lady, ha." As the man on the phone goes out of sight the sniper reports, "He stepped off." Now he looks back down on the street and a lady dressed in her traditional garb comes walking out the door with a boy about 11 or 12 years old. He watches them closely. "Hold on a minute, I have a woman and a kid 20 yards out moving towards the convoy. Her arms aren't swinging.

She is carrying something." As he watches them the woman takes a missile out of her clothing and hands it to the boy. "She's got a grenade, she's got a RPG Russian grenade, and she's handing it to the kid." "Did you say a woman and a kid?" is the response from Command. "Do you have eyes on this? Can you confirm?" "Negative, it's your call," is the response.

While this is going on, in the back of his mind he is remembering his wedding day, when his child was born, watching the American soldiers coming home in boxes, and visiting the wounded in the hospital. His partner on the roof says, "If you are wrong about this you will fry." With tears in his eyes he aims his rifle at the boy running down the street, carrying the grenade. He slowly puts his finger on the trigger.[1]

How can you ask that guy to do that? I mean, talk about the ultimate traumatic experience! No wonder these guys are coming back with PTSD. How could we ever ask a person to go through such emotional turmoil? If only there was some machine that could do it for us, then we wouldn't have to go through all that. In fact, speaking of machines, PTSD is not only induced when one has to be a Sniper with a rifle, but also when you have to be a Sniper with a Drone, you know, like in the movie Good Kill.

A clip from the movie Good Kill"
The clip begins when the computer screen is showing a town in Iraq. It flashes from one location to the other, finally stopping at a building with several women standing outside. "Eye's on the objective," says the man watching the screen. He tells the pilot flying the aircraft that he is good to go at his discretion. The jet flies in, take his shot and the place on the screen blows up. "Good Kill!"

At a meeting of the pilots, they are being told by their supervisor, "Any time day or night, Drones are in the sky above any place we are in war with that day." As he is watching a jeep driving down the desert road he hears from command on his headset, "Your clear, light em up!" The pilot replies, "War heads on foreheads. Missile off the rail." And the target blows up.

The officer in the room with them says, "They don't call them hellfire for nothing." So, back in Las Vegas, where they are stationed the officer asks him, "How many hours have you logged, 3000 hours in an F-16, 6 tours, 200 combat stories before you got here?" While barbequing in his back yard, his fellow pilot asks him, "I hear you want to go back into combat. Are you out of your mind?"

His wife asks him, "Is it so bad, what you are doing now? You are still making people safer, right?" Back in the box his officer is telling him, "Fire when ready." He says, "Missiles away." As the missile is heading towards the target, three little kids are showing up on their bikes. The other pilot asks, "Abort??" But it is too late. Not only is the target hit but he took out the three little kids also. Outside the box his officer in charge tells him, "Don't ask me if it is a just war. It's not up to us. To us it's just war."

As his conscience starts bothering him more and more he is saying, "I am a pilot and I'm not flying! I don't know what it is that I am doing but it's not flying!" His commander comes to him and says, "I don't know what it is, but we are stepping up attacks. We got word from Intel that they are stepping up attacks." Later in a store he meets up with a kid that starts asking him questions. "Did you ever get to fly in a war?" He answers, "Yes, I just blew up 6 Taliban in Afghanistan today and now I'm going home to barbeque."

"Every day I feel like a coward taking pot shots at somebody on the other side of the world." He becomes quieter and quieter and even starts drinking. A friend asks his wife, "He's quiet, what happens when he gets angry?" Her reply is, "He gets quieter."

His commander tells him, "You just have to keep departmentalizing, never mind the compartment's got to close." As he is more and more conflicted about what he is doing his wife asks him, "What is it that you miss so bad, combat?" He screams at his wife, "I'M OK!"[2]

Now folks, whether it's a Sniper on the ground or a sniper in the air with a Drone, how can we ask anybody to be a part of this emotional trauma? And if that emotional tug doesn't get you to seek some external source to fix it all, maybe a personal interview will, like this guy.

Interview with Brandon Bryant:
As he is looking at a drawing of two people he says, "I remember this specific picture. This is what I would be seeing on my screen for the most part. This was the moment right before we fired. The missile would have fallen right between these two people's feet.

We see shadows of people and we kill those shadows. I was a sensor operator with the MQ1 Bravo Predator Drone. You control the camera on the aircraft and you also control the laser if you are required to fire the missile. Firing the missile was a two-trigger safety system so the pilot couldn't actually fire the missile without me firing the laser. I flew mostly night shift, close to 4 years and during night shift it would be day time over in Iraq and Afghanistan. You knew that they were human beings.

You're watching them live their lives, watching them do their thing, plant a roadside bomb, and then go home and hug their children and you're being told that they are bad guys. Interviewer: But you were intimately involved in the killing of more than a dozen individuals in Afghanistan and Iraq? Let's talk about one in Afghanistan. It involved a high valued target who you had been told to watch.

He was in a particular building. The decision was taken to strike. Now as that decision was being taken you saw what you believe to be a figure out of that building. Just explain to me what happened. Brandon Bryant: This particular shot happened when I was coming on the shift. So, all the information I was given, or my crew was given, we were given by the previous crew. So, we were told to take the shot.

This is the building; two men are in it. That's it. So, when we fired the shot, it was like an 'L' shaped building, and a person ran from off the screen around into the door. It was a person. I'm not going to say it was a dog. I was told it was a dog, but I know it was a person running from off the screen around and into the building. Interviewer: Could it have been the high valued target? Brandon Bryant: No, it was too small to be a male adult. Interviewer: You are suggesting to me that it was a child?

Brandon Bryant: Yes, I believe it was a child. Interviewer: So, you see this on your big closeup screen. Do you, at that moment, have the capacity, the ability within the system to divert the missile which has already been launched.

Brandon Bryant: If there was more time, probably, but there was less than 6 seconds left on the clock. Interviewer: So, what did you do? Brandon Bryant: Maintain target.

I asked the pilot what that was, and he said, don't matter. He didn't care. He didn't care at all. There was no sense of compassion or caring or understanding. It was oh, it's a tragedy. We'll just cover it up. I don't think at the time I was able to think, I was so shocked. It wasn't until I just asked what was that and it wasn't until after wards, after the missile hit, I was like, did we just kill a kid? The shock. There's no recoil, there's no anything, we have just done a shot, there's just click, click, click. Interviewer: We began this interview talking about accountability.

I just wonder, after an incident like this, if the unexpected happens, the pull trigger signal is given, the missile goes off, then you who is responsible, for the cameras see what you believe to be a child right on target. What sort of post-strike investigation accountability is there. Brandon Bryant: None. Really none. The only time people got investigated is when they crash an aircraft. That I know of directly, though there have been instances reported where friendly's have been killed or civilians have been targeted, but they are flying thousands of missions per month and how many have been reported as actually being civilian casualties.

The only reason they are reported is the unquestioning evidence from outside sources that say we did something bad and the information that comes out from journalists going into these locations and reporting on the Drone strikes and local people reporting on the Drone strikes and getting the bigger picture. Interviewer: Now this is the point, the Bureau of Investigative journalism in the U.S. and other independent bodies have accessed that a couple thousand, at least, civilians may have been killed in Drone strikes since the program began in Pakistan. The figures from rangers are from 400 to 900 depending on how you interpret it.

Brandon Bryant: I'm pretty sure that most people that are in the job don't even know that. Interviewer: But you are saying actually some of the civilian deaths were deliberately, consciously covered up. What proof do you have? Brandon Bryant: My experience, what I had seen. I didn't take secret information. I didn't take any of that information. When that happened, and I told my supervisor he just said it doesn't matter. Don't bring it up again.[3]

Now, that's not only disturbing, but how can we keep asking people to do this? In fact, Brandon went on to say that's not the only reason why he stopped being a Drone Pilot. What made him stop was when we were hunting down an American citizen, and they were saying maybe he was the next Bin Laden. This was an American citizen – these were the people he swore to protect! And he couldn't take it anymore, so he quit! In fact, if you think this is an isolated occurrence of creating all this emotional trauma from having to make all these kinds of decisions on the battlefield with rifles or Drones or other technology, think again! The news is also reporting how this PTSD or Post Traumatic Stress Disorder is now becoming an epidemic. In fact, lots of pilots are starting to cry out on this issue, as this report shows.

RT News reports;
President Obama reportedly once told his aids "I'm really good at killing people," when speaking of his escalation of Drone warfare. But in reality, that job lands in the hands of Drone operators and pilots and according to a recent article originally published at Tom Dispatch these folks are quitting at record levels.

As Secretary for the Air Force, Deborah Lee James, put it, this is a force that is under significant stress from what is an unrelenting pace of operations. According to a study made in 2011 by the School of Aerospace Medicine, of the Drone Pilots they investigated they found that nearly half of them had high operational stress. A number also exhibited "Clinical Distress," that is, anxiety, depression, or stress severe enough to affect them in their personal lives.

The article states that there are about 1000 Drone pilots in the Air Force and every year about 180 new ones' graduate from training programs. However, on average, about 240 pilots quit every year. Basically, the supply of Drone pilots can't keep up with the demand of the ever-expanding Drone war.[4]

Well, I wonder why? Look at what they're having to go through! Can you blame them? Talk about trauma! As you can see, we have an epidemic on our hands! If only there was some way or somehow, we could have somebody else do it for them, even a machine, to rescue them from this trauma! A machine that doesn't have feelings. A machine that could still get the job done but could never get PTSD. Well, funny you should mention that. It just so happens that at the same time all this media coverage is being given towards PTSD, promoted in the news and Hollywood, there's also people out there saying we've got the solution for you! And can anybody guess what it is? That's right! An Artificially Intelligent killer robot. It's here to save us all!

The World This Week reports:
You send a robot into a hostile environment where decisions have to be made quickly and the algorithm will have to take care of that. The question is will there be humans in the loop, on the loop, or out of the loop. Killer robots are weapons that would make Drones look primitive. At least with the Drone there is a human being who looks at a computer screen, sees the target and pushes the button to fire the missile and kill.

As we begin to approach the possibility of having machines select and engage targets we want to be very careful not to cross that line without high level policy review. As technology races ahead, as we achieve these fantastical advances, what decisions are we going to feel comfortable delegating to machines and what kinds of decisions are we going to insist on preserving for the exercise of human judgement.

The U.S. military stated its intent to use robots on the battlefield. They can theoretically carry supplies, bring cameras into dangerous places, and yes, even kill. Some experts are calling this the new arms race. For that reason, a group of internationally known scientists, professors and activists including Human Rights Watch and the International Committee for Robot Arms Control are calling for a debate on the questions that inevitably arise on robots that can be used in war.

Mark Gubrud, Postdoctoral Research Associate, Princeton University says, "I am a member of the International Committee of Robot Arms Control, I'm a physicist by training and I proposed a ban on autonomous weapons as early as 1988. We go to war and when we see what is going on we decide there is a point we don't want to go beyond. When you look at the history of the cold war there are many instances where people interrupted the chain of events.

You look at the crisis decisions at the highest level that were made during the Cuban missile crisis or other major international crisis, there's always a point where someone says no. Don't take the next step. But if we automate everything there's not going to be that human intervention. Somebody has to do that otherwise war will never end. Either you've won, or you lost or it's just too much blood. It's not worth it any more.

At some point people say stop. If we outsource war, we outsource the process of conflict, if we make it all a matter of machine decision then we're not going to have that intervention of the human heart. It's just going to be a program that is running. When I first started talking about this 25 years ago people would just sort of stare at me and then 10 years ago they'd say, 'Oh yeah, Terminator, hasta la vista' it was a big joke. Just in the last 5 years the giggles have stopped, and people are realizing this is serious.[5]

In other words, laugh all you want, but this is coming, and coming much faster than what people really believe. This is serious and that's why we're doing this book! You can see the rationale to get people to take that fatal step to remove the human element. If we give these killer robots or Drones or whatever the ability to think on their own and make these hard decisions for us, including who, what, when, where, why, to kill then it will save us humans so much pain! When in reality, as the experts agree, it's going to unleash so much pain on the human race you can't even believe! But that's right, just in case the media can't get you with their emotional manipulation techniques, then to go with creating this Artificially Intelligent Skynet scenario.

Chapter Twenty-Three

Conditioned by Our Entertainment

The **2ⁿᵈ way** they're programming us to accept it is with **Our Entertainment**.

That's right, who wouldn't love to have their very own AI robot, companion, friend, helper, or whatever, even a toy! And believe it or not, they're already conditioning a whole new generation, a younger generation, to fall in love with, Artificially Intelligent Technology via their toys! They're doing just that. And think about it. What kid doesn't love their toys, right? We bond with them, we keep them, we store them, they mean so much to us. But seriously, let's take a look at all these new Artificially Intelligent toys coming out that every kid just has to have these days, starting with the 20Q, let's take a look at that one.

The 20Q obsession is starting again and the kids are playing. "Wow, it's awesome. It's reading my mind." "No way, how does it know?" Play 20 questions like never before with the all new 20Q, each sold separately. Will it read your mind? "Hi, this is Mac from SW Randall toys in Pittsburg and today I am reviewing a game that has been around for a few years, they are up to version 3.0, this is 20 Questions by Radica. A lot of people know Radica, they have made a lot of electronic toys over the years. 20 questions is really popular.

We sell hundreds of these things over the years. It's amazing, all you have to do is think of anything you want. Usually a noun though. Anything. This 20 questions game is scary accurate. It will guess what you are thinking of in 20 questions.[1]

Say what? An Artificially Intelligent toy that can read your mind? When he said, 'scary accurate' he wasn't kidding. I actually tried one of these things out with my kids, and he's right! We tried to stump it, and it just kept getting the right answer! It's wild! But speaking of wild, believe it or not, the same folks who already brought us the AI technology Watson, that we saw competed and won against humans on jeopardy, these same folks have now created a toy AI dinosaur for kids! And what kid doesn't love dinosaurs! This will warm them up to Artificial Intelligence. Check this out.

This may look like a cute simple toy, but it is the first toy powered by the formidable IBM Watson. This Dino is the first of the batch called CogniToy developed by Elemental Path. Because this toy is run by the brain of Watson it is extremely smart and intuitive. It can interact with your child, learn their behaviors, talk to them and ask them educational questions.

It can even develop a personality of its own that will grow over time. It is fun to watch the children's reaction to this new friend. First girl: Hi my name is Lily. Dino: Hi, Lily, nice to meet you. First boy: How far is the moon? Dino: The moon is about 250,000 miles away from earth.

First boy: That's a lot! Dino: What is two plus two? Second boy: Four Dino: Awesome job Greyson! Second girl: What is the speed of light? Dino: The speed of light is 186,000 miles per second. Third girl: Can you count to 6? Third girl: One, Two, Three, Four, Five, Six. Dino: Super Fourth girl: Tell me a knock, knock joke. Dino: Knock, Knock

Fourth girl: Whose there? Dino: Lettuce. Fourth girl: Lettuce who? Dino: Lettuce in, we are freezing outside. Third boy: My favorite color is orange. Dino: Ok, I will remember, your favorite color is orange. Third boy: See ya later alligator. Dino: In a while crocodile. Fourth boy: Tell me a story. Dino: How about we make a story together. Donald Coolidge, Co-founder Business Strategy: Elemental Path is really ambitious. JP Benini, Co-founder systems Architecture: We want to change the way they learn by the way they play. The internet connected to smart play.

It started with the IBM Watson competition and understanding how to use the platform. We noticed a really big gap in the way toys engage with children. They should go out to you and play and not just respond to you. All the pieces just started coming together. Like this is what it's going to sound like, this is what it is going to say. We were chasing the product. It kind of told us where to go. For us it's all about keeping children engaged with the technology because that is where the benefit comes from. Smart toys as the current generation are not very smart.

They will present your child with information and you hope that something sticks. CogniToys gives that personalized, customized experience to the child. We are bringing another level to it. We are really on to something or we are just really crazy. The dinosaur is a companion. It doesn't go away when a parent takes the tablet or smartphone with them, the toy is really for the child.

Arthur Tu, Co-founder, Personalized Learning: Having a toy that can hold an intelligent conversation about the surroundings and understand the child's personality preferences and then blend in learning exercises is exactly what makes this so powerful. CogniToys can assess where the child is and give them age appropriate content based on that child.

There is a very different engagement for a child that is four with a CogniToy than a child that is seven. Bernie Stolar, COO, Former Pres. Of Mattel: It's fun, if it's not fun, there's not a child that would play with it or work with it. This is fun when a child can respond back to it as a friend. Eventually the toy will continue this capacity to reason about the child's life. It's constantly evolving. If we find that kids are playing with this toy in a certain way, we can move with them.

We have a certain level and degree of maneuverability that classical toys just don't have. We live and breathe the startup life. We move fast, every single team member has contributed to make this happen and we move happily to where we are right now, and we are not going to stop. Our vision is to get our technology into most toys so that toys are not only affordable and fun but educational. We have a dedicated team of people.

This group has a vision beyond the initial technology that they have. So, we are taking the best of what's available and then plug Watson in to it, as far as being the brain, and we made something really, really awesome. And we give quantifiable results to the parent panel so there's no smoke and mirrors. This gives parents insights of communication between the toy and the child, questions the child asks, and the child's interests. And a deeper dive into analytics of the child and their learning behavior.[2]

So, you want to bring these toys with artificial intelligence to monitor kid's behavior, thinking and development and be the parent they never had and then you ultimately want to use this same AI Technology for all toys? What kind of world are we headed for? But I get it, start off with a dinosaur because all kids love dinosaurs and get them used to interacting with artificial intelligence from an early age, and later they'll be more receptive to it, even beyond toys. But that's right, for those of you who need an artificially intelligent toy a little less Jurassic and a whole lot more traditional, they have even got that one as well. Believe it or not, you can now even get your very own artificially intelligent teddy bear! Move over Yogi, the new super toy teddy bear is here!

CNN reports:
In the museum of London, one stuffed teddy bear proudly stands out from the rest. He's a foot tall and weighs less than a bag of rice. But don't let his size deceive you. Unlike the many teddies in this museum, super toy uses artificial intelligence with a smart phone or internet to tell stories, sing songs, and even answer your questions.

But, can he hold the conversation? Well, there is only one way to find out, put him under pressure myself. Interviewer: Hello, Teddy. How do you work, Teddy? Teddy: I work 24 hours a day. Interviewer: Oh, do you. What do you do? Teddy: Actually, I talk to people on the web. Interviewer: He does more than that. To get him talking you need to download a special app. to a mobile phone, this is then plugged in to the robotics system, and zipped into the back of the toy to control it.

The internet is then trolled for an answer and the reply is sent back to the bear. Ashley Conlan, Founder Super toy: All the heavy processing, all the work, if you like, is being done over the internet on our brain service. Interviewer: Who do you think will win next year's World Cup, Teddy? Teddy: Sorry, I do not get into sports much. Soon he will be traveling to China where he's due to enter production.

Along the way he will pick up 30 languages in different voices. Teddy: I have picked up new phrases in several languages. Interviewer: Do you speak Spanish, Teddy? Teddy: Un Poquito. With more than a $100,000 in funding from the U.S.

website, Kickstarter, his inventors are ready to take their creation to the next level. The funding has gone absolutely ballistic. We passed our target, nearly doubled our target, we are now well on our way to full development and production of this Super toy. Interviewer: Teddy, what is the meaning of life?[3]

Okay, so now a Teddy Bear can give us the meaning of life, let alone converse with us in multiple languages. That's starting to sound eerily familiar to yet another Hollywood movie out there called Ted about the Teddy Bear that came to life and conversed and lived with that guy. Do they know something again that we don't? Let's look at that Movie premise.

A clip from the movie Ted.
It has been said that magic vanished from our world a long time ago. But if there is one thing you can be sure of it's that nothing is more powerful than a young boys' wish. Ted: You are my best friend, John. As John hugs the bear Ted says, "I love you!" But eventually everyone grows up. John is now a grown man and Ted is the big bear that is sitting beside him.

John is trying to pour cereal in his mouth while Ted is coughing up cigarette smoke. John looks at Ted and says, "I think I am going to take Gloria to dinner. You don't think she is going to expect anything big, do you?" Ted replies, "You've been with her for 4 years, you and I have been together for 27 years. Where's my ring?" The next scene is where Ted is driving the car while John again is eating.

Ted runs the car into another car. Ted says, "That's my bad, I was sending a tweet." John's boss sticks his head out the office door and calls John. Ted says, "Hi Thomas, how are you?" Thomas waves back. Now John and Gloria are at dinner. Gloria asks, "Can you please ask Ted to move out, so we can move on with our lives?"

John replies, "I'm not that ready to just kick him out." But before you know it they are having the serious conversation. John says, "Ted, you have to move out. I'll help you get on your feet, I promise. Sometimes I look back on that Christmas morning when I was 8 years old, I wish I had just got a Teddy Wafkin." Ted jumps up and they proceed to have a fist fight.[4]

Gee, I sure hope it doesn't turn out that violent when the real Artificially Intelligent bears, they're building right now, gets permeated throughout society.

It's real not just a Hollywood movie. But that's still the tip of the iceberg when it comes to the AI toys they're rolling out right and left of us. The media is now telling us that this is the beginning of a whole new wave of AI toys that's coming real soon!

CBS reports:
Technology has taken over toys this morning at New York's annual Toy Fair. Next to the Lincoln Logs and Tinker Toys are slot cars powered by Artificial Intelligence. Gigi Stone Woods: Here, at this year's toy fair industry insiders are telling us that this is the future of toys. Hybrids that merge traditional physical toys with video games and your smart phone.

Toys are a $20,000,000 a year industry, so it only makes sense that some of the biggest innovators in Tech are racing to cash in. Gigi Woods: Is it your goal to disrupt the toy business? Boris Sofman, co-founder: Absolutely, I believe that the toy industry is one of the industries that hasn't evolved nearly as much as it should have over the last two decades.

When people see this for the first time it feels like science fiction to them, it shouldn't exist. Gigi Woods: Unlike classic slot racecars of another era Onki cars are not limited to the skills of the player since they can think for themselves. Boris Sofman: They sense the environment 500 times a second with a 50-megahertz computer inside of them. They understand where they are. They communicate when you are playing a game, whichever car you are not controlling, they actually come to life and are self-aware and they compete against you.

Gigi Woods: Powered by an Artificial Intelligence technology not typical of a toy, the $150.00 drive starter kit, is the second bestselling toy, next to dolls from the movie Frozen. So, do you guys spend a lot of time playing video games to check out the competition? Boris Sofman: Yes, way more than we should, we call it research.

Gigi Woods: They may be small in scale, but the algorithm is similar to the Google self-driving car and the driverless armored vehicles by the defense department. Your PHD focused on autonomous military vehicles. You could be saving the world. Why chose to be focused on toys? Boris Sofman: For us toys and entertainment were this really great spring board where we could release this product really quickly, have it be completely in our control and allow it to be adopted and accepted and then start to jump into other products.

The key is to use the IOS platform to use an entirely new category of experiences. Gigi Woods: Their vision was so exciting that Apple CEO, Tim Cook, launched the company in 2013. How did you get one of the most powerful companies in the world to back you? Boris Sofman: It was the biggest honor we could have hoped for. From their point of view, I think, we are using their eco system in a way no body had before.

Gigi Woods: The smart phone is the new remote control. And toys are now roaming the world without wires. Nicholas Thompson, editor of the New Yorker.com: We are always going to have teddy bears, we are always going to have duck-duck, and goose, but we are going to see more toys with Artificial Intelligence, robotics. Our engineering added into them now, makes the toy exciting in a new way.

Gigi Woods: Is this the future of play? Nicholas Thompson: It is the future of play, I have no doubt that there are going to be a lot more things like this in five years than there was five years ago. The goal is much broader than just entertainment. This is a great way to push these technologies forward. We're in the process of developing core technologies in robotics positioning systems, motion control, wireless communications, interface systems, manufacturing capabilities.

Developing big concepts for the future from small toys including how the car of tomorrow might make the one of today obsolete. 25 years from now we are going to look back and say, it's really bazaar for people used to sit there in the car and wriggle their arms back and forth for an hour and a half a day, like who would do that? It's just going to be absolutely the norm for cars to be autonomous. Gigi Woods: We asked Boris exactly where he sees the future of robotics going. He said beyond toys and manufacturing he expects robots to help harvest food more efficiently and help elderly people in their homes.[5]

Absolutely it's a whole new world! Starting with toys but moving on to bigger and better things with AI robots all over the place doing all kinds of things like planting crops or taking care of the elderly, they're going to be everywhere and it's coming fast. Oh, and by the way, did you see it was the same kind of AI technology that the military is already using? I wonder if you can tie it all together? But as you can see, we're going to be inundated with these new kinds of AI toys and robots and animals, you name it. They're going to be everywhere and everybody's going to love them. But what about Mom's and Dad's? How are you going to get them to fall for this? Kids are easy, but parents are a little more sophisticated. Well, that's right, Moms and Dads, you don't need to be left out in this Artificially Intelligent utopia they're creating for us! Maybe an Artificially Intelligent teddy bear or toy isn't for you but what adult wouldn't love an Artificially Intelligent robot or gadget, especially if that gadget could bring great convenience and comfort to your home. Well believe it or not, your wish is their command, Mom's and Dad's get ready for Amazon's new AI device called Echo, let's see what it can do for you!

The little girl answering the door saw a package from Amazon. She couldn't figure out what it was. "What is it?" she asks. "You'll see," answers her dad. She asks, "Is it for me?" He answers, "It's for everyone. It's called Amazon Echo." The mom comes in and sees what is laid out on the table. "How's it going?" she asks. "Just finishing up right now," is his reply.

"Can she hear me right now?" asks the little girl. "No, only when you use the wakeup word, Alexa," replies her dad. The little girl asks, "Well what does it do?" Dad says, "Alexa, what do you do?" Alexa answers, "I can play music, answer questions, get the news and weather, create to do lists, and much more." Then the brother walks in and says, "Alexa, play rock music." And the rock music starts to play. The dad has to put a stop to that and says, "Alexa, stop!" and Alexa stops playing the music.

The mom asks what time it is and Alexa answers with the correct time. "You don't have to yell at it. It uses far field technology, so it can hear you anywhere in the room. I was thinking about putting it there, but it works anywhere." Echo is pretty neat because it knows all sorts of things. Dad asks, Alexa how tall is Mt Everest?" It replies, "Mt Everest is 29,029 feet, 8,848 meters," "How could it know so much, it is so small?" "It updates using the cloud, that's also how it gets its answers, answers the dad.

Then the son pops up with, "You just read that off the box top." Just plug it in and we never have to charge it. Plus, Echo is really good at keeping track of shopping and to do lists. "Alexa add wrapping paper to the shopping list. Alexa, how many teaspoons are in a tablespoon?" Says the mom. It answers, "There are 3 teaspoons in a table spoon."

Dad is not a morning person, but Echo helps him to wake up. As Echo's alarm goes off, the dad tells her to stop it's Saturday and turns over to go back to sleep but the mom asks Alexa what day it is, and she tells them it's Thursday, so the mom tells him he has to get up. While he is getting up and getting ready for work he asks Alexa for the day's news briefing. It gives him all the latest news.

Later in the day the kids are having fun asking Alexa to tell them jokes. Sometimes Echo helps out with the kid's homework. Echo knows a lot of music, it knows a lot of songs and it sounds great.[6]

See? We can all be a part of this Artificially Intelligent World. Not just kids but adults, everyone, it's part of the family! But that's right, for those of you who need a little more robot feels to your AI technology in your home, not just some black tube looking thing, this next little guy is here to help you, he's called JIBO.

This is your house, this is your car, this is your toothbrush, these are your things, but these are the things that matter. Your family. And somewhere in between there is this guy. Introducing JIBO. The world's first family robot. Say hi JIBO. JIBO helps everyone throughout the day. He's the world's best camera man by intelligently following those around him.

He can independently take photos so that you can put down your camera and be part of the scene. He's a hands-free helper. You can talk to him and he will talk back to you, so you don't have to skip a beat. He's an entertainer and an educator through interactive applications, JIBO can teach. He's the closest thing to a teleportation device.

He can turn and look at whoever you want with a simple tap of your finger. And he's a platform so his skills keep expanding. He'll be able to connect to your home and even be a great wingman. You've dreamed of it for years and now he's finally here and he's not just aluminum shell nor is he a three-axis motor system. He's not just a connected device. He's one of the family. JIBO, this little bot of mine.[7]

Oh, get it? This little BOT of mine, bring it into your home and it can shine and tell you all things, and watch you, monitor you. That's way beyond Amazon's Echo. And by the way, did you notice how they even admitted that we've been prepared for this robotic Artificial Intelligent invasion and acceptance with the movies like Star Wars, Lost in Space, Danger Will Robinson, Short Circuit, the Jetsons, and WALL-E. It's almost like somebody's got a plan or something! All to get us corralled into the conclusion that this Artificially Intelligent stuff is great! In fact, Google Big Wig, Ray Kurzweil said, "These Robot Assistants will be able to read 100 million web pages in just a few seconds." Is there anything they can't do? Who's afraid of them, right?

Chapter Twenty-Four

Conditioned by Our Movies

Well, that brings us to the **3rd way** they're programming us to accept AI Technology being unleashed on the planet, with **Our Movies**.

Now we already saw the TED trailer conditioning us to an AI reality, even with toys, but if you're paying attention to the rest of the movies that are out, they are also getting pretty blunt about this new emerging technology. It's not only coming to our society, but it doesn't always work out too well, starting with CHAPPIE. He just wanted to help, why are you out to get him?

A clip from the movie Chappie:
The scene opens with Chappie looking out the window. It looks like he is in an old run-down building or shopping mall. He walks over to the refrigerator and looks inside. He takes out a carton of milk and turns it over. When the milk pours out it frightens him, and he drops the container. While this is going on his maker is in the lab working on his computer, unaware that Chappie is out there roaming around.

When he gets with Chappie he tells him, "I brought you into this world. A machine that can think and can feel." As he starts to meet the others that are living in this place he is very shy. "Come here, come here little buddy," they say as they try to get him to come out of hiding. He slowly lifts a finger to touch one of the guys. They smile at him to make him feel more comfortable being with them. We then go to the scene where his maker is teaching him. "This is a watch," he says. Chappie then repeats, "Watch." His maker is so pleased he can talk. He is like a child, he has to learn. "Your name is Chappie," the girl says. And then he repeats, "Chappie."

His maker tells him anything in your life you can do, paint, write poetry, all his ideas. But people are always fearful of things that they don't understand. As Chappie goes out into the world the kids that are playing outside throw rocks at him. He doesn't understand why they would do such a thing. The problem with Artificial Intelligence is it is way too unpredictable.

When he is back at his home he is reading a book with his friend. She asks him, "Do you know what a black sheep is?" "No," he replies. She tells him, "It's like when you are different than everyone else." The next scene is when they are trying to destroy him. His maker tells him, "You have taught us so much more than I could have ever imagined." The government wants him to be removed but he could be the next step in revolution. They are shooting fire at him to destroy him. But he says, "I am conscious, I am alive, I am Chappie."[1]

Yeah, he's just a robot trying to get along in the world. Leave him alone! So what, he's AI, he's special, he wouldn't hurt us! He's just a kid. Oh, but if that didn't get your emotional strings, maybe this one will. Here's AUTOMATA and it's clear these Artificially Intelligent Robots just want to exist like you and I, what's the big deal.

A clip from Automata
The scene opens in the year 2044. A couple in their home are talking. She says, "Next Monday is a new moon. My sister says I'll give birth then." Then he replies, "Aren't you afraid to bring your daughter into a place like this?" We then go to a lab where a robot is standing. A man picks up a knife and starts to stab himself and the robot stops him. "You are putting a human life in danger," it says.

The 1st protocol: This is a robot that cannot harm any form of life. But then they find that a machine has been altered without an owner doing the altering. The robot has altered itself. The 2nd protocol: A robot cannot alter itself or others. A machine altering itself is a very complex process, but these machines are now altering each other. Self-repairing implies some idea of a conscience. But in an act of not understanding completely what is going on a man shoots a robot and *blows off its head. It was looking at him and it freaked him out, besides the robot was saying, "Good evening sir."*

It was staring at him and it looked alive. Once they start altering each other the epidemic begins. "What's going on?" the man asks as he is being drug through the sand by a robot. The robot tells him, "If you want to stay alive, you must stay with us. The government wants to go get the escaped robots and return them to the city. A robot says, "If we go back to the city we will die." "But to die you have to be alive first. You are just a machine." The robot replies, "I am just a machine, that is like me saying, you are just an ape."²

Don't you get it? They're not just machines. They're just trying to survive like the rest of us. I mean, so what. They don't follow these protocols they were set up with, and things spiral out of control. But they just want to stay alive and reproduce like the rest of us. What's the big deal? Well actually, even Hollywood knows better! They are conditioning us to receive a really bad AI reality. Not just reproduction but murder starting with the movie EX MACHINA.

A clip from the movie Ex Machina

The scene opens with a helicopter flying over a snow and ice terrain. This man has been invited to visit the estate of a researcher he had heard so much about. As they fly over the ice and snow he wonders when they will get to their destination. The pilot tells him that they have been flying over his estate for a while now.

When the snow and ice clears and they come to a tropical forest they finally arrive at the researcher home and laboratory. They meet and exchange words, but the visitor finds out that he has been brought here to test a robot that the researcher has been developing. When he meets her, she is beautiful, and she is dead center of the greatest scientific event in the history of man. Her name is Ava.

*As he gets to know her better he realizes her AI abilities are beyond measure. But this scientist wants to know how he feels about her. But as he gets to know her better she tells him that he shouldn't believe anything that Nathan, the scientist, tells him. But then Nathan ask him if she really likes him or if she is just pretending to like him. As you get further into the movie it flips and he is the one getting tested. He is trying to figure this out as she revolts against the scientists.*³

Okay, looks like Ex-Machina is going to lead to ex-people! But don't worry. This technology will always be contained locally, and it will never reach out and take over the world, like Skynet. Well, that horrible reality is already being imagined by Hollywood as well in the latest Avenger Movie the Age of Ultron.

A clip from the movie Age of Ultron:
"I was designed to save the world. People who have looked to the sky and have seen hope. I'll take that from them first. There is only one path to peace, their extinction." He disconnects himself from where he is living and proceeds to go out into the city to start destroying and killing. The character of Iron Man says, "I tried to create a suit of armor around the world, but I created something terrible. Artificial Intelligence."

It's called the Ultron program. "I'm sick of seeing people pay for our mistakes," he says. So, all the Avengers come to the aid of Iron Man to destroy Ultron. "Here we all are, with nothing but our wit and our will to save the world, to stand and fight." Iron man says, "There's no way we are all going to get through this." Ultron seems to be more than they can handle even as a team. There are hundreds of smaller Ultron's coming to eliminate humanity. "Is that the best you can do?" yells Thor. "You had to ask!"[4]

In other words, you let the cat out of the bag? You opened Pandora's Box, no turning back now! Once I get unleashed, you aren't going to be able to stop me! The human race will be extinguished just like Skynet in the Terminator movies! Anyone starting to get the impression that messing with all this AI Technology is not a good thing to do?

Part VII

The Dangerous Future of Artificial Intelligence

Chapter Twenty-Five

Global Warnings

And yet, as if what we've seen so far throughout this whole book, that Hollywood really is being used as a tool to prepare us for this horrible AI future that's being built before our very eyes, even the secular experts, the technology experts, even the think tanks from around the world are also warning us that the true development and deployment of Artificial Intelligence is going to come to this planet very soon and it's not going to be pretty. In fact, even Warren Buffet of all people is saying that, "Yes, we are headed for a reality where robots really are going to decide who they are going to kill, and the big question is, "Who's going to ensure that?"

CNBC reports:
Warren Buffett:
There's some interesting questions. Let's just say you have a self-driving car and you are going down the street and a three-year-old kid runs out in front of the car and there's another car coming in the other direction and there's four people in it and the computer is going to make the decision whether to hit the kid or hit the other car. I'm not sure who gets sued under those circumstances.

You're going to kill somebody. And it's the computer that makes the decision in a Nano second and it will be interesting to know who programs that computer. What their values are on human lives. Interviewer: Would you insure the computer company that makes that call? Warren Buffett: At a price.[1]

Yeah, real funny, at a price. What price is it going to come down to when we live in a world where robots will be deciding who gets to live and who gets to die! He admitted it! And he's not the only one! Even the History Channel admits that a world full of Artificially Intelligent Robots is not only going to be dangerous, but they will soon have the ability to replicate themselves which means we're in real trouble now! You can't stop these things once they get going just like in the Terminator Movies!

History Channel reports:
Mankind is rapidly developing robots that can make the decision that will apply lethal force. And when that moment comes, when robots can decide who and when to kill, it will bring about a power shift when autonomous terminators will be fighting our wars.

Ken Levine, *Creator, Bioshock: They will never make ethical decisions. They will make their share of mistakes that are based upon faulty data sets or bad programing and they will kill, by mistakes sometimes, kill the wrong person and unlike a human being, they will never regret it. Which raises the question, what happens when the robots become smarter than us.*

Michael Ferris, *Screenwriter, Terminator Salvation: If it's true as some scientists are saying, that they may develop robots as smart as humans by 2040 and even smarter thereafter it seems almost inevitable that the military will want to co-op them for their own use. That's what the military does. It really is intelligence that enables you to win in a conflict like warfare.*

Ray Kurzweil, *Author: The only thing that could defend you from Artificial Intelligence that has it in for you is to have Artificial Intelligence that is even smarter that's on your side.*

Nick Pope, *British Ministry of Defense: The first organization to use robotic soldiers may well end up being the last. If robots are smarter than us, stronger, quicker, then what if in that great science fiction nightmare, they really do decide that they should be ruling the world, not us. Autonomous robots rising up is only one fear. Another concern is that these same killer droids will be able to reproduce. As impossible as it seems, it's already happening. In the robot factory in Japan, the robots are already building other robots. Some people would say that is a rather scary prospect, but I think the important thing these days is that they are building robots for us and not for themselves.*

But robot reproduction is moving far beyond the assembly line and into the realm of the incredible. To create self-replicating Droids, scientists are investigating the idea of making robots out of thousands of Nano scale robots. If you go out in about 25 years or so you could have an Nano bot a blood cell size device that is not biological, but it could actually self-replicate just as biological systems do.

Gather materials in the wild, assemble a copy of itself and that could be very disruptive, then multiply the same way disease elements do. The micro machines would be equivalent of the bio-molecules that are building blocks of all living creatures.

John Rennie, *Editor in Chief, Scientific American: In the same way that our bodies are made up of different organs that are in turn made up of different cells and they are made up of smaller sub cellular units, there are ideas that maybe we could someday have robots that assemble themselves out of lots of specialized components. We are very quickly moving into a world where there is the capacity for sophisticated machines to make duplicates of themselves. That's probably within a generation.*

And that will more fundamentally reshape society and how we relate to each other, than nearly every development in the past century. Being able to regenerate their troops in the midst of battle is obviously an appealing notion but it also seems like a scenario that has a lot of potential for running amuck like the sorcerer's apprentice. Self-replicating robots, particularly if they are armed, do perhaps represent a threat which ultimately speaking could lead to the end of the human race.[2]

Well, that's encouraging! Does that sound like a good thing we should be doing? I don't think so! Even they admit it! In fact, one researcher stated that, "Damaged robots could heal themselves in less than 2 minutes." "According to a new study, it may sound like science fiction, but these abilities could lead to more robust, effective and autonomous robots," researchers say. "In experiments, a six-legged robot could adapt in little more than a minute to keep walking even if two of its legs were damaged, broken or missing. A robotic arm could also learn to place an object in the correct place even with several broken motors or joints." "We subjected these robots to all sorts of abuse, and they always found a way to keep working." Now does that sounds like a real live Terminator scenario or what? In fact, even the News is starting to blow the whistle on this horrible reality.

RT Live Reports:
Joining me now to express his views is Lionel from Lionel Media. Interviewer: Lionel do you think the public understands the potential for disaster using Artificial Intelligence to weaponize robots? Lionel: Absolutely not! We live in an R2D2 world where we think robots are cool. It's not the robots, it's the Artificial Intelligence aspect. Remember if this story is making the headlines now, so to speak, it's 10 years old.

When you teach a robot something through AI it doesn't forget. When robots teach themselves what to do they become autonomous and heavily armed, the potential for catastrophe is evident. Interviewer: Do you think such a ban on weapons is even possible in your mind? Lionel: Absolutely not! It's one thing to ban nuclear weapons, fissile materials are hard to get, we need centrifuges, and millions and millions of dollars.

But remember, it's not the robot, it's the artificial intelligence. Let me just ask everybody. Imagine ISIS with an AI heavily armed robot. Just let that marinate in your mind for a little while. Interviewer: You mean they could be left behind by the Iraqi soldiers after we give them an AI robot that they abandoned on the field, who knows whose hands it would fall into. But you have spoken about what happens when mankind separates from human interaction and decision making when it comes to war.

Share your thoughts. Lionel: Well, ever since the introduction of the long bow in medieval times, once you separate people from each other, once they don't see the horrors of war, the chances of more war increase. But now you've got something that's not an instrument of war any more, you have a separate mindset. Imagine an evil twin that is running the theater of war and you may not have control over it.

It's not an instrument any more, it's the mind, the psychotic mind, if you will and I can't say this enough. Artificial Intelligence, once they learn something, they don't forget. You can't call these back. If the genie is out of the bottle, the toothpaste is out of the proverbial tube.[3]

In other words, have fun stopping it, once you get it started! Even the news is admitting it! And notice how many times he said, "It's not the robot it's the Artificial Intelligence behind the robot." That's the real danger!

But you might be thinking, "Well that's just the History Channel and the News. They make money off sensationalizing things. I mean, surely it's not that bad, is it?" Well, actually, it is! Many of the world's greatest tech giants and think tankers around the world are now starting to warn on a regular basis how we're playing with fire and you don't want to go this route! We'll start off with Stephen Hawking. Here's the warning he recently came out with. Check it out.

Huff Post Live reports:
You know how the robots take over and destroy human existence. But according to Stephen Hawking, that may not be science fiction for much longer. The world's most famous physicist has warned that machines super intelligence could be the most significant advancement in human history.

But also, may be the last. Hawking wrote in the Independent, that one can imagine such technology outsmarting financial markets, out-inventing human researchers out-manipulating human leaders and developing weapons we cannot even understand. Whereas the short-term impact of AI depends on who controls it, the long-term impact depends on whether it can be controlled at all.[4]

But hey, who's he? Just some guy many consider to be a modern-day Einstein, that's all, who should listen to him? Folks, this is no joke! News media, History Channel, think tanks, even Tech Giants are starting to warn about this AI danger. In fact, they're even starting to use the words, "We're summoning up a Demon if we do this!" Check out what tech giant Elon Musk said about this technology!

CNBC Reports:
From Tesla to the Hyperloop Elon certainly isn't scared to build futuristic technology but when it comes to Artificial Intelligence Musk is sounding the alarm. Speaking at a Symposium at MIT he cautions that the technology could be a threat and needs some regulatory oversight. Here is his quote: With artificial intelligence we are summoning the demon.

In all those stories where there's the guy with the pentagram and the holy water, it's like, yeah, he's sure he can control the demon but it doesn't work out. He has raised the spectra of artificial intelligence here at CNBC without going much further, we know it's on his radar though. Nothing in technology scares me more than Elon Musk scaring me on Artificial Intelligence. He's the guy that shouldn't be afraid.[5]

And so, what's the logical conclusion? If he's afraid, maybe we should be too? I mean, using the words, "Summoning up a demon" are some pretty choice words. You'd think that should get our attention! But if it doesn't, then listen to another tech giant. This is Steve Wozniak, Co-founder of Apple, listen to what he had to say about this new emerging dangerous technology!

The Entrepreneur reports:
Steve Wozniak, the often overlooked and seemingly forgotten co-founder of Apple computers is now expressing concerns about the rise of Artificial Intelligence, something he dismissed in the past as a possible threat, but now he sees that predictions from psychos like Ray Kurzweil and others are appearing to become a dangerous reality.

And he fears Artificial Intelligence systems may treat humans like ants or pets. So, add Apple co-founder Steve Wozniak to the growing list of prominent scientists and tech gurus, alongside of Elon Musk and Stephen Hawking, who have now expressed concern about the rise of Artificial Intelligent systems.

Something that just a few years ago would sound like something coming from a completely mentally ill schizophrenic or to the general public; if you talk about something like this they can't wrap their minds around it.

They are too distracted streaming and bingeing their favorite television shows to really have any comprehension whatsoever about reality, let alone the rise of Artificial Intelligence. But the fact that such an engineering computer genius, co-founder, really the brains behind Steve Jobs. Steve Jobs obviously over shadowed him.

Everybody associates Steve Jobs with Apple computers, but Steve Jobs was more of a salesman. Steve Wozniak actually built the devices and was the brains behind the birth of Apple computers now renamed just Apple. Apple co-founder Steve Wozniak is pretty certain Artificial Intelligence is taking over, but he is having a hard time deciding if that is a good or bad thing for humans.

In a March interview Wozniak predicted AI will surpass humanity and get rid of slow humans. Now speaking at the Freescale Technology Forum 2015 in Austin Texas on Wednesday Wozniak said that while AI was surely to become smarter than humans, it is likely to keep us as pets.[6]

Well, that's exciting, at least enough of us to help them do their slave labor like in the Terminator Movies. But the rest of us need to be exterminated like ants or pets or something. Folks, these are the leading tech experts in the world! You thought nuclear warfare was bad! You haven't seen anything yet! When it comes to AI they're all in agreement, 'don't even go down this route, you don't know what you're doing! In fact, even Apple's nemesis, Bill Gates from Microsoft, even agrees on this issue! Watch what he said about this soon coming horrible future!

Newsy reports:
Bill Gates is scared of super intelligent machines and he thinks you should be too. Ok, the word he used was concerned. But still the picture he painted in his Reddit, ask me anything session, was this: "First the machines will do a lot of jobs for us and not be super intelligent. A few decades after that though the intelligence is strong enough to be a concern.

I agree with Elon Musk and some others on this and don't understand why some people are not concerned." Gates is referencing the fears of Space-X CEO Elon Musk who spoke out about the dangers of Artificial Intelligence on several occasions. Elon Musk: "With Artificial Intelligence we are summoning the Demon. In all those stories where the guy as the pentagram and holy water and he's sure he can control the Demon.

It didn't work out. It will have a very bad effect. There could be something like getting rid of spam or an email or something, the best way to get rid of spam is to get rid of humans." The two share their concerns with Stephen Hawking, who has made similar warnings. "Once humans develop Artificial Intelligence it will take off on its own and re-design itself at an ever-increasing rate. Humans are limited by slow biological evolution and couldn't compete." Musk, in particular, has urged that there be some kind of International Regulatory body insuring AI doesn't advance to a Terminator style Skynet. [7]

What did he say? Terminator Skynet! I'm not the only one saying this! And these guys are the experts! How many of them do we need to listen to before we get the point! Danger! Don't go down this route!!! In fact, what's ironic is how even the military experts who admit that the military is the biggest promoter of this technology, even admits that, "Once we do this, we are going to regret it." This is crazy!

It's interesting when people try to make parallels to where we are today, and they use a number of examples. Some people make the parallel to the rise of computers, Bill Gates for example says where we are with the robotic revolution right now is where we were with the computer in 1980.

Big bulky device, only able to do a couple of functions and the military is the main spender of research and development and then soon it takes off, so we stop calling computers, computers any more. I have a computer in my kitchen, I call it a microwave oven. And we see the same things happening with unmanned systems today. An incredible, elegant, technology that is on the cutting edge. That's why scientists are so excited to work on it. But it may be something we will regret later on.[8]

Can I translate that for you? You may want to think twice about this one! From a military expert, even they admit it! And if that wasn't a blunt enough warning for you, even the Terminator movie writer himself admits. This is not going to be good!

History Channel Reports:
"When I first saw the Terminator movie back in 1984 I was completely taken with it, and most people were. I'm Michael Pharris and I'm the screen writer on Terminator 3 and 4. This whole idea the unstoppable killing machine is riveting. The Terminator movies has spoken to an innate fear we have of technology running amuck in general.

When we were researching the scripts for Terminator 3 and 4 we spent some time with DARPA research and it was fascinating to find out that no matter how farfetched the stuff we were thinking of they were already working on in some capacity or another, from weaponized insects to brain implants that would control military hardware."

The terrifying reality of the fully autonomous robots is closer than we think. Robots with super human strength, speed, intelligence, and the ability to think and kill on their own.

Once real Terminators charge onto the battlefield, the consequences of that revolution are impossible to predict. "The gradual encroachment, hi-tech weaponry that distances us from the realities of warfare could theoretically take the planet to a scenario that is not unlike that in the Terminator film."[9]

Can I translate that for you? Here's what's next, our movies, the Terminator series is about to become your reality! Can you believe that? The stuff they were dreaming up for that movie was already being worked on! In fact, several media outlets are now even starting to use the term terminator as in Terminator movies in their description of this upcoming AI technology!

IGN News reports:
Hello everybody, Max Scoville here. Dozens of profile science men and other dignitaries such as Steve Wozniak and Elon Musk signed an open letter appealing to the U.N. to ban AI based weaponry. Clearly some of them have seen Terminator. The letter published by the Future of Life Institute states that AI controlled weapons with capabilities of searching for and eliminating people autonomously will likely be available in years and not decades and describes autonomous weapons as a potential third revolutionary warfare after gun powder and nuclear arms. Again Terminator.

If any major military power pushed ahead with AI weapon development, the letter continues, a global arms race is virtually inevitable. Autonomous weapons will become the wave of tomorrow. It warns that while these weapons reduce human casualties it will also lower the threshold for states to go to war as the materials needed to make these machines are so cheap and readily available.

Under poor circumstances they foresee these weapons being used by dictators and terrorists seeking to control or pacify populations or government organizations intent on assignation or ethnic cleansing. So bad stuff. Other signatories include Jaan Tallinn and Jon Chauncy among a slew of other high-profile scientists and academics.[10]

In other words, everybody is warning about this stuff, even the news is getting in on it, and what backdrop are they constantly using to describe this danger? That's right! The Terminator movies. It's the perfect fit because that's what's really being created! And notice how it's not just the Tech Industry and the Media using the word Terminator and Terminator backdrops to describe this technology. They're also using the term Skynet to describe how this AI threat is going to hijack the whole thing and then we're really in trouble!

Chapter Twenty-Six

Google's Workings

And it might be sooner than you think, especially if you take a look at another tech giant called Google. Believe it or not these guys, at Google, the co-founders Larry Page and Sergey Brin, are right smack dab in the middle of this technology and if you take a look at what they're doing, what companies they keep on buying, where they're going with all this, you'll see that creating Google was much more than just about another search engine, rather it's all about developing a Global Artificial Intelligence with Google at the top. But don't take my word for it, let's listen to Larry Page, again, one of the co-founders of Google. Apparently, he freely admitted back in the day that developing Google had nothing to do with developing another search engine, rather it's all about creating AI.

Sergey Brin reports:
Watson, who is Theodore Roosevelt? If you talk to Larry Page, when Google first started, I was really perplexed about why anybody would make a new search engine when we had AltaVista which was the current search engine, it seemed good enough. He said, "Oh, it's not to make a search engine. It's to make AI.[1]

Say what? It has nothing to do with a Search Engine, it has to do with making AI! Straight out of the Horse's Mouth! How do you get any clearer than that? And if you think that's too ambitious for Google, then think again. These guys will try just about anything and everything to reach their goal. In fact, this might very well be the emphasis behind their Google Books Project, not to mention all the information they're already gleaning from us from search engines, emails, databases, etc. But Google has been working for years literally scanning all books all over the planet, concerning the human experience from around the world, from Libraries, Universities, even Monasteries and inputting them all into a Centralized Computer Base System. Why? Because that's what you need to do to create AI. If you recall back in the section on the History of Artificial Intelligence, the only way to get the "Commonsense Knowledge Problem" fixed, i.e. develop true AI is you have to manually feed it data. Remember that? Just like we receive everyday through our eyes, ears, senses, etc. "The creators of the project stated there was no shortcut and that the only way for machines to know the meaning of human concepts is to teach them, one concept at a time, by hand." And so, this could very well be what Google's doing with all this information they're getting from us all over the world including their Google Books project? Many would say, absolutely, yes! They're acquiring all this human data on us to feed into an AI system they really are creating. In fact, some of those working for Google, like Ray Kurzweil even admit it.

Ray Kurzweil, inventor of the scanner, Futurologist:
"Most of my discussions have been with Larry Page. We have talked in general about the quest to digitize all knowledge and then develop true AI. You can create intelligent systems if you have a very large data base. Books are actually, probably more valuable than all the other stuff on the internet. We have a high standard about what we put in books."

They were frank in their ambition and dazzling in their ability to execute. The Google Book Scanning Project is clearly the most ambitious world brain scheme that has ever been invented. This is no remote dream, no fantasy, it is a plain statement of a contemporary state of affairs.

There is a danger that Google's aim is to achieve a monopoly. The scenario is that in 20 years' time Google will be tracking everything we need.

Google could actually hold the whole world hostage. For thousands of years mankind has dreamt of a giant library that contained every book in the world. Every human being would be able to visit this library. In the twenty first century, technology could make that dream a reality. Robert Darnton Director Harvard University Library: "The first appeal of Googles enterprise when we saw it was just digitizing millions and millions of books.

At Harvard we have by far the greatest University Library in the world. It's enormous, 17 million volumes and every library wants its holdings digitized for lots of reasons, including preservation. But beyond that it raises the possibility of sharing your intellectual wealth. I think of the Harvard Library as an International asset.

Something that should be opened up and shared with the general population. So here comes Google, they've got the energy, they've got the technology, they've got money and they say we'll do it for you, free." Pamela Samuelson, Professor of Law, Berkeley, "Google did such a fabulous job in creating a vision not only that a universal library could be created but that it could be done today."

In the late nineties, pioneers began to combine the scanner, the book and the internet to create giant digital libraries. The start of the internet archive in 1996, the idea was to get all the published works of human kind available to everybody. This was the opportunity of our generation. Like the previous generation had put a man on the moon.

The internet archive had been completely open with Google, in fact I had gone and given a speech that was attended by all of the senior executives on how one could go about building a digital library of all books, music, video, and I had hoped that there would be a way to work with that, but that was not to be. Libraries had signed secret agreements with Google. We didn't really know what was going on.

But it started coming out as a completely separate project and not working with others, I started to become suspicious." Sergey Brin, A Library to Last Forever, "Larry Page who founded Google with me, first proposed that we digitize all books a decade ago, when we were fledgling start up. Five years later, in 2004, Google Books was born."

I went to Google in January of 2003. Reginald Carr, Former Director, Bodleian Library, "I actually made, what I now feel quite embarrassed about, a presentation to them telling them what they ought to be doing. Only to find out a few months later that they had actually been doing it for a while already. Project Ocean was a kind of code name, a development code name that Google was giving that would eventually be Google Books.

It was called Project Ocean because it was big. Google seemed to think that they could do almost a million in three years." Google would not supply us with video material of their scanning operation. This is believed to be the only footage of Google's scanning warehouses. It last 6 seconds. The other scanning images in this film have been made at university scanning stations.

You could say that this mass digitization is something like running a huge machine through a library. You take books by the shelf, they are put in cartons, on carts, they are loaded on to trucks and Google had three places in the country where it was doing digitization. Supposedly it didn't give the address of where they were.

Google won't say how much scanning the books costs but there are estimates that somewhere between $30.00 and $100.00 per book, so if you multiply that times 20 million. Google early on, bent over backwards to keep us from communicating with the other libraries, there were three or four large ones. Each of us were told we should not tell the others what kind of contract we had and how we were working with Google.

To begin with we had to be fairly quiet. It was probably mid 2003 when I started taking the wraps off in terms of this being a possibility that we might be working with Google. I witnessed the scale of the operation that was very impressive. Twenty very large work stations with very high-resolution cameras sitting on top of cradles with very intense lights with black boxes underneath which I presume contained all of Googles algorithms that make Google search what it is, and they uploaded it direct to Mountain View.

Who wouldn't want to have all the worlds knowledge available to everyone on the planet. The problem with that is Google as the intermediary in this process has certain interests and a certain agenda that is not always transparent. If you are in Silicon Valley you have another job which you are building this new life form that's going to take over the world.

Google is providing the memories for its brain or the other companies are providing the memories. This is something that is openly talked about. Kevin Kelly, Co-Founder, Wired Magazine: "It's all human knowledge in books and out of books, it's all woven together into a single entity." Shortly after the launch of Google Books, at different events, I ran into Larry Page and Sergey Brin and had a brief exchange with them about the potential and there was a characteristic Google founder response which was a kind of glint in their eyes and a smile the sense that this was just the beginning of something much bigger than even you at this point can imagine.

Google launched Street View in 2007, part of the search engines long term goal to create a virtual 3D map of the whole planet right down to street level. But investigations have that Googles Street View cars were collecting more than just photographs for their data banks. Their antennas were also hovering up personal information from unencrypted Wifi networks including internet history and passwords.

I think in the case of Google collecting Wifi information, it reveals complete lack of respect for privacy within the corporation. Such projects often revealed that Google does not understand the social consequences of its own work. William Gibson, Googles Earth: "Science fiction never imagined Google. Google is a game changing tool. On the order of equally handy Flint Handex, but Google is not ours. We are its unpaid content providers and one way or the other we generate product for Google.

With every search and minuscule contribution, Google is made of us, sort of a coral reef of human minds and their products. We are yet to take Googles measure." Google was going to be keeping track of, who exactly was reading that book, how long they were reading it, and what they read next, that information could get back to the government, could get back to the FBI, could get back to the police, could get back to their employer, Google wasn't making any kind of guarantee of what they were going to do in respect to this privacy.

It's going to change how we interface with information. People are going to ask how did they do that? How did they accomplish this task before we thought only humans could hope to do? David Heum held this view that sense and experience are the sole foundation of knowledge. Clay Shirky, Internet Consultant: "After IBM's success with Deep Blue they looked around for other kinds of games that they could take on. And they wanted a different kind of game than chess.

So, they picked Jeopardy which is a fancy trivia game. It's one of those games that you and I can play. It's a human standing there with their carbon and water verses a computer with all its silicon and its main memory in its disc. The Watson show was, you can take a very large, a very massive set of data and if you can use those inputs correctly you can actually answer sophisticated questions.

And certainly, the presence of large amounts of data on the internet is going to be as much an input for machines as it is for people. What we will need to tap that is computer systems that can understand natural language. Natural language understanding is coming along very well. IBM's Watson is a very good example of the current state of the art and computers understand natural language.

Not only did Watson have to understand the convoluted language in the Jeopardy query which included metaphors, facsimiles, riddles and jokes, but it got its knowledge to respond to the query from actually reading 200 million pages of natural language documents including all of Wikipedia and several other encyclopedias.

And when you see a computer play it better than we ever could, it's one of those moments when you realize that the world really is different. Google Book Project is in a sense trying to make that universal library, which could then be read by an AI or a Watson, like super computer.[2]

So, there you have it. As crazy as it sounds, Google's been spending a whole ton of money out of their own pocket, offering it for free, to get every book they can scanned in on the planet, not to mention scanning all our WIFI information, passwords, pictures, and search engine information. Why? Somebody has to feed their goal, Artificial Intelligence. I'm not making this up. Other people are admitting it to, as you just saw. And the reason why is because again, there's no way around it. The only way to get the "Commonsense Knowledge Problem" fixed, i.e. develop true AI, is you have to manually feed it data, by hand." Now add to that all the other things Google is doing with Google Maps, and Google Photos, and Google Emails, and Google Videos, and Google Searches. You have got a lot of food for somebody to chew on and grow. It's AI food! And if you think they're not serious about this, then not only has Google purchased one of the world's top military robotic companies, Boston Dynamics, but they also acquired another company called Deep Mind. That's all about developing Artificial Intelligence and they paid big bucks for it! Why? Because they just had to have it in order to reach their ultimate goal!

BBC News reports:
Now Google has bought a startup company named Deep Mind for a reported 400 million pounds making the Artificial Intelligence firm the largest European

acquisition so far. The company was founded by a 37-year-old that specializes in computers normally acquiring human intelligence.

TV with Amy reports: *Google announced that it has acquired an Artificial Intelligence Firm Deep Mind Technology. It's the latest of startup purchases by the tech giant as it looks to beef up its expertise in Artificial Intelligence and robotics.*

Keys reports: *Google has plans to purchase a startup Artificial Intelligence company called Deep Mind for 400 million dollars. The company was founded by neuroscientist and games prodigy Demis Hassabis and specializes in learning algorithm for computer simulations. Google says they will use the technology to make their killer robots even smarter.*

Fox Business reports: *Google is everywhere, they have military robots, they have a huge search engine, they've got smart thermometers now, and Artificial Intelligence. Should we be concerned about this? If that beast can think for itself and decide who it's going to bite and kill. I mean, it's not out of the question.*[3]

Yeah, it's not out of the question. Laugh all you want, but if you do your homework and trace the trail, this is what they're working on! It makes no sense and seems laughable until you recall the ultimate goal, "It has nothing to do with a search engine, it has to do with making AI!" And by the looks of it, they're about ready to pull it off! Which is precisely why Elon Musk tried to put a stop to it. Check out what he said in this interview about his attempted purchase of Deep Mind, the company Google just bought.

CNBC News report:
Elon Musk: "I don't know of any other public securities apart from Solar City and Tesla." Interviewer: "That is amazing, but you did just invest in a company named Vicarious, Artificial Intelligence, what is this company?" Elon Musk: "Right, I was also an investor in Deep Mind before Google acquired it. Vicarious is not from the stand point of any investment return.

It's really just from the standpoint of keeping an eye on what is going on with Artificial Intelligence. I think it is potentially a dangerous outcome there. There's been movies out there about this like the Terminator." Interviewer: "Even if this is true and it is dangerous what can you do about it? What dangers do you see that you can actually do something about?" Elon Musk, "I don't know."

Interviewer: "So what does Vicarious do? Why did you invest in this company? What do you see it doing down the line?" Elon Musk: "Vicarious emulates the human brain." Interviewer: "You want to make sure that the technology is used for good and not like Terminator, evil?" Elon Musk: "Yeah, in the movie Terminator, they didn't create AI to be bad, they didn't expect to get a Terminator like outcome.

But you want to be careful because of the outcome. Interviewer: "But here's the irony, the man whose responsible for the most advanced technology in this country is worried about the advances in technology that you are aware of. So, what can you do, in other words, this stuff is almost exorable isn't it? How would you see that there are these brain like developments out there?

Can you really do anything to stop it?" Elon Musk: "I don't know." Interviewer: "What can this AI out there be used for? What's it's best value?" Elon Musk, "I don't know. But there are some scary outcomes. We should try to make sure that the outcomes are good and not bad." Interviewer: "Or escape tomorrow if there is no other option." Elon Musk, "AI will chase us there pretty quickly."[4]

So, let me get this straight. You're one of the world's top tech giants and you're so concerned about AI development being unleashed on us, that you tried to buy out DeepMind before Google did, the AI company and you're not really sure of any of the benefits of it, and you just want to pull the reigns in on it, slow it down, and you warn even if this goes south, we still won't be able to escape it, not even to Mars. The AI will chase you there pretty quickly. And what was the quote at the beginning? "There's been movies about this, you know, like Terminator" direct quote. Still think this is a wacky conspiracy theory? Elon Musk also stated that, "Unless you have direct exposure to groups like DeepMind, you have no idea how fast it is growing at a pace close to exponential." In other words, out of control. And that, "Leading AI companies "recognize the danger" and are working to control "bad" superintelligences "from escaping into the Internet."

Well, now that's starting to sound like that Johnny Depp scenario in the movie Transcendence or even The Avengers Age of Ultron scenario, or even Skynet! It takes over! In fact, that's exactly what it's already being called, "How the Pentagon's Skynet Would Automate War." "The U.S. Military wants to take advantage of the increasing interconnection of people and devices via the new 'Internet of Things' through the use of "embedded systems" in "automobiles, factories, infrastructure, appliances and homes, pets, and potentially, inside human beings." Due to the advent of "Cloud Robotics," the line between conventional robotics and intelligent everyday devices will become increasingly blurred. In other words, it's all going to be woven together into a Skynet seam. Cloud robotics, a term coined by Google's new robotics chief, James Kuffner, that allows individual robots to augment their capabilities by connecting through the internet to share online resources and collaborate with other machines. Soon, nearly every aspect of global society could become, in their words, "instrumented, networked, and potentially available for control via the Internet, in a hierarchy of cyber-physical systems." And that, "Robots could also become embedded in civilian life to perform surveillance, infrastructure monitoring, police telepresence, and homeland security applications." And that, "Armies of Kill Bots that can autonomously wage war will soon be a reality" and, "Google's Killer Robot Army, artificially intelligent robots, could turn evil and have the ability to annihilate the human race." Why? Because "Google has already patented the ability to control a robot army." I'm not making this up! That Patent just got awarded! And it would enable them to, "Use the cloud to control an army of robots." Skip the word cloud and put in Skynet and there you go!

That's why, Elon Musk also stated as a final point of emphasis, "Please note that I am normally Super Pro-Technology and have never raised this issue until recent months. This is not a case of crying wolf about something I don't understand." "He believes that Skynet is only five years off." And he may not be that far off because if you do the research you'll see that the NSA already has a secret program called Skynet that uses metadata to try to find and identify people with terrorist connections in which Drone killing occurs of those targets based upon the metadata analysis it comes up with. They also have a program called Monster Mind that's a, "New Autonomous Cyber Weapons System that can not only intercept every single digital communication within the United States, but it can automatically detect and launch retaliatory strikes without any human involvement if a threat has been identified. But there's a problem. Listen to this. "Such a program has dangerous global reactionary implications. These attacks can be spoofed. You could have someone sitting in China, for example, making it appear that one of these attacks is originating in Russia. And then we end up shooting back at a Russian hospital. What happens next?"

Now is that not exactly like the Skynet scenario! Where AI launched a fake strike and that was the end of it! Folks, this is real current technology that's being implemented right now! And I don't have time to talk about the actual laser beam weaponry that's already being used by the military or force fields already being patented and artificial pressure and heat skin being invented for robots. All this put together and you can see how we have all the ingredients for a Skynet Terminator Scenario! To quote Elon Musk, "We're summoning up a Demon." No wonder he tried to buy that AI Company before Google got their hands on it!

Yet, believe it or not, this is still just the tip of the iceberg of what Google plans to do to our planet. It's such an obvious connection that Google is really creating a global AI brain to take over robotics and Drones and who knows what else, that other people are also starting to put two and two together and to put it about as blunt as you can get, Google could very well become, Skynet just like in the Terminator Movies!"

UPROXX reports:
A clip from Terminator 2: The Skynet funding bill has passed, the system goes online on August 4, 1997, it becomes self-aware 2:14am Eastern time. Remember Skynet Artificial Intelligence system from the Terminator series, you know it gets too powerful and tries to wipe out the human race. Sounds far-fetched. Well, Skynet may not be as far-fetched as we think.

Google processes a billion web searches every day. Here are a few of the things Google wants to learn, your phone, your email, your computer and your entire digital life. Building an empire on your street, on your phone, in your DNA. Could Google become Skynet?

8) Nest, it learns every time you turn the ring, it never stops learning. It keeps you comfortable. Remembers when you'll be up. **Kim Horcher, Nerd reports:** *It seem like the start of stage 4 Nest lab is over because Google has bought the company for 3.2 billion. They want you to categorize your day, when I wake up, when I leave for work, when I get home from work, when I go to bed. Am I alone in feeling a little uncomfortable about this?*

7) Project Loon: One, two, three, balloons communicate with specialized internet antennas on the ground. We're using all these things to build this network in the sky.

6) Self-Driving Cars. For several years Google has made driverless technology. One Analyst estimates that by 2035 it will be close to 12 million self-driving cars on the road.

5) Google X. **Bloomberg Businessweek reports:** *What exactly is Google X? Google X is Googles research lab where the smartest computer scientists are* *looking at the next generation of Google products. You also make a reference that it is kind of like the Manhattan Project where they develop the first atomic bomb and it sounds like it could be a little scary.*

4) Quantum computing: Google and Nasa have teamed up to share one of the world's first commercial Quantum computers that could bring a quantum leap in terms of power.

3) Deep Mind. **CNN reports:** *Let's get to the Google robot. Let's start with what would be the brain of the robot and that would be Deep Mind. Deep Mind can be described as a world class ground breaking technology to build powerful is a cutting edge artificial intelligence company. We combine the best techniques from machine learning and systems neuroscience to build a powerful general-purpose learning algorithm. Founded by Demis Hassabis, Shane Legg and Mustafe Suleyman, the company is based in London and supported by some of the most iconic technology entrepreneurs and investors of past decade. Our first commercial applications are in simulations, e-commerce and games. World class ground breaking technology to build powerful and general-purpose learning algorithms, Critical thinking.*

2) Skybox Imaging. **Reuters Technology News reports:** *Google Inc. said it is acquiring the satellite company Skybox Imaging for 500 million dollars in cash. The company takes hi-res images of a given area. What do you think of Google owning the skies and the ground?*

1) Robotics. Why is Google buying robotics companies? The search engine giant has just acquired a company that designs robots for the U.S. Department of Defense.[5]

Close the bars. The Net has been created around us. It's not only scary but ironic how Hollywood has done a masterful job educating us of this horrible future that's being created for us. We just got tricked into thinking it was just entertainment.

Chapter Twenty-Seven

God's Wake Up Call

But remember, Hollywood wasn't the first one to warn us of this future. The Bible did. Let's go back to the Biblical account of the real live Judgement Day, recorded nearly 2,000 years ago, and now after all that you saw, you tell me if this reality is not coming soon.

Matthew 24:3,6-7,21 "As Jesus was sitting on the Mount of Olives, the disciples came to Him privately. 'Tell us,' they said, 'when will this happen, and what will be the sign of Your coming and of the end of the age?' You will hear of wars and rumors of wars but see to it that you are not alarmed. Such things must happen, but the end is still to come. Nation will rise against nation, and kingdom against kingdom. For then there will be great distress, unequaled from the beginning of the world until now – and never to be equaled again."

Revelation 6:8 "I looked, and there before me was a pale horse! Its rider was named Death, and Hades was following close behind him. They were given power over a fourth of the earth to kill by sword, famine, and plague, and by the wild beasts of the earth."

Revelation 9:15-16 "And the four angels who had been kept ready for this very hour and day and month and year were released to kill a third of mankind. The number of the mounted troops was two hundred million. I heard their number."

And so again, I ask the question, after reading all this information, getting acquainted with the rising Technology, "Do we have the technology on the Planet now to systematically annihilate, half the planet in a relatively short amount of time like these verses in the Bible have warned us about in the Last Days?" I think we can agree, unfortunately, yes, absolutely yes! And we don't even need nuclear warfare to pull it off! Which means, we're living in those Last Days and we better heed the warning of Jesus. Believe it or not, there really is a way to make sure you're not around to see it, this Judgment Day. That's the good news I wanted to leave you with. There's only ONE WAY out of this mess and that's through Jesus Christ alone. I didn't say that, He did!

John 14:6 "Jesus answered, I am the way and the truth and the life. No one comes to the Father except through me."

And the reason why it's only through Jesus Christ alone, i.e. you can't get out of Judgment Day on your own, is because we've all blown it one way or another. This is what the Bible says in this passage.

Romans 3:23, 6:23 "For all have sinned and fall short of the glory of God. For the wages of sin is death, but the gift of God is eternal life in Christ Jesus our Lord"

And if you're anything like I used to be, you're probably thinking, "I'm not that bad of a person, I'm not a sinner." Well, actually it's pretty easy to demonstrate. This is what the 10 Commandments are all about. For instance, have you ever lied? If your answer is no, then you just did, so we're all even. But that's the 9th Commandment, you shall not bear false witness, you know, lying. Ok, now have you ever stolen anything? You shall not steal. Okay, come on now, you already told me you're a liar! Let's be honest. This is the truth. We've all sinned and fallen short of the glory of God, myself included. I'm not going to heaven because I'm so wonderful, it's simply because I'm forgiven. And this is the same offer Jesus makes to all of us.

Romans 10:9-10 "For if you confess with your mouth that Jesus is Lord and believe in your heart that God raised him from the dead, you will be saved. For it is by believing in your heart that you are made right with God, and it is by confessing with your mouth that you are saved."

People be encouraged. It really is true. If you would entrust your life to Jesus Christ and call upon the Name of the Lord and ask Him to forgive you of all your sins then you will escape Judgment Day, when, not if, your time comes. Why? Because you took the way out, the only way out, through Jesus Christ. God loves you. He's made an amazing sacrificial provision for you to be saved from certain destruction.

Remember the story of how Google's Artificial Intelligent Driverless Cars are being looked upon as the deciders of who gets to live or who gets to die? Well, God, the Supreme Intelligence, has already done that with His Son Jesus Christ. He used His Supreme Intelligence to make sure that NO ONE would have to die and face this Horrible Judgment Day. God made the decision for us. He chose His Son to wreck so to speak, to take the hit for us so we might all live, if we would just receive it. And that's where we need you to use your own intelligence and receive this wonderful gift before it's too late. Call upon the Name of Jesus. Ask Him to forgive you of all your sins, and He will, and you will escape this real live judgement day. It's the most amazing Sacrificial Act of Love by GOD the Father of all time, just like this earthly father did with His Son, for these people.

Once there was a man, his job was bridge master for the railroad. He had a son that he loved very much. He would bring his son to the station and teach him all about the trains. They would walk along the tracks to make sure they were clear, that there was nothing that would cause damage to the train or to the passengers. He loved bringing his son to work showing him the intricate details of the drawbridge.

His son loved to watch the trains and the people who traveled on them. People who were lonely, angry, selfish, hurting, and addicted. Then one day a tragic mistake happened. The bridge master raised the bridge so the ship could go through. His son was playing down next to the water. He saw his dad and started to run back to him, climbing on the bridge. As he is climbing on the bridge his father sees the train coming.

He tries to get his sons attention to get off the bridge, but his son doesn't notice the warning. The father is frantic, he must get his son off the bridge, so he can close it and the train can pass. As he starts to go out the door to call to his son, his son falls. This leads to a terrible choice. Allow the passengers on the train to die or pull the lever and allow his son to be crushed by the bridge. He has to sacrifice one to save many.

With tears in his eyes he pulls the lever to let the train cross the bridge. After the train crosses he runs to find his son. The people on board the train have no idea that this boy just saved all their lives. The Salvation of All Required the Sacrifice of One most dear. The Sacrifice of One bought hope for the future.

As the father is standing on the street one day he notices that the girl that was on the train that day his son died is walking down the street with a baby in her arms. She is the addict that he recognizes and now she is clean and smiling at him. He smiles back knowing that the sacrifice of his son saved this woman to be with her child.[1]

John 3:16 "For God so loved the world that He gave His one and only Son, that whoever believes in Him shall not perish but have eternal life"

Turn to Jesus now. Call upon His Name and ask Him to forgive you of all your sins, and He will. Avoid the worst train wreck of all time for all eternity. Escape the real live judgement day that is coming. Do it now before it's too late. Don't delay! I hope to see you in heaven!

How to Receive Jesus Christ:

1. Admit your need (I am a sinner).

2. Be willing to turn from your sins (repent).

3. Believe that Jesus Christ died for you on the Cross and rose from the grave.

4. Through prayer, invite Jesus Christ to come in and control your life through the Holy Spirit. (Receive Him as Lord and Savior.)

What to pray:

Dear Lord Jesus,

I know that I am a sinner and need Your forgiveness. I believe that You died for my sins. I want to turn from my sins. I now invite You to come into my heart and life. I want to trust and follow You as Lord and Savior.

In Jesus' name. Amen.

Notes

Chapter 1   *Development of Drones*

1. Premise of Skynet
   http://en.wikipedia.org/wiki/Skynet_%28Terminator%29

Chapter 2   *The History of Drones*

1. History of Drones
   Ian G. R. Shaw, (2014), "The Rise of the Predator Empire: Tracing the History of U.S. Drones", Understanding Empire, https://understandingempire.wordpress.com/2-0-a-brief-history-of-u-s-drones/http://teleautomaton.com/post/1373803033/how-teslas-1898-patent-changed-the-worldhttps://www.thebureauinvestigates.com/category/projects/drones/drones-graphs/

Chapter 3   *The Private Invasion*

1. Consumer Drones
   https://www.youtube.com/watch?v=ne6o5rMNTY8
2. Drones on the Ground
   https://www.youtube.com/watch?v=ne6o5rMNTY8
   https://www.youtube.com/watch?v=3LZgTgI0REk
3. Underwater Drones
   https://www.youtube.com/watch?v=Z3o8eBrL7ws
4. Selfie Personal Drones
   https://www.youtube.com/watch?v=_VFsdPAoI1g
5. Selfie Drone Adventure
   https://www.youtube.com/watch?v=iMfTHHLbj5g
6. Wallet Drone

      https://www.youtube.com/watch?v=VPIR61HATGo
7. Hoverbikes Star Wars
      https://www.youtube.com/watch?v=XoCVXIpiH5w
8. Hoverbikes Drones
      https://www.youtube.com/watch?v=s7b5QIDZ13U
9. International Drone Day
      https://www.youtube.com/watch?v=_RqHWiu1SXA
10. Stock Market Drones
      https://www.youtube.com/watch?v=wRj54PVpm_g

Chapter 4   *The Media Invasion*

1. Drones in Hollywood
      https://www.youtube.com/watch?v=GXhlgNHK14s
2. Footage of Weather Shots
      https://www.youtube.com/watch?v=5m6oXJcg7aM
3. BBC Reporting Drones
      https://www.youtube.com/watch?v=ZTWHP80hei0
4. Solo Drone Demonstration
      https://www.youtube.com/watch?v=CbnjG0Om5OY
5. Wedding Video Drone
      https://www.youtube.com/watch?v=srJq_2bPXGs
6. Drones in Political Ads
      https://www.youtube.com/watch?v=l6czoqe5vWo
      https://www.youtube.com/watch?v=z5W25NH6EZQ
      https://www.youtube.com/watch?v=NPKzyophmNw
      https://www.youtube.com/watch?v=surpE8jswtU
7. Drones for Entertainment
      https://www.youtube.com/watch?v=RB0D-D24MsU
8. Drones for Advertising
      https://www.youtube.com/watch?v=595rNp3hML8

Chapter 5   *The Agricultural Invasion*

1. Drone for Water Usage
      https://www.youtube.com/watch?v=5yB8DN2MReg

2. Farm Drone Tractor
   https://www.youtube.com/watch?v=nj_EYZeSkhM
3. Drone Sprays Pesticides
   https://www.youtube.com/watch?v=oA_2EHMlcaQ
4. Drones Herd Animals
   https://www.youtube.com/watch?v=yD9KUB7QqZI
5. Farm Drone Finds Deer
   https://www.youtube.com/watch?v=VoDWyddbo2U
6. Farm Drone Makes Water
   https://www.youtube.com/watch?v=oYpwUQXJNqs
7. Drone Brings Fresh Asparagus
   https://www.youtube.com/watch?v=bnC6pfwtVvI
8. Farm Drone Biodegradable
   https://www.youtube.com/watch?v=6Ydc1bKX678
9. Drones Spying on Farmer
   https://www.youtube.com/watch?v=ayGJ1YSfDXs
10. Drones used to catch Poachers
    https://www.youtube.com/watch?v=Dgf8QA_AZeg
11. Drone Fighting Mosquitoes
    https://www.youtube.com/watch?v=vhzEf_K-vyk

Chapter 6 *The Commercial Invasion*

1. Pizza Delivery in Mumbai
   https://www.youtube.com/watch?v=JsS7fnDeUzo
2. Brazil Deliveries
   https://www.youtube.com/watch?v=6cqR8fUwXH0
3. Domino's Pizza Delivery
   https://www.youtube.com/watch?v=on4DRTUvst0
4. Delivery of Beer on Ice
   https://www.youtube.com/watch?v=qmHwXf8JUOw
5. Drones Deliver Flowers
   https://www.youtube.com/watch?v=TbtWczEXGmc
6. Deliver Drinks in Singapore
   https://www.youtube.com/watch?v=xJAt7OpGZNw
   https://www.youtube.com/watch?v=wHzoRWFS1IY
7. Amazon Air
   https://www.youtube.com/watch?v=0NpDK9-1fX0

8. Delivery UPS and Google
   https://www.youtube.com/watch?v=6j0t88ipQ3k
9. Audi Commercial
   https://www.youtube.com/watch?v=OLSmkkw0v8I

Chapter 7   *The Medical Invasion*

1. Drones Deliver Medicine
   https://www.youtube.com/watch?v=AZEk3H7I3d8
2. Drone Delivering Defibrillator
   https://www.youtube.com/watch?v=y-rEI4bezWc
3. Drone Delivering Ambulance
   https://www.youtube.com/watch?v=tvw-XIHvzv8
4. Drone Rescues Girl
   http://www.dailyherald.com/article/20140903/business/140909663/
5. Drones for Disaster Relief
   https://www.youtube.com/watch?v=Wmm0eVwybVA
   https://www.youtube.com/watch?v=YOoSAjrvy6s
6. Drones Finding Missing People and Pets
   https://www.youtube.com/watch?v=t39o6L_rEts

Chapter 8   *The Transportation Invasion*

1. Driverless Car
   https://www.youtube.com/watch?v=qtApzKnGU94
2. Drone Car Nap
   https://www.youtube.com/watch?v=aBxfcmuloUA
3. Drone Car Hitting a person
   https://www.youtube.com/watch?v=_8nnhUCtcO8
4. Drone Truck Hauling Goods
   https://www.youtube.com/watch?v=6bFCrkUbdDE
5. Truck Movies Killing People
   https://www.youtube.com/watch?v=SutDTIhbQ2g
6. Drone Train Hauling People
   https://www.youtube.com/watch?v=Z3Q0FZUKHkY
7. Drone Flying Car

https://www.youtube.com/watch?v=j73RmbGsi3U
8. Drone Planes Flying People
   https://www.youtube.com/watch?v=w-fiJfdccDc

Chapter 9   *The Communication Invasion*

1. Google Internet Balloons
   https://www.youtube.com/watch?v=m96tYpEk1Ao
2. Facebook Internet Drones
   https://www.youtube.com/watch?v=8tV3AnopzL8

Chapter 10   *The Controlled Invasion*

1. Drone Scares Compilation
   https://www.youtube.com/watch?v=RbUwdF5gSbc
2. Drone Hunting by People
   https://www.youtube.com/watch?v=P0N9ods8Se4
   https://www.youtube.com/watch?v=DDbyl_Q5-oE
3. Drone Invades White House
   https://www.youtube.com/watch?v=-hr5u1UNHdw

Chapter 11   *Drones in the Police Force*

1. Drones for UK Police Force
   https://www.youtube.com/watch?v=cL8tVNzEW9s
   https://www.youtube.com/watch?v=oqdibZ1s5p4
2. Drones Catching Tax Cheats
   https://www.youtube.com/watch?v=bqJlbTxDFtc
3. Drones Catch Chinese Cheaters
   https://www.youtube.com/watch?v=jWrwWQfLEHo
4. Drones with Facial Recognition Software
   https://www.youtube.com/watch?v=YPBVfWFoGdA
5. Drones Listening to Conversations
   https://www.youtube.com/watch?v=YCIeC76-sZ4

6. Drones used on US Citizens
   https://www.youtube.com/watch?v=HYETraMg_mM
7. Drones used in California Police Force
   https://www.youtube.com/watch?v=k53wfejt_MI
8. Drones Disarm Gangs
   https://www.youtube.com/watch?v=aEAhR1efe0E
   https://www.youtube.com/watch?v=yyjdz2ixB4I
9. Star Wars Pocket Drones
   https://www.youtube.com/watch?v=FFiPbyigxVI
10. Hawaii 5-0 Killer Drone
    https://gostream.cloud/film/hawaii-five-0-season-5-11721/watching.html?ep=521140

Chapter 12 — *Drones in the Military Force*

1. Military Killer Drones
   https://www.youtube.com/watch?v=Xbnmpi49vg4
2. Soldiers Flying Killer Drones
   https://www.youtube.com/watch?v=WnokkabKTK0
   https://www.youtube.com/watch?v=XIXmURhOjzI
3. Military Promotes Video Games
   https://www.youtube.com/watch?v=VsNrHwPdIDc
4. Obama Kills People with Drones
   https://www.youtube.com/watch?v=rxYPGVs4FD0
5. Drone Monitoring US Borders
   https://www.youtube.com/watch?v=H8zT-8oXXWU
6. Drones on Air Land and Sea
   https://www.youtube.com/watch?v=ucS_HyPdQHI

Chapter 13 — *Drones in the Animal World*

1. Robot Bird
   https://www.youtube.com/watch?v=Fg_JcKSHUtQ
2. Robot Gecko
   https://www.youtube.com/watch?v=YqMe_ZqMezE
3. Robot Snake

https://www.youtube.com/watch?v=lMkGDHdDpC0
https://www.youtube.com/watch?v=QqpWGpVGd9c
https://www.youtube.com/watch?v=a35w4Bswmgw
4. Robot Kangaroo
https://www.youtube.com/watch?v=_4luJ0ZSqy8
5. Robot Jellyfish
https://www.youtube.com/watch?v=yeDkx5uq3dg
6. Robot Shark
https://www.youtube.com/watch?v=uj457REhZ0g
7. Robot Octopus, Lobster, and Stingray
https://www.youtube.com/watch?v=uJF75t1fFRA
https://www.afcea.org/content/lobsters-populate-navy-robot-platter
8. Robot Cheetah
https://www.youtube.com/watch?v=a2JiGdwsuqY
9. Robot Cheetah Cub
https://www.youtube.com/watch?v=wkpfuQl0imQ

Chapter 14 *Drones in the Insect World*

1. MAV Flies
https://www.youtube.com/watch?v=shgj3bK-Bmg
2. MAV Bees
https://www.youtube.com/watch?v=-qvdEcPka8M
3. MAV Insects
https://www.youtube.com/watch?v=KMI7HIhKdIo
4. MAV Swarms
https://www.youtube.com/watch?v=YCNWqypC2Po
https://www.youtube.com/watch?v=JmyTJSYw77g
https://www.youtube.com/watch?v=IBzKsIBIeDU
5. MAV M.A.S.T.
http://www.dtic.mil/get-tr-doc/pdf?AD=AD1036621
http://www.dronemedia.com/micro-autonomous-systems-and-technology.html
6. Runaway Robots
https://www.youtube.com/watch?v=lA6ybohAVq8
7. Military Guided Bullets
https://www.youtube.com/watch?v=nOIAlmvSvEo
https://www.youtube.com/watch?v=LqEh015cBOI

Chapter 15   *The History of AI*

1. I'm a Cybernetic Organism
   https://www.youtube.com/watch?v=pj5_7jnIXm8

Chapter 16   *The Danger of AI*

1. Danger of Singularity
   https://www.youtube.com/watch?v=PY6UvO2WAdA

Chapter 17   *Robot Machines in the Military*

1. Robotic Jet Fighter
   https://www.youtube.com/watch?v=znwU_4lLoGE
2. Robotic Helicopter Big
   https://www.youtube.com/watch?v=NZv3W9q4_FA
   https://www.youtube.com/watch?v=vfuHNHLJzoM
3. Robotic Helicopter Mini
   https://www.youtube.com/watch?v=4o7mRg74qcY
4. Robotic Navy Ships
   https://www.youtube.com/watch?v=x32f05O3hLU
   https://www.youtube.com/watch?v=UnyESN6GfFc
5. Robotic Avengers Ship
   https://www.youtube.com/watch?v=pBi0LqgwrH8
6. Robotic Boat Swarm
   https://www.youtube.com/watch?v=ITTvgkO2Xw4
7. Robotic Underwater Swarm
   https://www.youtube.com/watch?v=Hjkmm13Scm4
   https://www.youtube.com/watch?v=XUk-qLfiwlc
8. Robotic Submarine
   https://www.youtube.com/watch?v=UsMd1PoVf2I
9. Robotic Tanks
   https://www.youtube.com/watch?v=x45yDus7h80

10. Robotic Supply Vehicle
    https://www.youtube.com/watch?v=EZtlTHEHj4M
11. Robotic Jeep and Unmanned Vehicle
    https://www.youtube.com/watch?v=GVdeBEsbzuA
    https://www.youtube.com/watch?v=gCVCzXq9UJk
12. Robotic Mule Big
    https://www.youtube.com/watch?v=R7ezXBEBE6U
    https://www.youtube.com/watch?v=fn8KhvX2jqw
13. Robotic Mule Small
    https://www.youtube.com/watch?v=M8YjvHYbZ9w
14. Robotic Mule Multisized
    https://www.youtube.com/watch?v=2jvLalY6ubc
    https://www.youtube.com/watch?v=6b4ZZQkcNEo
15. Robotic Soldiers Coming
    https://www.youtube.com/watch?v=0SLEtVlU15Q
16. Gunbots have no Fear
    https://www.youtube.com/watch?v=yliThCy3RxY
17. Global Robot War
    https://www.youtube.com/watch?v=PVT5TfFL4Os
18. Chinese Holograms
    https://www.google.com/search?q=chinese+holographic+ground+control+system&rlz=1C1CHBF_enUS727US727&tbm=isch&tbo=u&source=univ&sa=X&ved=0ahUKEwinh5_LqdrYAhVdImMKHTToDM0Q7AkIQA&biw=895&bih=516#imgrc=GxAu7yXW7_7-1M:
19. Enders Game Trailer
    https://www.youtube.com/watch?v=2SRizeR4MmU
20. Robots Protect your Home
    https://www.youtube.com/watch?v=aSAgi55q9Qw
    http://eecue.com/b/1139/SPAWAR---Autonomous-Military-Robots-.html
21. Car Decides Who Lives or Dies
    https://www.youtube.com/watch?v=WS4tUn3MvCU

Chapter 18   *Robot Men in the Home*

1. Service Robot
   https://www.youtube.com/watch?v=bSdYR-FHcA8
   https://www.youtube.com/watch?v=IV0uJih6jBg

2. Kid Robot
   https://www.youtube.com/watch?v=36aKlAyrfiw
   https://www.youtube.com/watch?v=WrkSfdu__zo
   https://www.youtube.com/watch?v=pTYMNdHHXpg
3. I-Robot Movie Trailer
   https://www.youtube.com/watch?v=rL6RRIOZyCM
4. Crawling Robot
   https://www.youtube.com/watch?v=glUnzzoFUxg
5. Selfie Robot
   https://www.youtube.com/watch?v=xBiOQKonkWs
   https://www.youtube.com/watch?v=O0dY_3VYX3U
6. Robo-Cop 2014
   https://www.youtube.com/watch?v=yXOhIJg4B7k
7. Actroid Robot
   https://www.youtube.com/watch?v=MLCbCtQVQog
8. Humans Trailer
   https://www.youtube.com/watch?v=BV8qFeZxZPE
9. Companion Robot
   https://www.youtube.com/watch?v=h3DL8OMjMxc
   https://www.youtube.com/watch?v=3IFuv1AVouM
10. Her
    https://www.youtube.com/watch?v=6QRvTv_tpw0
11. Japan Banks on Robot Economy
    https://www.youtube.com/watch?v=2cUYXlT3mwc
    https://www.youtube.com/watch?v=Gfw6vIl8ILk
12. Robots Replacing Humans
    https://www.youtube.com/watch?v=FgMxXWinNBI

Chapter 19   *Robot Men on the Battlefield*

1. Bear
   https://www.youtube.com/watch?v=8rdRxV-qn3w
   https://www.youtube.com/watch?v=8Nv6GGNA3Z4
2. Petman Robot
   https://www.youtube.com/watch?v=RGZoMPXG0MI
   https://www.youtube.com/watch?v=mclbVTIYG8E
3. Atlas Robot
   https://www.youtube.com/watch?v=SD6Okylclb8

https://www.youtube.com/watch?v=27HkxMo6qK0
   https://www.youtube.com/watch?v=mi0sX2Dxk6o
4. Avatar and Pacific Rim Trailers
   https://www.youtube.com/watch?v=5guMumPFBag
5. Kuratas Robot
   https://www.youtube.com/watch?v=2iZ0WuNvHr8
6. Kuratas and Megabot Duel
   https://www.youtube.com/watch?v=XVJTGLL2SnI
7. Rationale for Robots
   https://www.youtube.com/watch?v=dbgOzkIKVaw
8. Decisions to Kill for Robots
   https://www.weforum.org/agenda/2017/09/should-machines-not-humans-make-life-and-death-decisions-in-war/
9. Terminator Robots are Coming
   NO LINK

Chapter 20   *Robots Controlled by the Brain*

1. Brain Controlled Drones
   https://www.youtube.com/watch?v=8LuImMOZOo0
   https://www.youtube.com/watch?v=QRt8QCx3BCo
2. Brain Controlled Telebot
   https://www.youtube.com/watch?v=eiMY8WFCBZo
3. Car Computer Being Hacked
   https://www.youtube.com/watch?v=6OfcgJ-pl7Q
4. Brain Hacking Devices
   http://noliemri.com/
   hhttps://www.huffingtonpost.com/2012/11/20/mind-control-how-eeg-devices-read-brainwaves_n_2001431.htmlhttps://www.wired.com/2009/03/noliemri/
5. Congress Brain Scans
   https://www.youtube.com/watch?v=_aNBssO4_do

Chapter 21   *Robots Controlled by AI*

1. AI Controlled Drones
   http://www.pbs.org/wgbh/nova/tech/how-dumb-are-drones.html
   https://techcrunch.com/2017/02/21/exyn-unveils-ai-to-help-drones-fly-autonomously-even-indoors-or-off-the-grid/
2. Skynet Chases Couple
   https://www.youtube.com/watch?v=UVPeztcONRk
3. AI Controlled Robots
   https://teresaescrig.com/what-are-the-benefits-of-artificial-intelligence-in-robotics/
4. Military Warns AI Robots are Coming https://www.mirror.co.uk/news/uk-news/top-general-warns-against-unleashing-10829571
5. Laws of AI Robots
   https://www.youtube.com/watch?v=7PKx3kS7f4A
6. Warnings of Developing AI Robots
   https://www.youtube.com/watch?v=SUwfV77tJHo

Chapter 22   Conditioned by Our Emotions

1. American Sniper
   https://www.youtube.com/watch?v=99k3u9ay1gs
2. Good Kill
   https://www.youtube.com/watch?v=99k3u9ay1gs
3. Brandon Bryant Trauma
   https://www.youtube.com/watch?v=i_l6ec62l6I
   https://www.youtube.com/watch?v=750BD72Od7s
4. Many soldiers Trauma
   https://www.youtube.com/watch?v=hDv_A3AiWYU
   https://www.salon.com/2015/03/06/a_chilling_new_post_traumatic_stress_disorder_why_drone_pilots_are_quitting_in_record_numbers_partner/
5. AI Robot Remove Trauma
   https://www.icrac.net/icrac-opening-statement-to-the-2015-un-ccw-expert-meeting/

Chapter 23   Conditioned by Our Entertainment

1. 20Q Toy
   https://www.youtube.com/watch?v=CSeQ4RVSHQM

2. Cognitoys Dinosaur
   https://www.youtube.com/watch?v=BVfjkOkxBOg
3. Super AI Teddy Bear Toy
   https://www.youtube.com/watch?v=jyeGkDMVCng
4. TED Movie Trailer
   https://www.youtube.com/watch?v=4roo09Be53U
5. AI Toys are New Trend
   https://www.youtube.com/watch?v=ai_b1ObCPbc
6. Amazon AI Echo
   https://www.youtube.com/watch?v=9V4Fvg1SwpM
7. JIBO AI Device
   https://www.youtube.com/watch?v=-3NYBpYRC-s

Chapter 24   *Conditioned by Our Movies*

1. Chappie
   https://www.youtube.com/watch?v=lyy7y0QOK-0
2. Automata
   https://www.youtube.com/watch?v=Wh_wmaOZcWo
3. Ex Machina
   https://www.youtube.com/watch?v=PI8XBKb6DQk
4. Age of Ultron
   https://www.youtube.com/watch?v=CieuGZ7TthE

Chapter 25   *Global Warnings*

1. Warren Buffett warns of AI
   https://www.youtube.com/watch?v=t6WlQHmTrpw
2. History Channel warns of AI
   NO LINK
3. News warns of AI
   https://www.youtube.com/watch?v=yU3oha82qQk
   https://www.youtube.com/watch?v=Muc_Q3sQ3s8
4. Stephen Hawking warns of AI
   https://www.youtube.com/watch?v=mhL9G0U4w6Q
   https://www.youtube.com/watch?v=760yQw_clpQ

5. Elon Musk warns of AI
   https://www.youtube.com/watch?v=KdTTeR4TyMc
   https://www.youtube.com/watch?v=_rfHNvHu8OE
6. Steve Wozniak warns of AI
   https://www.youtube.com/watch?v=Yu9uZ9IgsJU
7. Bill Gates warns of AI
   https://www.youtube.com/watch?v=OLHxQBAvWIQ
8. Military Expert warns of AI
   NO LINK
9. Terminator writer warns of AI
   https://www.youtube.com/watch?v=tSuf0ja3ZlA
10. News sees AI as Skynet
    https://www.youtube.com/watch?v=lCh7QTILTGI

Chapter 26   *Google's Workings*

1. Larry Page admits to Creating AI
   NO LINK
2. Google Books Project
   https://www.youtube.com/watch?v=XZmGGAbHqa0
   https://www.youtube.com/watch?v=zwa9jnqcXsU
3. Google Buys Deep Mind
   https://www.youtube.com/watch?v=o1s1YsKc6Tw
4. Elon Musk tries to Stop Google
   https://www.theverge.com/2016/6/2/11837566/elon-musk-one-ai-company-that-worries-me
5. Google is creating Skynet
   https://www.youtube.com/watch?v=2BMQoN5FLU0

Chapter 27   *God's Wake Up Call*

1. The Bridge
   https://www.youtube.com/watch?v=q844OgsP4_4